MUIRHEAD LIBRARY OF PHILOSOPHY

AN admirable statement of the aims of the Library of Philosophy was provided by the first editor, the late Professor J. H. Muirhead, in his description of the original programme printed in Erdmann's *History of Philosophy* under the date 1890. This was slightly modified in subsequent volumes to take the form of the following statement:

'The Muirhead Library of Philosophy was designed as a contribution to the History of Modern Philosophy under the heads: first of Different Schools of Thought—Sensationalist, Realist, Idealist, Intuitivist; secondly of different Subjects—Psychology, Ethics, Political Philosophy, Theology. While much had been done in England in tracing the course of evolution in nature, history, economics, morals and religion, little had been done in tracing the development of thought on these subjects. Yet "the evolution of opinion is part of the whole evolution".

'By the co-operation of different writers in carrying out this plan it was hoped that a thoroughness and completeness of treatment, otherwise unattainable, might be secured. It was believed also that from writers mainly British and American fuller consideration of English Philosophy than it had hitherto received might be looked for. In the earlier series of books containing, among others, Bosanquet's *History of Aesthetic*, Pfleiderer's *Rational Theology since Kant*, Albee's *History of English Utilitarianism*, Bonar's *Philosophy and Political Economy*, Brett's *History of Psychology*, Ritchie's *Natural Rights*, these objects were to a large extent effected.

'In the meantime original work of a high order was being produced both in England and America by such writers as Bradley, Stout, Bertrand Russell, Baldwin, Urban, Montague, and others, and a new interest in foreign works, German, French and Italian, which had either become classical or were attracting public attention, had developed. The scope of the Library thus became extended into something more international, and it is entering on the fifth decade of its existence in the hope that it may contribute to that mutual understanding between countries which is so pressing a need of the present time.'

The need which Professor Muirhead stressed is no less pressing today, and few will deny that philosophy has much to do with enabling us to meet it, although no one, least of all Muirhead himself, would regard that as the sole, or even the main, object of philosophy. As Professor Muirhead continues to lend the distinction of his name to the Library of Philosophy it seemed not inappropriate to allow him to recall us to these aims in his own words. The emphasis on the history of thought also seemed to me very timely; and the number of important works promised for the Library in the very near future augur well for the continued fulfilment, in this and other ways, of the expectations of the original editor.

H. D. LEWIS

MUIRHEAD LIBRARY OF PHILOSOPHY

General Editor: H. D. Lewis

Professor of History and Philosophy of Religion in the University of London

The Analysis of Mind by BERTRAND RUSSELL
Brett's History of Psychology edited by R. S. PETERS
Clarity is Not Enough by H. D. LEWIS
Coleridge as a Philosopher by J. H. MUIRHEAD
The Commonplace Book of G. E. Moore edited by C. LEWY
Contemporary American Philosophy edited by G. P. ADAMS and W. P. MONTAGUE
Contemporary British Philosophy first and second Series edited by J. H. MUIRHEAD
Contemporary British Philosophy third Series edited by H. D. LEWIS
Contemporary Indian Philosophy edited by RADHAKRISHNAN and J. H. MUIRHEAD 2nd edition
The Discipline of the Cave by J. N. FINDLAY
Doctrine and Argument in Indian Philosophy by NINIAN SMART
Essays in Analysis by ALICE AMBROSE
Ethics by NICOLAI HARTMANN translated by STANTON COIT 3 vols
The Foundations of Metaphysics in Science by ERROL E. HARRIS
Freedom and History by H. D. LEWIS
The Good Will: A Study in the Coherence Theory of Goodness by H. J. PATON
Hegel: A Re-examination by J. N. FINDLAY
Hegel's Science of Logic translated by W. H. JOHNSTON and L. G. STRUTHERS 2 vols.
History of Aesthetic by B. BOSANQUET 2nd edition
History of English Utilitarianism by E. ALBEE
History of Psychology by G. S. BRETT edited by R. S. PETERS abridged one volume edition 2nd edition
Human Knowledge by BERTRAND RUSSELL
A Hundred Years of British Philosophy by RUDOLF METZ translated by J. H. HARVEY, T. E. JESSOP, HENRY STURT
Ideas: A General Introduction to Pure Phenomenology by EDMUND HUSSERL translated by W. R. BOYCE GIBSON
Imagination by E. J. FURLONG
Indian Philosophy by RADHAKRISHNAN 2 vols revised 2nd edition
Identity and Reality by EMILE MEYERSON

Muirhead Library of Philosophy

EDITED BY H. D. LEWIS

IN DEFENCE OF FREE WILL

AND OTHER PHILOSOPHICAL ESSAYS

by the same author
SCEPTICISM AND CONSTRUCTION
ON SELFHOOD AND GODHOOD

IN DEFENCE OF FREE WILL

WITH OTHER PHILOSOPHICAL ESSAYS

BY

C. A. CAMPBELL

Emeritus Professor of Logic and Rhetoric
Glasgow University

LONDON: GEORGE ALLEN & UNWIN LTD
NEW YORK: HUMANITIES PRESS INC

PRINTED IN GREAT BRITAIN
in 11 on 12pt Imprint type
BY UNWIN BROTHERS LIMITED
LONDON AND WOKING

PREFACE

In common (I imagine) with most other philosophers who have been a longish while in the business, I find that I have in my time produced a good many papers for which I now feel no affection whatsoever. None of these, naturally, finds a place in the present volume. For them to have appeared in print once was enough—very possibly more than enough. The papers I have chosen as most suitable for republication from these that still give me reasonable satisfaction have at least the qualification, for what it is worth, that they do all seem to myself to have made on philosophical problems of importance some constructive suggestions that were worth making at the time and have not lost their relevance since. How far others will agree with this hardly disinterested assessment is a different matter, and I confess to a good deal of hesitancy about putting the question to the test. I should have been still more hesitant, however, were it not for the favour already shown to a number of these papers by various recent compilers of anthologies and text-books (particularly in the U S A).

A general consideration which has further encouraged me is that, unless I am sadly mistaken, there has gradually come about in this country over the past dozen or so years a distinctly more hospitable climate of philosophic thought than that which prevailed when most of these papers were first published. Several factors have contributed to this state of affairs, but I should myself accord definite pride of place to two. The first is the recognition, now almost universal, that the Verifiability Principle of Meaning can claim plausibility only after suffering modifications so severe as to divest it of its revolutionary implications. The second is the scepticism that is now generally felt about the more far-reaching of the vast claims originally made for linguistic analysis as an instrument of philosophical investigation. In both cases dogmatic subscription to the extreme view made it almost a duty (as well as a pleasure) to dismiss unread the greater part of the work of those philosophers who remained obstinately 'non-subscribers'. But with the outmoding of these extreme views there has emerged, it seems to me, a real prospect that, before so very long, the pursuit of philosophy in these islands will have become again the more broadly based and mutually co-operative enterprise that it once was.

The lowering of barriers is still at an early stage; but one might instance, as especially full of promise for the future, how much there now is in common between current attitudes towards linguistic analysis. There must be very few philosophers at the present time who do not acknowledge, in practice as well as in theory, *both* that linguistic analysis has a very important part to play in tackling philosophic problems, *and* that, for fully effective treatment of many of these problems, there must be at least supplementation by other, more traditional forms of attack. Inevitably, and properly, sharp differences of opinion remain within the general consensus. (Mutual co-operation does not exclude, on the contrary it is an indispensable condition of, informed mutual criticism.) But the key question now is not whether linguistic analysis has a valuable function in philosophy—that has already been settled. It is rather as to the precise nature and extent of its profitable employment in solving specific problems. And this question, it is becoming increasingly clear, is one which can be decided only by philosophers addressing themselves to these specific problems unshackled by inhibiting methodological presuppositions one way or the other.

Save for the correction of occasional misprints, I have not altered in any way the original wording of these papers. I have, however, judged it desirable to omit, in the altered circumstances of publication, the concluding Section in the original version of Paper I and the opening paragraph in that of Paper II: the former because there was nothing of substance said there that is not said more adequately, and in a more appropriate context, in Paper II; and the latter because its interest was purely local and personal, not philosophical.

Papers I, IV, VI, and VII of this volume first appeared in *Mind* (1951, 1935, 1950, and 1936); Papers III and XI in *Proceedings of the Aristotelian Society* (1939–40 and 1944–45); Papers X and XIII in *The Philosophical Quarterly* (1960 and 1953); Paper VIII in *The Hibbert Journal* (1949); Paper IX in *Analysis* (1958); Paper V was delivered before The British Academy as the Hertz Annual Philosophical Lecture for 1948, and subsequently published in their *Proceedings*; Paper II was delivered as an Inaugural Lecture on assuming the Glasgow University Chair of Logic and Rhetoric in 1938, and subsequently published by Jackson, Son & Co., Glasgow; Paper XII was a contribution to *Theories of the Mind*, a volume edited by Dr Jordan M. Scher and published in 1962 by The Free Press of Glencoe, a Division of the Macmillan Company. I gratefully acknowledge the permission to reprint given by the several editors, publishers and institutions concerned.

My thanks are due also to my friends Professor W. G. Maclagan and Dr Eva Schaper, of Glasgow University, for valuable help at various stages in the preparation of the book.

Callander   C. A. CAMPBELL
January 1967.

CONTENTS

PART I
PHILOSOPHY OF MORALS

IS 'FREE WILL' A PSEUDO-PROBLEM?

I

In the days when the Verifiability Principle was accepted by its
devotees as a secure philosophical truth, one could understand,
though one might not agree with, the sweeping claim that many
of the traditional problems of philosophy had been shown to be
mere 'pseudo-problems'. It was easy to see how, given the
Principle's validity, most of the leading questions which agitated
our forefathers in metaphysics, in ethics, and in theology, automatically become nonsensical questions. What is perplexing,
however, is that despite the pretty generally acknowledged
deterioration in the Principle's status to that of a convenient
methodological postulate, the attitude to these same questions
seems to have changed but little. To admit that the Verifiability
Principle is not an assured truth entails the admission that a
problem can no longer be dismissed as meaningless simply on the
ground that it cannot be stated in a way which satisfies the
Principle. Whether or not a problem is meaningless is now something that can only be decided after critical examination of the
particular case on its own individual merits. But the old antipathies
seem in large measure to have survived the disappearance of their
logical basis. One gets the impression that for at least many
thinkers with Positivist sympathies the 'liquidation' of a large, if
unspecified, group of traditional philosophic problems is still
established fact. If that impression is mistaken, well and good.
One may then hope for an early recrudescence of interest in
certain problems that have too long suffered the consequences of an
unhappy *tabu*. If the impression is correct, a real service would be
done to philosophy if it were plainly stated which of the traditional
problems are still regarded as pseudo-problems, and what are the
reasons, old or new, for passing this sentence upon them. The
smoke of old battles, perhaps understandably, darkens the philosophic air, to the considerable inconvenience of all concerned.
Fortunately, however, the obscurity complained of is not

totally unrelieved. We do know of one traditional problem that is definitely on the black list of the *avant garde*—the problem of 'Free Will': and we do have pretty adequate information about the reasons which have led to its being placed theron. This, so far as it goes, is satisfactory. A plain obligation now lies upon philosophers who still believe that 'Free Will' is a genuine problem to explain just where, in their opinion, the case for the prosecution breaks down. To discharge this obligation is the main purpose of the present paper.

There will be a clear advantage in making our start from the *locus classicus* of the 'pseudo-problem' theory, if *locus classicus* there be. And I think that there must be something of the sort. At any rate, the casual, and indeed slightly bored, tones in which so many contemporary philosophers allude to the traditional problem, and their contentment to indicate in only a sketchy manner the reasons why it no longer exists, strongly suggest that *somewhere* the matter has in their eyes been already effectively settled. At least one important 'document in the case' is, I suspect, Chapter VII of Moritz Schlick's *Problems of Ethics*, first published in 1931. This chapter, the title of which is 'When is a Man Responsible?' and the first section of which bears the heading 'The Pseudo-problem of Freedom of the Will', presents in concentrated form, but with some show of systematic argument, most of the considerations upon which later writers appear to rely. It will be worth our while, therefore, to try to see just why Professor Schlick is so sure (and he is *very* sure indeed) that 'Free Will', as traditionally formulated, is a pseudo-problem, begotten by mere confusion of mind.

II

I shall first summarize, as faithfully as I can, what I take to be the distinctive points in Schlick's argument.

The traditional formulation of the problem, Schlick points out, is based on the assumption that to have 'free will' entails having a will that is, at least sometimes, exempt from causal law. It is traditionally supposed, quite rightly, that moral responsibility implies freedom in *some* sense: and it is supposed, also quite rightly, that this sense is one which is incompatible with compulsion. But because it is further supposed, quite *wrongly*, that to be subject to causal or natural law is to be subject to compulsion,

the inference is drawn that the free will implied in moral responsibility is incompatible with causal continuity. The ultimate root of
the error, Schlick contends, lies in a failure to distinguish between
two different kinds of Law, one of which does indeed 'compel', but
the other of which does *not*.[1] There are, first, *pre*scriptive laws, such
as the laws imposed by civil authority, which presume contrary
desires on the part of those to whom they are applied; and these
may fairly be said to exercise 'compulsion'. And there are, secondly,
*de*scriptive laws, such as the laws which the sciences seek to
formulate; and these merely state what does as a matter of fact
always happen. It is perfectly clear that the relation of the latter,
the natural, causal laws, to human willing is radically different
from the 'compulsive' relation of prescriptive laws to human
willing, and that it is really an absurdity to talk of a species of
natural law like, say, psychological laws, *compelling* us to act in
this or that way. The term 'compulsion' is totally inept where, as
in this case, there are no contrary desires. But the traditional
discussions of Free Will, confusing descriptive with prescriptive
laws, fallaciously assume 'compulsion' to be ingredient in Law as
such, and it is contended accordingly that moral freedom, since it
certainly implies absence of compulsion, implies also exemption
from causal law.

It follows that the problem of Free Will, as traditionally stated,
is a mere pseudo-problem. The statement of it in terms of exemption from causal law rests on the assumption that causal law
involves 'compulsion'. And this assumption is demonstrably false.
Expose the muddle from which it arises and the so-called
'problem' in its traditional form disappears.

But is it quite certain that the freedom which moral responsibility implies is no more than 'the absence of compulsion'? This
is the premise upon which Schlick's argument proceeds, but
Schlick is himself well aware that it stands in need of confirmation
from an analysis of the notion of moral responsibility. Otherwise
it might be maintained that although 'the absence of compulsion'
has been shown not to entail a contra-causal type of freedom, there
is nevertheless some *other* condition of moral responsibility that
does entail it. Accordingly Schlick embarks now upon a formal
analysis of the nature and conditions of moral responsibility

[1] *Problems of Ethics*, Ch. VIII. Section 2. (All references are to the English
translation by David Rynin, published in New York in 1939.)

designed to show that the *only* freedom implied by moral responsibility is freedom from compulsion. It was a trifle ambitious, however, even for a master of compression like Professor Schlick to hope to deal satisfactorily in half a dozen very brief pages with a topic which has been so extensively debated in the literature of moral philosophy: and I cannot pretend that I find what he has to say free from obscurity. But to the best of my belief what follows does reproduce the gist of Schlick's analysis.

What precisely, Schlick asks, does the term 'moral responsibility' mean in our ordinary linguistic usage?[1] He begins his answer by insisting upon the close connection for ordinary usage between 'moral responsibility' and *punishment* (strictly speaking, punishment and *reward*: but for convenience Schlick virtually confines the discussion to punishment, and we shall do the same). The connection, as Schlick sees it, is this. In ordinary practice our concern with the responsibility for an act (he tells us) is with a view to determining *who is to be punished for it*. Now punishment is (I quote) 'an educative measure'. It is 'a means to the formation of motives, which are in part to prevent the wrong-doer from repeating the act (reformation), and in part to prevent others from committing a similar act (intimidation)'.[2] When we ask, then, 'Who in a given case is to be punished?'—which is the same as the question 'Who is responsible?'—what we are really wanting to discover is some agent in the situation upon whose motives we can bring to bear the appropriate educative influences, so that in similar situations in future his strongest motive will impel him to refrain from, rather than to repeat, the act. 'The question of who is responsible' Schlick sums up, 'is . . . a matter only of knowing who is to be punished or rewarded, in order that punishment and reward function as such—be able to achieve their goal'.[3] It is not a matter, he expressly declares, of trying to ascertain what may be called the 'original instigator' of the act. That might be a great-grand-parent, from the consequence of whose behaviour vicious tendencies have been inherited by a living person. Such 'remote causes' as this are irrelevant to questions of punishment (and so to questions of moral responsibility), 'for in the first place their actual contribution cannot be determined, and in the second place they are generally out of reach'.[4]

[1] *Loc. cit.*, Ch. VII, Section 5.   [2] *Ibid.*, p. 152.
[3] *Ibid.*, p. 153.   [4] *Ibid.*, p. 153.

It is a matter for regret that Schlick has not rounded off his discussion, as one had hoped and expected he would, by formulating a precise definition of moral responsibility in terms of what he has been saying. I think, however, that the conclusion to which his argument leads could be not unfairly expressed in some such way as this: 'We say that a man is morally responsible for an act if his motives for bringing about the act are such as we can affect favourably in respect of his future behaviour by the educative influences of reward and punishment'.

Given the truth of this analysis of moral responsibility, Schlick's contention follows logically enough that the only freedom that is required for moral responsibility is freedom from compulsion. For what are the cases in which a man's motives are *not* capable of being favourably affected by reward and punishment?—the cases in which, that is, according to Schlick's analysis, we do *not* deem him morally responsible? The only such cases, it would seem, are those in which a man is subjected to some form of external constraint which prevents him from acting according to his 'natural desires'. For example, if a man is compelled by a pistol at his breast to do a certain act, or induced to do it by an externally administered narcotic, he is not 'morally responsible'; or not, at any rate, in so far as punishment would be impotent to affect his motives in respect of his future behaviour. External constraint in one form or another seems to be the sole circumstance which absolves a man from moral responsibility. Hence we may say that freedom from external constraint is the only sort of freedom which an agent must possess in order to be morally responsible. The 'contra-causal' sort of freedom which so many philosophers and others have supposed to be required is shown by a true analysis of moral responsibility to be irrelevant.

This completes the argument that 'Free Will', as traditionally formulated, is a pseudo-problem. The only freedom implied by moral responsibility is freedom from compulsion; and as we have rid ourselves of the myth that subjection to causal law is a form of compulsion, we can see that the only compulsion which absolves from moral responsibility is the external constraint which prevents us from translating our desires into action. The true meaning of the question 'Have we free will?' thus becomes simply 'Can we translate our desires into action?' And this question does not constitute a 'problem' at all, for the answer to it is not in doubt. The obvious answer is 'Sometimes we can, sometimes we can't, according to the specific circumstances of the case'.

III

Here, then, in substance is Schlick's theory. Let us now examine it.

In the first place, it is surely quite unplausible to suggest that the common assumption that moral freedom postulates some breach of causal continuity arises from a confusion of two different types of law. Schlick's distinction between descriptive and prescriptive law is, of course, sound. It was no doubt worth pointing out too, that descriptive laws cannot be said to 'compel' human behaviour in the same way as prescriptive laws do. But it seems to me evident that the usual reason why it is held that moral freedom implies some breach of causal continuity, is not a belief that causal laws 'compel' as civil laws 'compel', but simply the belief that the admission of unbroken causal continuity entails a *further* admission which is directly incompatible with moral responsibility; viz. the admission that no man could have acted otherwise than he in fact did. Now it may, of course, be an error thus to assume that a man is not morally responsible for an act, a fit subject for moral praise and blame in respect of it, unless he could have acted otherwise than he did. Or, if *this* is not an error, it may still be an error to assume that a man could not have acted otherwise than he did, in the sense of the phrase that is crucial for moral responsibility, without there occurring some breach of causal continuity. Into these matters we shall have to enter very fully at a later stage. But the relevant point at the moment is that these (not prima facie absurd) assumptions about the conditions of moral responsibility have very commonly, indeed normally, been made, and that they are entirely adequate to explain why the problem of Free Will finds its usual formulation in terms of partial exemption from causal law. Schlick's distinction between prescriptive and descriptive laws has no bearing at all upon the truth or falsity of these assumptions. Yet if these assumptions are accepted, it is (I suggest) really inevitable that the Free Will problem should be formulated in the way to which Schlick takes exception. Recognition of the distinction upon which Schlick and his followers lay so much stress can make not a jot of difference.

As we have seen, however, Schlick does later proceed to the much more important business of disputing these common assumptions about the conditions of moral responsibility. He offers us an analysis of moral responsibility which flatly contradicts these assumptions; an analysis according to which the only freedom demanded by morality is a freedom which is compatible with Determinism. If this analysis can be sustained, there is certainly no problem of 'Free Will' in the traditional sense.

But it seems a simple matter to show that Schlick's analysis is untenable. Let us test it by Schlick's own claim that it gives us what we mean by 'moral responsibility' in ordinary linguistic usage.

We do not ordinarily consider the lower animals to be morally responsible. But *ought* we not to do so if Schlick is right about what we mean by moral responsibility? It is quite possible, by punishing the dog who absconds with the succulent chops designed for its master's luncheon, favourably to influence its motives in respect of its future behaviour in like circumstances. If moral responsibility is to be linked with punishment as Schlick links it, and punishment conceived as a form of education, we should surely hold the dog morally responsible? The plain fact, of course, is that we don't. We don't, because we suppose that the dog 'couldn't help it': that its action (unlike what we usually believe to be true of human beings) was simply a link in a continuous chain of causes and effects. In other words, we do commonly demand the contra-causal sort of freedom as a condition of moral responsibility.

Again, we do ordinarily consider it proper, in certain circumstances, to speak of a person no longer living as morally responsible for some present situation. But *ought* we to do so if we accept Schlick's essentially 'forward-looking' interpretation of punishment and responsibility? Clearly we cannot now favourably affect the dead man's motives. No doubt they could *at one time* have been favourably affected. But that cannot be relevant to our judgment of responsibility if, as Schlick insists, the question of who is responsible 'is a matter only of knowing who is to be punished or rewarded'. Indeed he expressly tells us, as we saw earlier, that in asking this question we are not concerned with a 'great-grand-parent' who may have been the 'original instigator', because, for one reason, this 'remote cause' is 'out of reach'. We cannot bring the appropriate educative influence to bear upon it. But the plain fact, of course, is that we do frequently assign moral responsibility for present situations to persons who have long been inaccessible to any punitive action on our part. And Schlick's position is still more paradoxical in respect of our apportionment of responsibility for occurrences in the distant past. Since in these cases there is no agent whatsoever whom we can favourably influence by punishment, the question of moral responsibility here should have no meaning for us. But of course it has. Historical writings are studded with examples.

Possibly the criticism just made may seem to some to result from taking Schlick's analysis too much *au pied de la lettre*. The absurd consequences deduced, it may be said, would not follow if we interpreted Schlick as meaning that a man is morally responsible where his motive is such as can *in principle* be favourably affected by reward or punishment—whether or not we who pass the judgment are in a position to take such action. But with every desire to be fair to Schlick, I cannot see how he could accept this modification and still retain the essence of his theory. For the essence of his theory seems to be that moral responsibility has its whole meaning and importance for us in relation to our potential control of future conduct in the interests of society. (I agree that it is hard to believe that anybody *really* thinks this. But it is perhaps less hard to believe to-day than it has ever been before in the history of modern ethics.)

Again, we ordinarily consider that, in certain circumstances, the *degree* of a man's moral responsibility for an act is affected by considerations of his inherited nature, or of his environment, or of both. It is our normal habit to 'make allowances' (as we say) when we have reason to believe that a malefactor had a vicious heredity, or was nurtured in his formative years in a harmful environment. We say in such cases 'Poor chap, he is more to be pitied than blamed. We could scarcely expect him to behave like a decent citizen with *his* parentage or upbringing.' But this extremely common sort of judgment has no point at all if we mean by moral responsibility what Schlick says that we mean. On *that* meaning the degree of a man's moral responsibility must presumably be dependent upon the degree to which we can favourably affect his future motives, which is quite another matter. Now there is no reason to believe that the motives of a man with a bad heredity or a bad upbringing are either less or more subject to educative influence than those of his more fortunate fellows. Yet it is plain matter of fact that we do commonly consider the degree of a man's moral responsibility to be affected by these two factors.

A final point. The extremity of paradox in Schlick's identification of the question 'Who is morally blameworthy?' with the question 'Who is to be punished?' is apt to be partially concealed from us just because it is our normal habit to include in the meaning of 'punishment' an element of 'requital for moral transgression' which Schlick expressly denies to it. On that account we commonly think of 'punishment', in its strict sense, as implying moral blameworthiness in the person punished. But if we remember to mean by punishment what Schlick means by it, a purely 'educative measure', with no retributive ingredients, his identification of the two questions loses such plausibility as it might otherwise have. For clearly we often think it proper to 'punish' a person, in *Schlick's* sense, where we are not at all prepared to say that the person is morally blameworthy. We may even think him morally commendable. A case in point would be the unmistakably sincere but muddleheaded person who at the cost of great suffering to himself steadfastly pursues as his 'duty' a course which, in our judgment is fraught with danger to the common weal. We should most of us feel entitled, in the public interest, to bring such action to bear upon the man's motives as might induce him to refrain in future from his socially injurious behaviour: in other words, to inflict upon him what Schlick would call 'punishment'. But we should most of us feel perfectly clear that in so 'punishing' this misguided citizen we are not proclaiming his moral blameworthiness for moral wickedness.

Adopting Schlick's own criterion, then, looking simply 'to the manner in which the concept is used',[1] we seem bound to admit that constantly people do assign moral responsibility where Schlick's theory says they shouldn't, don't assign moral responsibility where Schlick's theory says they should, and assign degrees of moral responsibility where on Schlick's theory there should be no difference in degree. I think we may reasonably conclude that Schlick's account of what we mean by moral responsibility breaks down.

The rebuttal of Schlick's arguments, however, will not suffice of

[1] *Loc. cit.*, Ch. VII, Section 5, p. 151.

itself to refute the pseudo-problem theory. The indebtedness to Schlick of most later advocates of the theory may be conceded; but certainly it does not comprehend all of significance that they have to say on the problem. There are recent analyses of the conditions of moral responsibility containing sufficient new matter, or sufficient old matter in a more precise and telling form, to require of us now something of a fresh start. In the section which follows I propose to consider some representative samples of these analyses—all of which, of course, are designed to show that the freedom which moral responsibility implies is not in fact a contra-causal type of freedom.

But before reopening the general question of the nature and conditions of moral responsibility there is a *caveat* which it seems to me worth while to enter. The difficulties in the way of a clear answer are not slight; but they are apt to seem a good deal more formidable than they really are because of a common tendency to consider in unduly close association two distinct questions: the question 'Is a contra-causal type of freedom implied by moral responsibility?' and the question 'Does a contra-causal type of freedom anywhere exist?' It seems to me that many philosophers (and I suspect that Moritz Schlick is among them) begin their enquiry with so firm a conviction that the contra-causal sort of freedom nowhere exists, that they find it hard to take very seriously the possibility that it is *this* sort of freedom that moral responsibility implies. For they are loth to abandon the commonsense belief that moral responsibility itself is something real. The implicit reasoning I take to be this. Moral responsibility is real. If moral responsibility is real, the freedom implied in it must be a fact. But contra-causal freedom is not a fact. Therefore contra-causal freedom is not the freedom implied in moral responsibility. I think we should be on our guard against allowing this or some similar train of reasoning (whose premises, after all, are far from indubitable) to seduce us into distorting what we actually find when we set about a direct analysis of moral responsiblity and its conditions.

IV

The pseudo-problem theorists usually, and naturally, develop their analysis of moral responsibility by way of contrast with a view which, while it has enjoyed a good deal of philosophic support,

I can perhaps best describe as the common view. It will be well to remind ourselves, therefore, of the main features of this view.

So far as the *meaning*, as distinct from the *conditions*, of moral responsibility is concerned, the common view is very simple. If we ask ourselves whether a certain person is morally responsible for a given act (or it may be just 'in general'), what we are considering, it would be said, is whether or not that person is a fit subject upon whom to pass moral judgment; whether he can fittingly be deemed morally good or bad, morally praiseworthy or blameworthy. This does not take us any great way: but (*pace* Schlick) so far as it goes it does not seem to me seriously disputable. The really interesting and controversial question is about the *conditions* of moral responsibility, and in particular the question whether freedom of a contra-causal kind is among these conditions.

The answer of the common man to the latter question is that it most certainly *is* among the conditions. Why does he feel so sure about this? Not, I argued earlier, because the common man supposes that causal law exercises 'compulsion' in the sense that prescriptive laws do, but simply because he does not see how a person can be deemed morally praiseworthy or blameworthy in respect of an act which he could not help performing. From the stand-point of moral praise and blame, he would say—though not necessarily from other stand-points—it is a matter of indifference whether it is by reason of some external constraint or by reason of his own given nature that the man could not help doing what he did. It is quite enough to make moral praise and blame futile that in either case there were no genuine alternatives, no open possibilities, before the man when he acted. He could not have acted otherwise than he did. And the common man might not unreasonably go on to stress the fact that we all, even if we are linguistic philosophers, do in our actual practice of moral judgment appear to accept the common view. He might insist upon the point alluded to earlier in this paper, that we do all, in passing moral censure, 'make allowances' for influences in a man's hereditary nature or environmental circumstances which we regard as having made it more than ordinarily difficult for him to act otherwise than he did: the implication being that if we supposed that the man's heredity and environment made it not merely very *difficult* but actually *impossible* for him to act otherwise than he did, we could not properly assign moral blame to him at all.

Let us put the argument implicit in the common view a little more sharply. The moral 'ought' implies 'can'. If we say that A morally ought to have done X, we imply that in our opinion, he could have done X. But we assign moral blame to a man only for failing to do what we think he morally ought to have done. Hence if we morally blame A for not having done X, we imply that he could have done X even though in fact he did not. In other words, we imply that A could have acted otherwise than he did. And that means that we imply, as a necessary condition of a man's being morally blameworthy, that he enjoyed a freedom of a kind not compatible with unbroken causal continuity.

v

Now what is it that is supposed to be wrong with this simple piece of argument?—For, of course, it must be rejected by all these philosophers who tell us that the traditional problem of Free Will is a mere pseudo-problem. The argument looks as though it were doing little more than reading off necessary implications of the fundamental categories of our moral thinking. One's inclination is to ask 'If one is to think morally at all, how else than this *can* we think?'.

In point of fact, there is pretty general agreement among the contemporary critics as to what is wrong with the argument. Their answer in general terms is as follows. No doubt A's moral responsibility does imply that he could have acted otherwise. But this expression 'could have acted otherwise' stands in dire need of analysis. When we analyse it, we find that it is not, as is so often supposed, simple and unambiguous, and we find that in *some* at least of its possible meanings it implies *no* breach of causal continuity between character and conduct. Having got this clear, we can further discern that only in one of these *latter* meanings is there any compulsion upon our moral thinking to assert that if A is morally blameworthy for an act, A 'could have acted otherwise than he did'. It follows that, contrary to common belief, our moral thinking does *not* require us to posit a contra-causal freedom as a condition of moral responsibility.

So much of importance obviously turns upon the validity or otherwise of this line of criticism that we must examine it in some detail and with express regard to the *ipsissima verba* of the critics.

In the course of a recent article in *Mind*,[1] entitled 'Free Will and Moral Responsibility', Mr Nowell Smith (having earlier affirmed his belief that 'the traditional problem has been solved') explains very concisely the nature of the confusion which, as he thinks, has led to the demand for a contra-causal freedom. He begins by frankly recognizing that 'It is evident that one of the necessary conditions of moral action is that the agent "could have acted otherwise" ' and he adds 'it is to this fact that the Libertarian is drawing attention'.[2] Then, after showing (unexceptionably, I think) how the relationship of 'ought' to 'can' warrants the proposition which he has accepted as evident, and how it induces the Libertarian to assert the existence of action that is 'uncaused', he proceeds to point out, in a crucial passage, the nature of the Libertarian's error:

'The fallacy in the argument (he contends) lies in supposing that when we say "A could have acted otherwise" we mean that A, *being what he was and being placed in the circumstances in which he was placed*, could have done something other than what he did. But in fact we never do mean this.'[3]

What then *do* we mean here by 'A could have acted otherwise'? Mr Nowell Smith does not tell us in so many words, but the passage I have quoted leaves little doubt how he would answer. What we really mean by the expression, he implies, is not a *categorical* but a *hypothetical* proposition. We mean 'A could have acted otherwise, *if he did not happen to be what he in fact was*, or *if he were placed in circumstances other than those in which he was in fact placed*'. Now, *these* propositions, it is easy to see, are in no way incompatible with acceptance of the causal principle in its full rigour. Accordingly the claim that our fundamental moral thinking obliges us to assert a contra-causal freedom as a condition of moral responsibility is disproved.

Such is the 'analytical solution' of our problem offered (with obvious confidence) by one able philosopher of to-day, and entirely representative of the views of many other able philosophers. Yet I make bold to say that its falsity stares one in the face. It seems perfectly plain that the hypothetical propositions which Mr Nowell Smith proposes to substitute for the categorical proposition

[1] January 1948.   [2] *Loc. cit.*, p. 49.   [3] *Loc. cit.*, p. 49.

cannot express 'what we really mean' in this context by 'A could have acted otherwise', for the simple reason that these hypothetical propositions have no bearing whatsoever upon the question of the moral responsibility of *A*. And it is *A* whose moral responsibility we are talking about—a definite person *A* with a definitive character and in a definitive set of circumstances. What conceivable significance could it have for our attitude to A's responsibility to know that someone with a *different* character (or *A* with a different character, if that collocation of words has any meaning), or A in a different set of circumstances from those in which A as we are concerned with him was in fact placed, 'could have acted otherwise'? No doubt this supposititious being *could* have acted otherwise than the definitive person A acted. But the point is that where we are reflecting, as we are supposed in this context to be reflecting, upon the question of *A*'s moral responsibility, our interest in this supposititious being is precisely *nil*.

The two hypothetical propositions suggested in Mr Nowell Smith's account of the matter do not, however, exhaust the speculations that have been made along these lines. Another very common suggestion by the analysts is that what we really mean by 'A could have acted otherwise' is 'A could have acted otherwise *if he had willed, or chosen, otherwise*'. This was among the suggestions offered by G. E. Moore in the well-known chapter on Free Will in his *Ethics*. It is, I think, the suggestion he most strongly favoured: though it is fair to add that neither about this nor about any other of his suggestions is Moore in the least dogmatic. He does claim, for, I think, convincing reasons, that 'we *very often* mean by "could" merely "would, *if* so-and-so had chosen" '.[1] And he concludes 'I must confess that I cannot feel certain that this may not be all that we usually mean and understand by the assertion that we have Free Will'.[2]

This third hypothetical proposition appears to enjoy also the support of Mr C. L. Stevenson. Mr Stevenson begins the chapter of *Ethics and Language* entitled 'Avoidability-Indeterminism' with the now familiar pronouncement of his School that 'controversy about freedom and determinism of the will . . . presents no permanent difficulty to ethics, being largely a product of confusions'. A major confusion (if I understand him rightly) he takes to lie in the meaning of the term 'avoidable', when we say 'A's

----

[1] *Ethics*, p. 212.   [2] *Loc. cit.*, p. 217.

action was avoidable'—or, I presume, 'A could have acted otherwise'. He himself offers the following definition of 'avoidable'— ' "A's action was avoidable" has the meaning of "If A had made a certain choice, which in fact he did not make, his action would not have occurred" '.[1] This I think we may regard as in substance identical with the suggestion that what we really mean by 'A could have acted otherwise' is 'A could have acted otherwise *if* he had chosen (or willed) otherwise'. For clarity's sake we shall here keep to this earlier formulation. In either formulation the special significance of the third hypothetical proposition, as of the two hypothetical propositions already considered, is that it is compatible with strict determinism. If this be indeed all that we mean by the 'freedom' that conditions moral responsibility, then those philosophers are certainly wrong who hold that moral freedom is of the contra-causal type.

Now this third hypothetical proposition does at least possess the merit, not shared by its predecessors, of having a real relevance to the question of moral responsibility. If, e.g., A had promised to meet us at 2 p.m., and he chanced to break his leg at 1 p.m., we should not blame him for his failure to discharge his promise. For we should be satisfied that he *could not* have acted otherwise, even if he had so chosen; or *could not*, at any rate, in a way which would have enabled him to meet us at 2 p.m. The freedom to translate one's choice into action, which we saw earlier is for Schlick the *only* freedom required for moral responsibility, is without doubt *one* of the conditions of moral responsibility.

But it seems easy to show that this third hypothetical proposition does not exhaust what we mean, and *some*times is not even *part* of what we mean, by the expression 'could have acted otherwise' in its moral context. Thus it can hardly be even part of what we mean in the case of that class of wrong actions (and it is a large class) concerning which there is really no question whether the agent could have acted otherwise, *if* he had chosen otherwise. Take lying, for example. Only in some very abnormal situation could it occur to one to doubt whether A, whose power of speech was evinced by his telling a lie, was in a position to tell what he took to be the truth *if* he had so chosen. Of *course* he was. Yet it still makes good sense for one's moral thinking to ask whether A, when lying, 'could have acted otherwise': and we still require an

[1] *Ethics and Language*, p. 298.

affirmative answer to this question if A's moral blameworthiness is to be established. It seems apparent, therefore, that in this class of cases at any rate one does *not* mean by 'A could have acted otherwise', 'A could have acted otherwise *if* he had so chosen'.

What then *does* one mean in this class of cases by 'A could have acted otherwise'? I submit that the expression is taken in its simple, categorical meaning, without any suppressed 'if' clause to qualify it. Or perhaps, in order to keep before us the important truth that it is only as expressions of *will* or *choice* that acts are of moral import, it might be better to say that a condition of A's moral responsibility is that he could have *chosen* otherwise. We saw that there is no real question whether A who told a lie could have acted otherwise *if* he had chosen otherwise. But there is a very real question, at least for any person who approaches the question of moral responsibility at a tolerably advanced level of reflection, about whether A could have *chosen* otherwise. Such a person will doubtless be acquainted with the claims advanced in some quarters that causal law operates universally: or/and with the theories of some philosophies that the universe is throughout the expression of a single supreme principle; or/and with the doctrines of some theologians that the world is created, sustained and governed by an Omniscient and Omnipotent Being. Very understandably such world-views awaken in him doubts about the validity of his first, easy, instinctive assumption that there are genuinely open possibilities before a man at the moment of moral choice. It thus becomes for him a real question whether a man could have chosen otherwise than he actually did, and, in consequence, whether man's moral responsibility is really defensible. For how can a man be morally responsible, he asks himself, if his choices, like all other events in the universe, could not have been otherwise than they in fact were? It is precisely against the background of world-views such as these that for reflective people the problem of moral responsibility normally arises.

Furthermore, to the man who has attained this level of reflection, it will in *no* class of cases be a sufficient condition of moral responsibility for an act that one could have acted otherwise *if* one had chosen otherwise—not even in these cases where there *was* some possibility of the operation of 'external constraint'. In these cases he will, indeed expressly recognize freedom from external constraint as a *necessary condition*, but not as a *sufficient* condition. For he will be aware that, even granted *this* freedom, it is still conceivable that the agent had no freedom to choose otherwise than he did, and he will therefore require that the latter sort of freedom be added if moral responsibility for the act is to be established.

I have been contending that, for persons at a *tolerably advanced level of reflection*, 'A could have acted otherwise', as a condition of A's moral responsibility, means 'A could have chosen otherwise'. The qualification italicized is of some importance. The unreflective or unsophisticated person, the ordinary 'man in the street', who does not know or much care what scientists and theologians and philosophers have said about the world, sees well enough that A is morally responsible only if he could have acted otherwise, but in his intellectual innocence he will, very probably, envisage nothing capable of preventing A from having acted otherwise except some material impediment—like the broken leg in the example above. Accordingly, for the unreflective person, 'A could have acted otherwise', as a condition of moral responsibility, *is* apt to mean no more than 'A could have acted otherwise *if* he had so chosen'.

It would appear, then, that the view now favoured by many philosophers, that the freedom required for moral responsibility is merely freedom from external constraint, is a view which they share only with the less reflective type of layman. Yet it should be plain that on a matter of this sort the view of the unreflective person is of little value by comparison with the view of the reflective person. There are some contexts, no doubt, in which lack of sophistication is an asset. But this is not one of them. The question at issue here is as to the kind of impediments which might have prevented a man from acting otherwise than he in fact did: and on this question knowledge and reflection are surely prerequisites of any answer that is worth listening to. It is simply on account of the limitations of his mental vision that the unreflective man interprets the expression 'could have acted otherwise', in its context as a condition of moral responsibility, solely in terms of external constraint. He has failed (as yet) to reach the intellectual level at which one takes into account the implications for moral choices of the world-views of science, religion, and philosophy. If on a matter of this complexity the philosopher finds that his analysis accords with the utterances of the un-

B

educated he has, I suggest, better cause for uneasiness than for self-congratulation.

This concludes the main part of what it seems to me necessary to say in answer to the pseudo-problem theorists. My object so far has been to expose the falsity of those innovations (chiefly Positivist) in the way of argument and analysis which are supposed by many to have made it impossible any longer to formulate the problem of Free Will in the traditional manner. My contention is that, at least so far as these innovations are concerned, the simple time-honoured argument still holds from the nature of the moral ought to the conclusion that moral responsibility implies a contra-causal type of freedom. The attempts to avoid that conclusion by analysing the proposition 'A could have acted otherwise' (acknowledged to be implied in *some* sense in A's moral responsibility) into one or other of certain hypothetical propositions which are compatible with unbroken causal continuity, break down hopelessly when tested against the touchstone of actual moral thinking. It is, I think, not necessary to defend the procedure of testing hypotheses in the ethical field by bringing to bear upon them our actual moral thinking. If there is any other form of test applicable, I should be much interested to learn what it is supposed to be. Certainly 'logical analysis' *per se* will not do. That has a function, but a function that can only be ancillary. For what we are seeking to know is the meaning of the expression 'could have acted otherwise' not *in the abstract*, but in the context of the question of man's *moral responsibility*. Logical analysis *per se* is impotent to give us this information. It can be of value only in so far as it operates within the orbit of 'the moral consciousness'. One may admit, with some qualifications, that on a matter of this sort the moral consciousness without logical analysis is blind: but it seems to me to be true without any qualification whatsoever that, on the same problem, logical analysis without the moral consciousness is empty.

IN DEFENCE OF FREE WILL

In casting about for a suitable topic upon which to address you to-day, I have naturally borne in mind that an inaugural lecture of this sort should be devoted to some theme of much more than merely esoteric import: to some theme, for preference, sufficiently central in character to have challenged the attention of all who possess a speculative interest in the nature of the universe and man's place within it. That is a principal reason why I have chosen to-day to speak on free will. Mighty issues turn, and turn directly, on the solution of the free will problem. It is in no way surprising that for centuries past it has exercised a fascination for thinkers both within and without the ranks of the professional philosophers that is probably not paralleled in the case of any of the other great problems of metaphysics.

There are, however, other considerations also which have governed my choice of subject. More particularly, I have been influenced by a conviction that the present state of philosophical opinion on free will is, for certain definitely assignable reasons, profoundly unsatisfactory. In my judgment, a thoroughly perverse attitude to the whole problem has been created by the almost universal acquiescence in the view that free will in what is often called the 'vulgar' sense is too obviously nonsensical a notion to deserve serious discussion. Free will in a more 'refined' sense—which is apt to mean free will purged of all elements that may cause embarrassment to a Deterministic psychology or a Deterministic metaphysics—is, it is understood, a conception which may be defended by the philosopher without loss of caste. But in its 'vulgar' sense, as maintained, for example, by the plain man, who clings to a belief in genuinely open possibilities, it is (we are told) a wild and even obnoxious delusion, long ago discredited for sober thinkers.

Now, as it happens, I myself firmly believe that free will, in something extremely like the 'vulgar' sense, is a fact. And I am anxious to-day to do what I can, within the limits of a single lecture, to justify that belief. I propose therefore to develop a statement of the Libertarian's position which will try to make clear why he finds himself obliged to hold what he does hold, and to follow this up with a critical examination of the grounds most in vogue among philosophers for impugning this position. Considerations of time will, I fear, compel a somewhat close economy in my treatment of objections. But I shall hope to say enough to instigate a doubt in some minds concerning the validity of certain very fashionable objections whose authority is often taken to be virtually final. And if no other good purpose is served, it will at least be of advantage if I can offer, in my positive statement, a target for the missiles of the critics more truly representative of Libertarianism than the targets at which they sometimes direct their fire—targets, I may add, upon which even the clumsiest of marksmen could hardly fail to register bull's-eyes.

Let us begin by noting that the problem of free will gets its urgency for the ordinary educated man by reason of its close connection with the conception of moral responsibility. When we regard a man as morally responsible for an act, we regard him as a legitimate object of moral praise or blame in respect of it. But it seems plain that a man cannot be a legitimate object of moral praise or blame for an act unless in willing the act he is in some important sense a 'free' agent. Evidently free will in some sense, therefore, is a pre-condition of moral responsibility. Without doubt it is the realization that any threat to freedom is thus a threat to moral responsibility—with all that that implies—combined with the knowledge that there are a variety of considerations, philosophic, scientific, and theological, tending to place freedom in jeopardy, that gives to the problem of free will its perennial and universal appeal. And it is therefore in close connection with the question of the conditions of moral responsibility that any discussion of the problem must proceed, if it is not to be academic in the worst sense of the term.

We raise the question at once, therefore, what are the conditions, in respect of freedom, which must attach to an act in order to make it a morally responsible act? It seems to me that the fundamental conditions are two. I shall state them with all possible brevity, for we have a long road to travel.

The first condition is the universally recognised one that the act must be *self*-caused, *self*-determined. But it is important to accept this condition in its full rigour. The agent must be not merely *a* cause but the *sole* cause of that for which he is deemed morally responsible. If entities other than the self have also a causal influence upon an act, then that act is not one for which we can say without qualification that the *self* is morally responsible. If in respect of it we hold the self responsible at all, it can only be for some feature of the act—assuming the possibility of disengaging such a feature—of which the self *is* the sole cause. I do not see how this conclusion can be evaded. But it has awkward implications which have led not a few people to abandon the notion of individual moral responsibility altogether.

This first condition, however, is quite clearly not sufficient. It is possible to conceive an act of which the agent is the sole cause, but which is at the same time an act *necessitated* by the agent's nature. Some philosophers have contended, for example, that the act of Divine creation is an act which issues necessarily from the Divine nature. In the case of such an act, where the agent could not do otherwise than he did, we must all agree, I think, that it would be inept to say that he *ought* to have done otherwise and is thus morally blameworthy, or *ought not* to have done otherwise and is thus morally praiseworthy. It is perfectly true that we do sometimes hold a person morally responsible for an act, even when we believe that he, being what he now is, virtually could not do otherwise. But underlying that judgment is always the assumption that the person has *come* to be what he now is in virtue of past acts of will in which he *was* confronted by real alternatives, by genuinely open possibilities: and, strictly speaking, it is in respect of these *past* acts of his that we praise or blame the agent *now*. For ultimate analysis, the agent's power of alternative action would seem to be an inexpugnable condition of his liability to moral praise or blame, i.e. of his moral responsibility.

We may lay down, therefore, that an act is a 'free' act in the sense required for moral responsibility only if the agent (*a*) is the sole cause of the act; and (*b*) could exert his causality in alternative ways. And it may be pointed out in passing that the acceptance of condition (*b*) implies the recognition of the inadequacy for moral freedom of mere 'self-determination'. The doctrine called 'Self-determinism' is often contrasted by its advocates with mere Determinism on the one hand and Indeterminism on the other, and pronounced to be the one true gospel. I must insist, however, that if 'Self-determinism' rejects condition (*b*), it cannot claim to be a doctrine of free will in the sense required to vindicate moral responsibility. The doctrine which demands, and asserts, the fulfilment of both conditions is the doctrine we call 'Libertarianism'. And it would in my opinion minister greatly to clarity if it were more widely recognized that for any doctrine which is not a species of Libertarianism to pose as a doctrine of 'free will' is mere masquerade.

And now, the conditions of free will being defined in these general terms, we have to ask whether human beings are in fact capable of performing free acts; and if so, where precisely such acts are to be found. In order to prepare the way for an answer, it is desirable, I think, that we should get clear at once about the significance of a certain very familiar, but none the less formidable, criticism of free will which the Self-determinist as well as the Libertarian has to meet. This is the criticism which bases itself upon the facts of heredity on the one hand and of environment on the other. I may briefly summarize the criticism as follows.

Every historic self has an hereditary nature consisting of a group of inborn propensities, in range more or less common to the race, but specific to the individual in their respective strengths. With this equipment the self just *happens* to be born. Strictly speaking, it antedates the existence of the self proper, i.e. the existence of the self-conscious subject, and it is itself the effect of a series of causes leading back to indefinitely remote antiquity. It follows, therefore, that any of the self's choices that manifests the influence of his hereditary nature is not a choice of which *he*, the actual historic self, is the sole cause. The choice is determined, at least in part, by factors external to the self. The same thing holds good of 'environment'. Every self is born and bred in a particular physical and social environment, not of his own choosing, which plays upon him in innumerable ways, encouraging this propensity, discouraging that, and so on. Clearly any of the self's choices that manifests the influence of environmental factors is likewise a choice which is determined, at least in part, by factors external to the self. But if we thus grant, as seems inevitable, that heredity and environment are external influences, where shall we find a choice in the whole history of a self that is not subject to external influence? Surely we must admit that every particular act of choice bears the marks of the agent's hereditary nature and environmental nurture; in which case a free act, in the sense of an act determined solely by the self, must be dismissed as a mere chimaera.

To this line of criticism the Self-determinist—T. H. Green is a typical example—has a stock reply. He urges that these factors, heredity and environment, are not, in so far as their operation in willing (and therefore in conduct proper) is concerned, 'external' to the self at all. For the act of willing, when we analyse it, reveals itself to be in its nature such that no end can be willed save in so far as it is conceived by the self as a good for the self. A 'native propensity' cannot function *as such* in willing. It can function only in so far as the self conceives its object as a good for the self. It follows that the self in willing is essentially *self*-determining; not moved from the outside, but moved always by its own conception of its own good. Inherited nature and environmental circumstance do play their part; but not as factors external to the self. They can function only in so far as their suggestions are, as it were, incorporated by the self in its conception of its own good. Consequently—so we are told—the threat to self-determination from the side of inheritance and environment disappears on an adequate analysis of the act of willing.

I am afraid, however, that this argument, though it contains important truth, cannot bear the heavy weight that is here imposed upon it. Let us grant that inheritance and environment can operate in willing only in the medium of the self's conception of its own good. But then let us ask, how is the self's conception of its own good constituted? Self-consciousness is required, of course: but mere self-conscious reflection *in vacuo* will not furnish the self with any conception of a personal good whatsoever. Obviously to answer the question in regard to any agent we are obliged to make reference to certain sheer external facts; viz., to the quality and strength of that person's inherited propensities, and to the nature of the influences that are brought to bear upon him from the side of environment. It seems certain, then, that the self's conception of its own good is influenced directly by its particular inheritance and environment. But to admit this surely involves the admission that external determination enters into choices. It may be true that the self's choices are always determined by its conception of its own good. But if what it conceives to be its own good is always dependent, at least partly, upon inheritance and environment, as external facts, then it is idle to deny that the self's choices are externally influenced likewise.

Indeed I cannot but regard the attempt to save self-determination by denying the externality of the influence of heredity and environment as a quite desperate expedient. It is significant that nobody really believes it in practice. The externality of these influences is taken for granted in our reflective practical judgments upon persons. On those occasions when we are in real earnest about giving a critical and considered estimate of a man's moral calibre— as, e.g., in any serious biographical study—we impose upon ourselves as a matter of course the duty of enquiring with scrupulous care into his hereditary propensities and environmental circumstances, with a view to discovering how far his conduct is influenced by these factors. And having traced these influences, we certainly do not regard the result as having no bearing on the question of the man's moral responsibility for his conduct. On the contrary, the very purpose of the enquiry is to enable us, by due appreciation of the *external* influences that affect his conduct, to gain as accurate a view as possible of that which can justly be attributed to the man's own *self*-determination. The allowances that we all of us do in practice make for hereditary and environmental influences in passing judgment on our fellows would be meaningless if we did not suppose these influences to be in a real sense 'external' to the self.

Now the recognition of this externality is, of course, just as serious a matter for the Libertarian as for the Self-determinist. For the Libertarian, as we saw, accepts condition (*a*) no less wholeheartedly than the Self-determinist does: i.e. that an act is free only if it is determined by the self and nothing but the self. But though we have not been *directly* advancing our course by these recent considerations, we have been doing so indirectly, by narrowing and sharpening the issue. We know now that condition (*a*) is not fulfilled by any act in respect of which inheritance or environment exerts a causal influence. For that type of influence has been shown to be in a real sense external to the self. The free act of which we are in search has therefore got to be one into which influences of this kind do not enter at all.

Moreover, one encouraging portent has emerged in the course of our brief discussion. For we noticed that our reflective practical judgments on persons, while fully recognizing the externality of the influence of heredity and environment, do nevertheless presuppose throughout that there *is something* in conduct which is genuinely self-determined; something which the agent contributes solely on his own initiative, unaffected by external influences; something for which, accordingly, he may justly be held morally responsible. That conviction may, of course, be a false one. But the fact of its widespread existence can hardly be without significance for our problem.

Let us proceed, then, by following up this clue. Let us ask, why do human beings so obstinately persist in believing that there is an indissoluble core of purely *self*-originated activity which even heredity and environment are powerless to affect? There can be little doubt, I think, of the answer in general terms. They do so, at bottom, because they feel certain of the existence of such activity from their immediate practical experience of themselves. Nor can there be in the end much doubt, I think, in what function of the self that activity is to be located. There seems to me to be one, and only one, function of the self with respect to which the agent can even pretend to have an assurance of that absolute self-origination which is here at issue. But to render precise the nature of that function is obviously of quite paramount importance: and we can do so, I think, only by way of a somewhat thorough analysis—which I now propose to attempt—of the experiential situation in which it occurs, viz., the situation of 'moral temptation'.

It is characteristic of that situation that in it I am aware of an end A which I believe to be morally right, and also of an end B, incompatible with A, towards which, in virtue of that system of conative dispositions which constitutes my 'character' as so far formed, I entertain a strong desire. There may be, and perhaps must be, desiring elements in my nature which are directed to A also. But what gives to the situation its specific character as one of moral temptation is that the urge of our desiring nature towards the right end, A, is felt to be *relatively* weak. We are sure that if our desiring nature is permitted to issue directly in action, it is end B that we shall choose. That is what is meant by saying, as William James does, that end B is 'in the line of least resistance' relatively to our conative dispositions. The expression is, of course, a metaphorical one, but it serves to describe, graphically enough, a situation of which we all have frequent experience, viz., where we recognize a specific end as that towards which the 'set' of our desiring nature most strongly inclines us, and which we shall indubitably choose if no inhibiting factor intervenes.

But inhibiting factors, we should most of us say, *may* intervene:
B*

and that in two totally different ways which it is vital to distinguish clearly. The inhibiting factor may be of the nature of another desire (or aversion), which operates by changing the balance of the desiring situation. Though at one stage I desire B, which I believe to be wrong, more strongly than I desire A, which I believe to be right, it may happen that before action is taken I become aware of certain hitherto undiscerned consequences of A which I strongly desire, and the result may be that now not *B* but *A* presents itself to me as the end in the line of least resistance. Moral temptation is here overcome by the simple process of ceasing to be a moral temptation.

That is one way, and probably by far the commoner way, in which an inhibiting factor intervenes. But it is certainly not regarded by the self who is confronted by moral temptation as the *only* way. In such situations we all believe, rightly or wrongly, that even although B *continues* to be in the line of least resistance, even although, in other words, the situation remains one with the characteristic marks of moral temptation, we *can* nevertheless align ourselves with A. We can do so, we believe, because we have the power to introduce a new energy, to make what we call an 'effort of will', whereby we are able to act contrary to the felt balance of mere desire, and to achieve the higher end despite the fact that it continues to be in the line of greater resistance relatively to our desiring nature. The self in practice believes that it has this power; and believes, moreover, that the decision rests solely with its self, here and now, whether this power be exerted or not.

Now the objective validity or otherwise of this belief is not at the moment in question. I am here merely pointing to its existence as a psychological fact. No amount of introspective analysis, so far as I can see, even tends to disprove that we do as a matter of fact believe, in situations of moral temptation, that it rests with our self absolutely to decide whether we exert the effort of will which will enable us to rise to duty, or whether we shall allow our desiring nature to take its course.

I have now to point out, further, how this act of moral decision, at least in the significance which it has for the agent himself, fulfils in full the two conditions which we found it necessary to lay down at the beginning for the kind of 'free' act which moral responsibility presupposes.

For obviously it is, in the first place, an act which the agent believes he could perform in alternative ways. He believes that it is genuinely open to him to put forth effort—in varying degrees, if the situation admits of that—or withhold it altogether. And when he *has* decided—in whatever way—he remains convinced that these alternative courses were really open to him.

It is perhaps a little less obvious, but, I think, equally certain, that the agent believes the second condition to be fulfilled likewise, i.e. that the act of decision is determined *solely* by his self. It appears less obvious, because we all realize that formed character has a great deal to do with the choices that we make; and formed character is, without a doubt, partly dependent on the external factors of heredity and environment. But it is crucial here that we should not misunderstand the precise nature of the influence which formed character brings to bear upon the choices that constitute conduct. No one denies that it determines, at least largely, what things we desire, and again how greatly we desire them. It may thus fairly be said to determine the felt balance of desires in the situation of moral temptation. But all that that amounts to is that formed character prescribes the nature of the situation *within* which the act of moral decision takes place. It does not in the least follow that it has any influence whatsoever in determining the act of decision itself—the decision as to whether we shall exert effort or take the easy course of following the bent of our desiring nature: take, that is to say, the course which, in virtue of the determining influence of our character as so far formed, we feel to be in the line of least resistance.

When one appreciates this, one is perhaps better prepared to recognize the fact that the agent himself in the situation of moral temptation does not, and indeed could not, regard his formed character as having any influence whatever upon his act of decision as such. For the very nature of that decision, as it presents itself to him, is as to whether he will or will not permit his formed character to dictate his action. In other words, the agent distinguishes sharply between the self which makes the decision, and the self which, as formed character, determines not the decision but the situation within which the decision takes place. Rightly or wrongly, the agent believes that through his act of decision he can oppose and transcend his own formed character in the interest of duty. We are therefore obliged to say, I think, that the agent *cannot* regard his formed character as in any sense a determinant of the act of decision as such. The act is felt to be a genuinely creative act, originated by the self *ad hoc*, and by the self alone.

Here then, if my analysis is correct, in the function of moral decision in situations of moral temptation, we have an act of the self which at least *appears to the agent* to satisfy both of the conditions of freedom which we laid down at the beginning. The vital question now is, is this 'appearance' true or false? Is the act of decision really what it appears to the agent to be, determined solely by the self, and capable of alternative forms of expression? If it is, then we have here a free act which serves as an adequate basis for moral responsibility. We shall be entitled to regard the agent as morally praiseworthy or morally blameworthy according as he decides to put forth effort or to let his desiring nature have its way. We shall be entitled, in short, to judge the agent as he most certainly judges himself in the situation of moral temptation. If, on the other hand, there is good reason to believe that the agent is the victim of illusion in supposing his act of decision to bear this character, then in my opinion the whole conception of moral responsibility must be jettisoned altogether. For it seems to me certain that there is no other function of the self that even looks as though it satisfied the required conditions of the free act.

Now in considering the claim to truth of this belief of our practical consciousness, we should begin by noting that the onus of proof rests upon the critic who rejects this belief. Until cogent evidence to the contrary is adduced, we are entitled to put our trust in a belief which is so deeply embedded in our experience as practical beings as to be, I venture to say, ineradicable from it. Anyone who doubts whether it is ineradicable may be invited to think himself imaginatively into a situation of moral temptation as we have above described it, and then to ask himself whether in that situation he finds it possible to *disbelieve* that his act of decision has the characteristics in question. I have no misgivings about the answer. It is possible to disbelieve only when we are thinking abstractly about the situation; not when we are living through it, either actually or in imagination. This fact certainly establishes a strong prima facie presumption in favour of the Libertarian position. Nevertheless I agree that we shall have to weigh carefully several criticisms of high authority before we can feel justified in asserting free will as an ultimate and unqualified truth.

Fortunately for our purpose, however, there are some lines of criticism which, although extremely influential in the recent past, may at the present time be legitimately ignored. We are not to-day confronted, for example, by any widely accepted system of metaphysic with implications directly hostile to free will. Only a decade or two ago one could hardly hope to gain a sympathetic hearing for a view which assigned an ultimate initiative to finite selves, unless one were prepared first to show reason for rejecting the dominant metaphysical doctrine that all things in the universe are the expression of a single Mind or Spirit. But the challenge so lately offered by monistic Idealism has in the present age little more significance than the challenge once offered by monistic Materialism.

Much the same thing holds good of the challenge from the side of physical science. Libertarianism is certainly inconsistent with a rigidly determinist theory of the physical world. It is idle to pretend that there can be open possibilities for psychical decision, while at the same time holding that the physical events in which such decisions manifest themselves are determined in accordance with irrevocable law. But whereas until a few years ago the weight of scientific authority was thrown overwhelmingly on the side of a universal determinism of physical phenomena, the situation has, as everybody knows, profoundly altered during the present century more especially since the advent of Planck's Quantum Theory and Heisenberg's Principle of Uncertainty. Very few scientists to-day would seek to impugn free will on the ground of any supposed implications of the aims or achievements of physical science. I am not myself, I should perhaps add in passing, disposed to rest any part of the case against a universal physical determinism upon these recent dramatic developments of physical science. In my view there never were in the established results of physical science cogent reasons for believing that the apparently universal determinism of inorganic processes holds good also of the processes of the human body. The only inference I here wish to draw from the trend of present-day science is that it removes from any *contemporary* urgency the problem of meeting one particular type of objection to free will. And it is with the contemporary situation that I am in this paper anxious to deal.

I may turn at once, therefore, to lines of argument which do still enjoy a wide currency among anti-Libertarians. And I shall begin with one which, though it is a simple matter to show its irrelevance to the Libertarian doctrine as I have stated it, is so extremely popular that it cannot safely be ignored.

The charge made is that the Libertarian view is incompatible with the *predictability* of human conduct. For we do make rough predictions of people's conduct, on the basis of what we know of their character, every day of our lives, and there can be no doubt that the practice, within certain limits, is amply justified by results. Indeed if it were not so, social life would be reduced to sheer chaos. The close relationship between character and conduct which prediction postulates really seems to be about as certain as anything can be. But the Libertarian view, it is urged, by ascribing to the self a mysterious power of decision uncontrolled by character, and capable of issuing in acts inconsistent with character, denies that continuity between character and conduct upon which prediction depends. If Libertarianism is true, prediction is impossible. But prediction *is* possible, therefore Libertarianism is untrue.

My answer is that the Libertarian view is perfectly compatible with prediction within certain limits, and that there is no empirical evidence at all that prediction is in fact possible beyond these limits. The following considerations will, I think, make the point abundantly clear.

(1) There is no question, on our view, of a free will that can will just anything at all. The range of possible choices is limited by the agent's character in every case; for nothing can be an object of possible choice which is not suggested by either the agent's desires or his moral ideals, and these depend on 'character' for us just as much as for our opponents. We have, indeed explicitly recognized at an earlier stage that character determines the situation within which the act of moral decision takes place, although not the act of moral decision itself. This consideration obviously furnishes a broad basis for at least approximate predictions.

(2) There is *one* experiential situation, and *one only*, on our view, in which there is any possibility of the act of will not being in accordance with character; viz. the situation in which the course which formed character prescribes is a course in conflict with the agent's moral ideal: in other words, the situation of moral temptation. Now this is a situation of comparative rarity. Yet with respect to all other situations in life we are in full agreement

with those who hold that conduct is the response of the agent's formed character to the given situation. Why should it not be so? There could be no reason, on our view any more than on another, for the agent even to consider deviating from the course which his formed character prescribes and he most strongly desires, *unless* that course is believed by him to be incompatible with what is right.

(3) Even within that one situation which is relevant to free will, our view can still recognize a certain basis for prediction. In that situation our character as so far formed prescribes a course opposed to duty, and an effort of will is required if we are to deviate from that course. But of course we are all aware that a greater effort of will is required in proportion to the degree in which we have to transcend our formed character in order to will the right. Such action is, as we say, 'harder'. But if action is 'harder' in proportion as it involves deviation from formed character, it seems reasonable to suppose that, on the whole, action will be of rarer occurrence in that same proportion: though perhaps we may not say that at any level of deviation it becomes flatly impossible. It follows that even with respect to situations of moral temptation we may usefully employ our knowledge of the agent's character as a clue to prediction. It will be a clue of limited, but of by no means negligible, value. It will warrant us in predicting, e.g., of a person who has become enslaved to alcohol, that he is unlikely, even if fully aware of the moral evil of such slavery, to be successful immediately and completely in throwing off its shackles. Predictions of this kind we all make often enough in practice. And there seems no reason at all why a Libertarian doctrine should wish to question their validity.

Now when these three considerations are borne in mind, it becomes quite clear that the doctrine we are defending is compatible with a very substantial measure of predictability indeed. And I submit that there is not a jot of empirical evidence that any larger measure than this obtains in fact.

Let us pass on then to consider a much more interesting and, I think, more plausible criticism. It is constantly objected against the Libertarian doctrine that it is fundamentally *unintelligible*. Libertarianism holds that the act of moral decision is the *self's* act, and yet insists at the same time that it is not influenced by any of those determinate features in the self's nature which go to constitute its 'character'. But, it is asked, do not these two propositions contradict one another? Surely a *self*-determination which is determination by something other than the self's *character* is a contradiction in terms? What meaning is there in the conception of a 'self' in abstraction from its 'character'? If you really wish to maintain, it is urged, that the act of decision is not determined by the self's character, you ought to admit frankly that it is not determined by the *self* at all. But in that case, of course, you will not be advocating a freedom which lends any kind of support to moral responsibility; indeed very much the reverse.

Now this criticism, and all of its kind, seem to me to be the product of a simple, but extraordinarily pervasive, error: the error of confining one's self to the categories of the external observer in dealing with the actions of human agents. Let me explain.

It is perfectly true that the standpoint of the external observer, which we are obliged to adopt in dealing with physical processes, does not furnish us with even a glimmering of a notion of what can be meant by an entity which acts causally and yet not through any of the determinate features of its character. So far as we confine ourselves to external observation, I agree that this notion must seem to us pure nonsense. But then we are *not* obliged to confine ourselves to external observation in dealing with the human agent. Here, though here alone, we have the inestimable advantage of being able to apprehend operations from the *inside*, from the standpoint of *living experience*. But if we do adopt this internal standpoint—surely a proper standpoint, and one which we should be only too glad to adopt if we could in the case of other entities—the situation is entirely changed. We find that we not merely can, but constantly do, attach meaning to a causation which is the self's causation but is yet not exercised by the self's character. We have seen as much already in our analysis of the situation of moral temptation. When confronted by such a situation, we saw, we are certain that it lies with our *self* to decide whether we shall let our character as so far formed dictate our action or whether we shall by effort oppose its dictates and rise to duty. We are certain, in other words, that the act is *not* determined by our *character*, while we remain equally certain that the act *is* determined by our *self*.

Or look, for a further illustration (since the point we have to make here is of the very first importance for the whole free will controversy), to the experience of effortful willing itself, where the act of decision has found expression in the will to rise to duty. In such an experience we are certain that it is our self which makes the effort. But we are equally certain that the effort does not flow from that system of conative dispositions which we call our formed character; for the very function that the effort has for us is to enable us to act against the 'line of least resistance', i.e. to act in a way *contrary* to that to which our formed character inclines us.

I conclude, therefore, that those who find the Libertarian doctrine of the self's causality in moral decision inherently unintelligible find it so simply because they restrict themselves, quite arbitrarily, to an inadequate standpoint: a standpoint from which, indeed, a genuinely creative activity, if it existed, never *could* be apprehended.

It will be understood, of course, that it is no part of my purpose to deny that the act of moral decision is in *one* sense 'unintelligible'. If by the 'intelligibility' of an act we mean that it is capable, at least in principle, of being inferred as a consequence of a given ground, then naturally my view is that the act in question is '*un*intelligible'. But that, presumably, is not the meaning of 'intelligibility' in the critic's mind when he says that the Libertarian holds an 'unintelligible' doctrine. If it were all he meant, he would merely be pointing out that Libertarianism is not compatible with Determinism! And that tautologous pronouncement would hardly deserve the title of 'criticism'. Yet, strangely enough, not all of the critics seem to be quite clear on this matter. The Libertarian often has the experience of being challenged by the critic to tell him *why*, on his view, the agent now decides to put forth moral effort and now decides not to, with the obviously intended implication that if the Libertarian cannot say 'why' he should give up his theory. Such critics apparently fail to see that if the Libertarian *could* say why he would already have given up his theory! Obviously to demand 'intelligibility' in this sense is simply to prejudge the whole issue in favour of Determinism. The sense in which the critic is entitled to demand intelligibility of our doctrine is simply this; he may demand that the kind of action which our doctrine imputes to human selves should not be, for ultimate analysis, meaningless. And in that sense, as I have already argued, our doctrine is perfectly intelligible.

Let us suppose, then, that the Determinist, confronted by the plain evidence of our practical self-consciousness, now recognizes his obligation to give up the position that the Libertarian doctrine is without qualification 'meaningless', and concedes that from the standpoint of our practical self-consciousness at any rate it is 'meaningful'. And let us ask what will be his next move. So far as I can see, his most likely move now will be to attack the value of that 'internal' standpoint, contrasting it unfavourably, in respect of its claim to truth, with the rational, objective, standpoint of 'pure philosophy'. 'I admit,' he may tell us, 'that there is begotten in the self, in the practical experience you refer to, a belief in a self-causality which is yet not a causality exercised through the self's character. But surely this must weigh but lightly in the balance against the proposition, which appeals to our reason with axiomatic certainty, that an act cannot be caused by a self if it has no ground in the determinate nature of that self. If the choice lies between either disbelieving that rational proposition, or dismissing the evidence of practical self-consciousness as illusion, it is the latter alternative which in my opinion any sane philosophy is bound to adopt.'

But a very little reflection suffices to show that this position is in reality no improvement at all on that from which the critic has just fallen back. For it is evident that the proposition alleged to be axiomatic is axiomatic, at most, only to a reason which knows nothing of acts or events save as they present themselves to an external observer. It obviously is *not* axiomatic to a reason whose field of apprehension is broadened to include the data furnished by the direct experience of acting. In short, the proposition is axiomatic, at most, only to reason functioning *abstractly*; which most certainly cannot be identified with reason functioning *philosophically*.

What is required of the critic, of course, if he is to make good his case, is a reasoned justification of his cavalier attitude towards the testimony of practical self-consciousness. That is the primary desideratum. And the lack of it in the bulk of Determinist literature is in my opinion something of a scandal. Without it, the criticism we have just been examining is sheer dogmatism. It is, indeed, dogmatism of a peculiarly perverse kind. For the situation is, in effect, as follows. From our practical self-consciousness we gain a notion of a genuinely creative act—which might be defined as an act which nothing determines save the agent's doing of it. Of such a character is the act of moral decision as we experience it. But the critic says 'No! This sort of thing cannot be. A person cannot without affront to reason be conceived to be the author of an act which bears, *ex hypothesi*, no intelligible relation to his character. A mere intuition of practical self-consciousness is the solitary prop of this fantastic notion, and surely that is quite incapable of bearing the weight that you would thrust upon it.' Now observe the perversity! The critic says, excluding the evidence of practical self-consciousness, the notion makes nonsense. In other words, excluding the only evidence there ever *could* be for such a notion, the notion makes nonsense! For, of course, if there should be such a thing as creative activity, there is absolutely no other way save an intuition of practical self-consciousness in which we could become aware of it. Only from the inside, from the standpoint of the agent's living experience, can 'activity' possibly be apprehended. So that what the critic is really doing is to condemn a notion as nonsensical on the ground that the only evidence for it is the only evidence there ever could be for it.

Up to the present I have deemed it advisable, in order better to cover the ground, to deal with typical rather than with individual criticisms of the Libertarian position. I wish, however, to depart from that precedent in one instance before I conclude. I am anxious to come to somewhat closer grips with the criticism which Professor C. D. Broad makes in an inaugural lecture published under the title 'Determinism, Indeterminism, and Libertarianism': a work which, short as it is, seems to me to offer incomparably the best elucidation of the problem of freedom that we have. Mr Broad's criticism does not, as I shall try to show, raise any really new point of principle. But its author's pre-eminence in contemporary philosophy, combined with the recency of this pronouncement, makes it desirable to give a rather particular attention to his views.

The business of elucidation—with which by far the greater part of his lecture is concerned—is in my opinion executed almost to perfection. I acquiesce with especial pleasure in the position Mr Broad adopts on three important aspects of the problem. (1) He takes as his starting-point the conditions implied in moral obligability; the only starting-point, as I believe, which will ensure that the freedom to be discussed will be the freedom which constitutes the real problem. (2) He is entirely clear that the freedom implied in moral obligability is a freedom in which there are genuinely open possibilities before the self: a freedom in which, to use Mr Broad's terminology, our volition is not merely 'conditionally' but 'categorically' substitutable: i.e. a freedom in which the agent 'could have done otherwise than he did' even though the whole set of conditions environing his decision remained constant. And (3) his analysis culminates in the frank recognition of what he calls the 'effortful factor' in willing as the crux of the whole problem. It is by reference to this that the Libertarian position has got to be defined. What the Libertarian wants to say, he tells us, is that where an effort of will is put forth to reinforce my desire for a course A, 'it is logically consistent with all the nomic, occurrent, dispositional, and background facts that no effort should have been made, or that it should have been directed towards reinforcing the desire for B instead of the desire for A, or that it should have been put forth more or less strongly than it actually was in favour of the desire for A'; and that, nevertheless, the putting forth of the effort was no mere *accident*, but was 'in a unique and peculiar way' determined '*by the agent or self*'.

Now up to this point, p. 43 of a book of less than fifty pages, I am, with only a few relatively unimportant reservations, in almost verbal agreement with what Mr Broad says. Yet I doubt whether even those who, unlike myself, are in sympathy also with Mr Broad's ultimate verdict will escape disappointment from the remaining few pages. The problem of free will has at this juncture been no more than stated. But for Mr Broad, apparently, the mere statement is virtually tantamount to a Determinist solution. In one single paragraph he now proceeds to offer his reasons for rejecting the Libertarian position as certainly false. Let me quote from it the passage on which this summary dismissal turns. 'The putting forth of an effort', he says, 'of a certain intensity, in a certain direction, at a certain moment, for a certain duration, is quite clearly an event or process, however unique and peculiar it may be in other respects. It is therefore subject to any conditions which self-evidently apply to every event, as such. Now it is surely quite evident that, if the beginning of a certain process at a certain time is determined at all, its total cause *must* contain as an essential factor another event or process which *enters into* the moment from which the determined event or process *issues*. I see no prima facie

objection to there being events that are not completely determined. But, in so far as an event *is* determined, an essential factor
in its total cause must be other events' (p. 44).

I wish to suggest, with all respect, that we have here merely
another manifestation of the cardinal fallacy of anti-Libertarian
criticism, the fallacy of bringing to the interpretation of human
action categories derived solely from the stand point of the
external observer.

For consider. 'It is surely quite evident', says Mr Broad, 'that if
the beginning of a certain process at a certain time is determined
at all, its total cause *must* contain as an essential factor another
event or process which *enters into* the moment from which the
determined event or process *issues*.' On this contention his whole
argument rests. On this, and this alone, depends his conclusion
that the act of moral decision is preconditioned, and therefore
not, as Libertarianism holds, creative. But *is* this contention
evident? It may seem evident with respect to those events to which
we stand in the relation solely of external observer. But that is not
the only relation in which we can stand to events. If the decision
to put forth or forbear from putting forth effort in the situation
of moral temptation is an event—and I agree that from one point
of view it may rightly be called so—it is an event which we can
know from within. And, as known from within, it is the *reverse* of
evident that its total cause must contain another event which
enters into the moment from which the determined event issues.
On the contrary, from the internal standpoint of the experiment
himself, it is evident that while the event which is the moral
decision is determined, in that the self is recognized as its author,
there is no *other* event concerned in the matter at all. What
determines my 'deed', in the act of moral decision, is felt to be
nothing but my doing of it. And this 'doing' is of course not some
other event antecedent to the deed itself. It is just the deed (or
decision) as *act*, which is the other side of the deed (or decision)
as *event*. It seems to me perfectly clear, therefore, that the proposition which Mr Broad says is 'quite evident' must in fact
appear to be a false proposition to any moral agent engaged in the
actual function of moral decision.

It will be seen, then, that my objection to Mr Broad's criticism
is identical in principle with the general objection which I urged
earlier. Mr Broad is not entitled to say that certain conditions of

the occurrence of an event as such are 'self-evidently' necessary, if that 'self-evidence' is achieved only by ignoring the testimony of our practical self-consciousness. This holds good, it seems to me, irrespective of any question as to the ultimate value of that testimony. The point is that if that testimony is relevant to the problem at all—and if it is not, I should very much like to know *why* it is not—then it *cannot* be 'self-evident' that the conditions Mr Broad alleges are necessary conditions. It may possibly be the case, though I do not believe it to be so, that Mr Broad's ultimate verdict is the correct one: that Libertarianism is a false theory, and the notion of 'categorical obligability' in consequence a delusive notion. But it is not the case that, in Mr Broad's words, 'Libertarianism is self-evidently impossible'. Mr Broad has helped enormously towards the solution of the free will problem by his masterly statement of the issues involved. But, if I am right, much laborious analysis and deliberation upon *pros* and *cons* (which to Mr Broad, for the reasons we have seen, appears as a work of mere supererogation) must ensue before we can possibly be in a position to say that the problem is 'solved' one way or the other.

And here, to my regret, my own too brief discussion must terminate. There is much more that I should have liked to say: much more, in my opinion, that badly requires to be said. I should have liked, perhaps above all, to have been able to give more space to an analysis of the experience we call 'effort of will', and to have attempted to expose the fallacies which seem to me to underlie all attempts to explain away that experience by resolving it into something other than itself. That, however, is a matter with which I have partially dealt on a previous occasion, and to which I propose to return under conditions more appropriate to the full-length treatment which can alone be of much service on a difficult psychological theme of this kind. Meantime I can only hope that the little I have been able to say may do something towards regaining for free will in the 'vulgar' sense a place in serious philosophical discussion: that it may do something—to use language of an appropriate vulgarity—towards putting Libertarianism 'on the map' once more. It is not, in my opinion, 'on the map' at all at present. It cannot be, when critics are so often content to make slogans and shibboleths do the work of analysis and argument; when a few satirical references to the 'mysterious fiat' of a 'pure ego' are regarded in so many quarters as a sufficient rejoinder to the Libertarian's claims. Prejudicial phrases like these have certainly a good deal of power. They are evocative of an acutely hostile emotional atmosphere. But, unless accompanied by the most careful analysis, they seem to me to stand for bad habits rather than for good reasons. And it would be no disservice to philosophy if they were extruded from the literature of the free will problem altogether.

THE PSYCHOLOGY OF EFFORT OF WILL

I should like to begin by emphasizing the word 'psychology' in the title of this paper. My whole concern will be with the *experience* of making what we call 'effort of will'—with its psychological nature, its psychological context, and its psychological antecedents. That psychological analysis of this experience must have an important bearing upon central problems of metaphysics, I am very far from doubting. But obviously we must first of all get a true view of the psychological facts before we can usefully study their metaphysical implications. As will become sufficiently clear, I think, from what follows, this is by no means so simple a matter as it has often been taken to be.

My paper will fall roughly into two Sections. The first, and longer, Section will be occupied with a critical consideration of the views of others, and its results will be almost wholly negative. In the second Section I shall attempt something in the way of positive construction. There are, however, some preliminary matters upon which a few words should be said before coming to actual grips with our problem.

In the first place, we want a general description of the experiential situation in which effort of will is located, sufficient at least for purposes of identification. For the term effort of will is at times rather carelessly used, and is allowed to denote psychical processes which we should certainly not, on due reflection, identify with efforts of will.

There is some confusion, for example, between effort of will and the activity of willing. It is important to be clear that these are quite distinct phenomena. No doubt there is an activity of a sort involved in all willing or choosing; but to be conscious of that activity is not necessarily to be conscious of exerting effort of will. If I am considering how I may most enjoyably spend the evening, and choose, as the occupation which seems most attractive, to read the latest P. G. Wodehouse, I am, indeed, conscious of *choosing*, but it would be sheer nonsense to say that I am conscious of making an effort of will. I am choosing the course which is also the course towards which I feel that my desiring nature most strongly inclines me; and wherever that is the case—as it probably is in some 99 per cent of our choices—I think we must all agree that we are not conscious in our choosing of exerting what we call effort of will.

It is fairly evident, I think, that we are conscious of making an effort of will *only* when we choose a course that is contrary to the course towards which we feel that our desiring nature most strongly inclines us. The most obvious case, accepted by most writers on the subject as typical, occurs when, as we say, we succeed in 'overcoming a temptation'. What we mean when we so speak seems clear enough. The 'temptation' consists in the fact that while believing a course X to be morally superior to a course Y, we are conscious of our desiring nature as inclining us more strongly to Y than to X. In William James's terminology, Y is felt by us to be 'in the line of least resistance', relatively to our desiring nature. In choosing X we seem to ourselves to be acting in the line of greater resistance—not necessarily, as is more commonly said, in the line of *greatest* resistance[1]—and to be succeeding in doing so by virtue of making this so-called effort of will whereby we somehow reinforce the energy of the weaker desire.

So far nothing has been said with which any psychologist is likely seriously to quarrel. The trouble begins when we attempt a closer study of the psychological nature of this ostensibly new energy which is added to that of the weaker desire. Is it a unique form of energy, as the agent himself is apt to suppose, different in kind from that energy of the desires which is the dynamic of at least most of our choices, and the antecedents of which can be traced with some show of scientific rigour to determinate elements in the agent's psychical make-up of instincts, emotions, sentiments and the like? Or is it, despite first appearances, reducible to some specific manifestation of the energy of desire in a determinate

[1] It is clear that we sometimes exert an effort of will in order to achieve an end recognized to be *higher* than that to which our desiring nature inclines us, but at the same time recognized not to be the *highest* end. In such cases it would seem that the latter, but not the former, end will be felt to be in the line of *greatest* resistance. The former end will be felt to be merely in the line of *greater* resistance—or perhaps just 'resistance'—relatively to our desiring nature. The point, however, is not of first importance, and in dealing later with certain psychological theories I shall use whatever form of words their advocates prefer.

context of circumstances which the psychologist can make plain to us? These are, broadly speaking, the alternatives between which the student of the problem has to choose.

There is not much doubt which of these alternatives has proved the more attractive to most psychologists. With James as almost the solitary exception, they have preferred the second alternative. Nor is this surprising. The psychologist is a scientist, and the scientist, as such, has a predilection for the discovery of as much law and order as possible in his subject-matter. Now, so long as choices are universally explicable in terms of desires, then, since desires themselves, in their various degrees of strength, are fairly intelligible, though often complex, products of determinate instincts, emotions and sentiments, there seems no serious obstacle in principle to regarding the psychical process of choice as a law-abiding member of a law-abiding system. If, on the other hand, choices can be influenced by some mysterious form of energy not reducible to that of desire, the causal continuity which the psychologist *qua* scientist desiderates is gravely threatened. It is thus not unnatural that the psychologist should be averse to the admission of this seemingly obstreperous element. He may even be commended, indeed, if he refuses to admit it until he has first tried out the alternative hypothesis for all that it is worth, and a little more.

And there is a further factor, I think, which has not been without its effect in determining the attitude of psychologists to our subject. Psychologists, until very recently, have also been philosophers, or, at the least, sufficiently interested in philosophy to be stirred by the prevailing currents of philosophic thought. Now in dealing with the problem of free will, the one thing upon which respectable philosophers of all parties have been agreed is that it is monstrous to admit as a subjective determinant of the will any element which has not intelligible roots in the character of the agent. An act of will which does not spring from the self's character, it is said, is obviously not the self's act at all. It is of no more use to the wise Libertarian than to the Determinist. This may fairly be said to have established itself as a philosophical cliché. It is also, as I believe, and as I have argued more than once elsewhere, a devastating error which has played havoc with the whole free will controversy. My purpose at the moment, however, is merely to point out that here, in the climate of philosophical opinion, there has been an additional encouragement to the psychologist to give a preference to one of the two rival hypotheses concerning the experience of will-effort. It is, I hope, not unfair to suggest that psychologists have often approached the analysis of the experience of will-effort with a rather definite expectation of finding that, even from the standpoint of psychology, there is nothing which lends countenance to the notion of a form of mental energy which, while not intelligibly rooted in character, can yet influence the act of choice.

One further word before commencing consideration of the more important of the psychological analyses which proceed along what, for the sake of a convenient label, we may call 'Determinist' lines. We ought to be clear at the outset about the fundamental requirement which any such analysis must fulfil. If the explanation it offers is really going to *explain*, it must give an account of the psychical factors involved, and of their relationship, such that any person who faithfully constructs this complex experience in imagination is able to say 'Yes, when these conditions are satisfied in my experience, I do find that I have the experience that I am accustomed to call "effort of will"'. Otherwise, the psychologist is not explaining the experience, but merely explaining it away. His explanation is really a type of *ignoratio elenchi*. Whether or not any of the theories we are now about to examine are free from this fatal defect remains to be seen.

MCDOUGALL'S VIEW

It is natural to take one's start from the theory advanced by Professor McDougall in his *Social Psychology*. No one, so far as I know, has offered so thorough an analysis from the Determinist standpoint, and his conclusions are both well known and, apparently, widely approved.

McDougall leaves us in no doubt as to the motive inspiring the analysis he is about to offer. The considerations which we have noticed as encouraging the tendency to a Deterministic analysis operate undisguisedly in Professor McDougall's mind. He is aware that the plain man tends to interpret his effort of will in Libertarian terms. But McDougall is convinced that the Libertarian must be wrong. For, he tells us, 'the acceptance of the Libertarian doctrine in its more extreme form'—by which

McDougall means primarily, I think, a Libertarianism for which
the self is not determined in all its choices at least by its own
character—'would be incompatible with any hope that a science of
society, in any proper sense of the word "science", may be
achieved'.[1] 'Some attempt must therefore be made', he goes on, 'to
show that the effort of volition is not the mysterious and utterly
incomprehensible process the extreme Libertarians would have it
to be; but that it is to be accounted for by the same principles as
other modes of human activity; that it involves no new principles
of activity and energy, but only a more subtle and complex inter-
play of these impulses which actuate all animal behaviour and in
which the ultimate mystery of mind and life resides.'[2]

How then does McDougall attempt to implement this undertaking?

Let us begin by reminding ourselves of the psychological
setting within which effort of will, whatever it may turn out to be,
is admitted to occur. McDougall would not, I think, dissent from
any item in the description we gave earlier, and he does, in fact,
accept almost in so many words James's statement of the situation
which we have ourselves followed. The essence of the situation
was, we saw, that in it the agent contemplates two mutually
exclusive courses, X and Y, towards the former of which, X, he has
a desire which he feels as weaker but believes to be higher, and
towards the latter of which, Y, he has a desire which he feels as
stronger but believes to be lower. The end Y is felt to be in the
line of least resistance, relatively to the agent's desiring nature.
It is the end towards which his desiring nature, as it stands, most
strongly inclines him. Towards the end X, on the other hand, his
desire is felt to be relatively weak. End X has, however, the additional claim upon the agent's interest of being the end believed to
be 'higher'—i.e. it is vested in his eyes with a certain moral
authority relatively to end Y.

So much is matter of common agreement. It is also agreed that
we do, in fact, sometimes choose X, even though it is felt to be in
the line of greater resistance; and that it is precisely in making
such choices that we are conscious of exerting effort of will. The
problem is to give an account of what happens in these 'effortful'
volitions. That the energy of the weaker desire is *somehow* 'reinforced' seems certain; and presumably the experience of effort is

---

[1] *Social Psychology*, p. 199.   [2] *Ibid*, p. 200.

the experience of that 'reinforcing'. But in what precisely does this reinforcing consist?

Stripped to its barest essentials, McDougall's account of it is as follows. At first we do desire Y, the lower end, more strongly than we desire X, the higher end. But prior to our actual choice certain new desires intervene and ally themselves with the desire for X. These new desires are excited from within the self-regarding sentiment, which is defined by McDougall as 'the system of emotional and conative dispositions that is organized about the idea of the self, and is always brought into play to some extent when the idea of the self rises to the focus of consciousness'.[1] The consequence of the increment of strength which the desire for X draws from these new desires—desires emanating from self-respect, pride, and the like—is that the desire for X is enabled to win the mastery over the desire for Y. It has become, in short, in virtue of these reinforcements, the stronger desire. Hence, so McDougall contends, the agent's choice of X becomes perfectly intelligible to us without our being obliged to acquiesce in the postulation of any mysterious new energy. Effortful volition is simply—to quote the definition at which McDougall eventually arrives—'the supporting or reinforcing of a desire or conation by the co-operation of an impulse excited within the self-regarding sentiment'.[2]

Now without doubt this theory of McDougall's has a good deal of plausibility. For my part, I should not at all deny that the process described by McDougall, and supported by a wealth of aptly chosen examples, does very often take place. Indeed, I should even admit that McDougall has here accurately described the most common way in which a moral agent, confronted by a temptation, succeeds in choosing the right. The trouble is that this way is just *not* the way that the agent adopts in those cases in which he seems to himself to be exerting effort of will. The psychical process which McDougall describes could not, it seems to me, give rise to the experience of effort of will. For consider. What happens, according to McDougall is that the desire which was originally the weaker becomes now, through the co-operation of desires emanating from the self-regarding sentiment, the stronger desire. Hence it must now be X, the 'higher' end, that is felt to be in the line of least resistance. But if X is now felt to be in the line of least

---

[1] *Social Psychology*, p. 213.　　　　[2] *Ibid*, p. 214.

resistance, how could one possibly suppose one's self to be *exerting an effort of will* in order to achieve it? Whatever else is involved in the experience of effortful willing, there is at least involved always the consciousness of acting contrary to the line of least resistance. Yet if McDougall's account be the true one, we are, after all, merely choosing what we most strongly desire, and we ought therefore to be conscious of acting not *against* but *in* the line of least resistance; unless, indeed, one cares to take refuge in the desperate assumption—to which I confess I can attach no intelligible meaning—that that which we most strongly desire may be felt by us as *not* that which we most strongly desire.

What McDougall has failed to see is that there are *two* ways— there is not just one way—in which a moral agent may seem to himself to overcome temptation. It is perfectly correct to say with McDougall that in a situation of moral temptation reflection upon the implications of the two opposed courses often brings into play new desires and aversions, more particularly desires and aversions emanating from the self-regarding sentiment, that these additional forces may have the effect of weighting the balance of the desiring situation in favour of the higher course, and that the agent is thereby enabled to choose the higher course. That is one way, and, as I have already granted, probably the most common way. The temptation in such cases is overcome, we may say, by ceasing to be a temptation. The lower end ceases to be felt by us as exerting a stronger attraction for our desiring nature than the higher end, and the willing of the latter accordingly takes place without any consciousness of effort. The other way in which we seem to ourselves to overcome temptation is by exerting effort of will. Whatever may be the ultimate analysis of this latter way, at least it seems certain that it cannot be coincident with that of the former way. McDougall has, as I think, confused the two, with the result that, having set out to explain what happens when we experience an effort of will in resisting temptation, what he actually gives us is an explanation of what happens when we resist a temptation without experiencing an effort of will.

Before we take final leave of McDougall's solution, it will be worth our while to notice a brief 'gloss' on that solution by Mr Wisdom in his *Problems of Mind and Matter*.

Wisdom accepts in principle McDougall's account of what happens when we act in the line of greater resistance. It is always a matter of the reinforcing of the weaker desire by certain other desires. But Wisdom draws attention to a fact not explicitly noticed by McDougall, e.g., that there are many cases in which the most careful introspection does not enable us to discover these new desires (or 'motives', as Wisdom prefers to call them) whose introduction is, on McDougall's theory, supposed to determine the decision. We must even admit, he contends, that 'we can sometimes be sure that the observable motives were not the complete cause of the decision'.[1] Ought we then to conclude that in these cases some factor is operative other than the motive of desire? Wisdom sees no reason to embrace this dangerous alternative. McDougall's theory will still hold if we incorporate into it a recognition of the existence of *unobservable* desires. For 'how do we know' asks Wisdom, 'that there is not some other motive which is *unobservable* and which yet affects one's decisions and one's acts? We cannot know this unless we assume that every desire affecting decision can be detected by introspection. And no one will maintain this; especially in view of the evidence which the psycho-analysts provide for motives undiscoverable by introspection.'[2]

The point seems to me fairly taken, and I imagine that McDougall would have accepted what Wisdom says here as a legitimate supplement to his own account. It is necessary to make clear, however, that, effective as Wisdom's appeal to sub-conscious desires is in rebutting one obvious criticism of McDougall's theory, it does not touch the particular criticism of it which I have just been advancing. The cardinal defect of McDougall's theory, I argued, was that whereas in exerting effort of will we seem to ourselves to be acting contrary to the line of least resistance, the process which McDougall describes would lead us to suppose ourselves to be acting along the line of least resistance. The use to which Mr Wisdom puts the notion of the subconscious does nothing to meet this objection.

On the other hand—and this is why I have deemed it desirable to make reference to Wisdom's view—it is possible to conceive of an extended use of the notion of the subconscious which might seem to hold out promise of a way of escape. For where the new, reinforcing desires are unobservable by the agent, may not the increment of power which they bring be unobservable likewise?

<hr>

[1] *Mind and Matter*, p. 129.   [2] *Ibid.*

And if so, will it not be the fact, in such cases at any rate, that the agent will still *feel* that he is acting along the line of greater resistance whereas in *fact* he is acting along the line of least resistance?

The suggestion is at first sight attractive. It seems to me pretty certain, however, that it will not do. A sufficient, though by no means the sole, objection to it is this; that while we certainly have abundant evidence, as Wisdom claims, of the operation in us of desires of whose particular nature we are not at the time aware, no one, to the best of my knowledge, had found evidence that these or any other desires operate in us without their *impulsive tendency* being *felt*. On the contrary, the chief evidence for the existence of sub-conscious desires seems to be just that we do sometimes feel a strong impulsive tendency towards a certain end where introspection reveals no overt desire capable of explaining it. There is, I think, little need to dwell on the matter. Perhaps no one will seriously deny that sub-conscious desires, like any other desires, affect the felt balance of the desiring situation. What I referred to on a previous page as the 'desperate assumption' that that which we most strongly desire may be felt by us as *not* that which we most strongly desire seems to me not to be rendered less desperate by an appeal to the sub-conscious.

STOUT'S VIEW

Professor Stout's psychological explanation of effort of will is to be found in the chapter on Voluntary Decision in his *Manual of Psychology*. His view has interesting points of difference from that of McDougall; but, like McDougall, he writes with the explicit aim of controverting the Libertarian interpretation sponsored by James, and he is equally convinced that action in the line of greater resistance does not, when carefully analysed, imply the introduction of any new psychical factor. His discussion of the topic is exceedingly brief, covering much less than three pages.[1]

The problem for Stout, as for McDougall, is what really happens when, as we say, we exert an effort of will and act against the line of least resistance? The key to the correct answer, he believes, lies in remembering that when a voluntary decision is once formed, 'opposing conative tendencies either cease to

---

[1] *Manual of Psychology*, 5th Edition, pp. 639–641.

operate, or they appear only as difficulties or obstacles in the way of carrying out our decision'. 'The disappearance of opposing tendencies, on the one hand,' he proceeds, 'or their persistence as obstacles, on the other, are the two alternatives which correspond to action in the line of least resistance and in the line of greatest resistance.' In cases of hard, 'effortful' volition, as when we voluntarily decide 'in opposition to some present organic craving', the volition is felt as effortful because of the persistence of the opposing tendencies. For, in Stout's words, 'the craving itself is maintained by organic conditions which continue to operate both in the very moment of decision and after the decision is made'. In cases of easy, effortless volition, as when we decide 'in favour of indulging the animal appetite', the volition is felt as effortless because (again in Stout's words) 'the counter-motives tend to disappear altogether, instead of persisting as obstacles. They are not maintained by organic conditions, nor are they obtruded on the mind by any other circumstance.'

This then, according to Stout, is all there is to the experience of effort of will. If he is right, there is evidently no reason to believe that in effortful willing the weaker desires triumph. The appearance to the contrary is due simply to our consciousness of the persistence of opposing tendencies, whereby we are deluded into imagining that we are acting contrary to the line of least resistance. Accordingly there is no ground here at all for postulating the introduction of a new form of psychical energy.

I do not think, however, that this theory will suffice. It does not really seem to be the case that persistence of opposing tendencies as obstacles during and after decision causes a volition to be experienced as effortful. For, although it is true that in all effortful volition opposing tendencies persist as obstacles, it is also true that in many cases of effort*less* volition opposing tendencies *also* persist as obstacles.

To take an example. If I am fleeing from an angry bull, my aching limbs and panting lungs may cry out for rest long before I reach a place of refuge. I am acutely conscious that organic tendencies oppose themselves as obstacles to my volition to keep on the run. But I am certainly *not* conscious of having to exert an effort of will to keep on the run. My aversion to the prospect of what will happen to me if I desist is quite enough, and is felt to be quite enough, to determine me to continue my flight in despite of

c

my physical cravings. A *muscular* effort, of course, I do exert. But muscular effort is very different from effort of will—a point to which I shall return. Effort of will, so far as I can see, there is none. Indeed, were anyone to suggest to me after such an adventure that it must have taken a great effort of will to keep moving, I might be pardoned for supposing him to be jesting.

Or take another instance. While listening with uncommon pleasure to a musical broadcast, I begin to feel thirsty. The thirst becomes acute, but I am aware that to get myself a drink will mean making a journey downstairs and interrupting my enjoyment of the recital. I continue to listen in, because much as I desire to quench my thirst, I desire still more to hear the music. 'The craving itself is maintained', as Stout would put it, and I ought therefore, if his theory is correct, to be conscious of exerting effort of will and of acting in the line of greatest resistance. But in actual fact I am conscious of nothing of the sort. I am, and I know that I am, following my strongest desire, doing that to which my desiring nature in the given situation most strongly inclines me, and the continuing operation of opposing conative tendencies does not in the least lead me to imagine that I make or maintain my decision by exerting effort of will.

I must conclude, therefore, that Stout's account of the matter will not meet the facts. Experience of effortful volition is not reducible to experience of volition in the face of persisting obstacles. The psychological explanation of the characteristic of 'effortfulness' is still to seek.

THOULESS'S VIEW

Dr R. H. Thouless in his *Social Psychology* has also devoted some little space to our problem. In the course of a general account of volition he tells us that 'the difficulty in the explanation of volitional action lies in the fact that, of two impulses, it is often the one which appears the weaker that is voluntarily adopted'.[1] He proceeds to consider, very briefly, the manner in which James and McDougall respectively have dealt with the difficulty and, in rejecting both of these accounts, to give us his own view of the matter.

That view appears to be that the problem is really meaningless

---

[1] *Social Psychology*, p. 244.

in the terms in which it is usually formulated. James and Mc-
Dougall both formulate the problem in terms of 'strong' and
'weak' impulses, and ask how we can choose the end of the weaker
impulse. But, Thouless contends, such a formulation is open to the
criticism 'that the strength and weakness of impulses can in no
wise be measured except by observing which of a pair of competing impulses finds expression in action'.[1] The implication
seems to be that it is nonsense to talk of stronger and weaker
impulses unless we are simply meaning by the 'stronger', that which
in fact prevails, and by the 'weaker', that which in fact does not
prevail. But if that *is* what we are meaning, then, of course,
quaestio cadit. There is no question of how the weaker impulse can
triumph in a volition. For it never does.

Thouless's view, if I have interpreted it correctly, is certainly
a paradoxical one. Unfortunately, it is stated with such brevity
that the critic may do less than justice to the reasons which underlie it. But so far as I understand his position, it appears to me to be
demonstrably false. Certainly we do not in practice wait until we
have made our choice, and can thus observe 'which of a pair of
competing impulses finds expression in action', before pro-
nouncing a confident judgment as to which of two competing
impulses is the stronger. If I say that I want to hear a certain
lecture this evening, but that I also want to go to the theatre, and
that my desire to go to the theatre is the stronger of the two
desires, this last clause has a perfectly intelligible meaning both for
me and for my hearers. I mean that, so far as my desiring nature is
concerned, I feel myself more strongly attracted to the theatre
than to the lecture, so that, should my desiring nature as it stands
be allowed to determine my choice, it is the theatre and not the
lecture which I shall choose to attend. And it is hard to see how
anyone can deny my ability to measure the relative strength of my
desires, prior to action, in this sense.

Why should Thouless suppose that this is not a proper way of
measuring the relative strength of desires? I am at a loss to find the
answer. Of course we do not always know in advance—nor claim
to know—which desire is the 'stronger' in the sense of being the
one that will in fact prevail. As we are well aware in many cases,
other factors may intervene to influence us before the act of
choice takes place. But we do know in advance, or certainly think

[1] *Social Psychology*, p. 247.

we know, which desire is the stronger in the sense of being the one which will prevail if no further factor intervenes. Nor is there the slightest empirical evidence, so far as I can see, to suggest that we are ever mistaken in thinking that we know this. Surely we have here a perfectly valid meaning of the term 'stronger desire', and a perfectly valid way of measuring it in advance?

I at any rate cannot regard it as seriously doubtful that we are able to measure in advance of action the relative strength of impulses in the way which James's and McDougall's formulation of the problem presupposes. It is true, of course, that there are rare occasions when we find it almost or quite impossible to say which of two competing impulses is the stronger. But that is not because we can apply to them no valid principle of measurement. It is because when we do apply to them our principle of measurement we find them to be approximately equal. We feel that the two ends exercise an equal attraction for us, so that (as we sometimes say on these occasions) 'we do not know how to choose between them'. That, so far as I can see, is the only kind of case in which there is a difficulty about knowing in advance which of two competing impulses is the stronger, and the difficulty is obviously completely compatible with the applicability of a valid principle of measurement.

This completes all that I think I can usefully say in this paper in the way of criticism of definitive theories. To complete the negative part of my programme, however, I must add a few words about certain mistaken views about effort of will, which although not as a rule supported by any explicit analysis, seem to be implied in a good many casual references to the subject.

I suspect, for example, that there is a certain amount of confusion of effort of will with both *muscular* effort and *intellectual* effort. It is not difficult to show that neither a volition involving the exertion of muscular effort nor a volition involving the exertion of intellectual effort is necessarily a volition involving effort of will. But I am not at all sure that this is always realized. I propose, therefore, to devote a little space to making clear that effort of will (as experienced) is distinct from either of these phenomena.

To take muscular effort first. If my child falls, and I pick her up, I am conscious of exerting muscular effort in picking her up. But it would be absurd to suggest that I am, in a normal case, exerting effort of will. In willing to pick her up I will to do what

I most strongly desire to do, i.e., I will along the line of least resistance. And that is precisely the kind of willing that is experienced as effort*less*. It is obvious, of course, that on occasion I do exert an effort of will in order to make a muscular effort. I may have to exert an effort of will, as well as muscular effort, in order to get out of bed on a December morning. And probably it is exclusive attention to cases of this sort that has led some persons to assume that the willing of a muscular effort is always a case of effort of will. But what such cases really indicate, of course, is simply that the willing of muscular effort is *sometimes* contrary to the line of least resistance, relatively to our desiring nature, just as *sometimes* it is along the line of least resistance.

The case of intellectual effort is amenable to parallel treatment. The chess-player is conscious of exerting intellectual effort in planning his next moves, but he would think it ridiculous if he were told he had to exert an effort of will in making this intellectual effort. His zest for the game sustains the intellectual effort, and precludes any need for exerting an effort of will. Intellectual effort *may*, of course, like muscular effort, require an effort of will to initiate or sustain it, e.g., when we are trying to read a difficult work which has little intrinsic interest for us, but which we feel we ought to master. Whether or not an intellectual effort does require an effort of will is, as in the case of muscular effort, simply a matter of whether or not it is felt to be against the line of least resistance.

There is one other thing which effort of will is *not*, of which we may remind ourselves before proceeding to the consideration of its positive features. It is not the activity characteristic of volition as such. That was made sufficiently clear, I think, at the beginning of my paper, and needs no further remark here.

I turn now to attempt what I can in the way of positive construction.

I may say at once that I am in substantial agreement with James's view of the matter. So far as I can see, effort of will, as we experience it, is an unique phenomenon, incapable of being analysed in terms of anything but itself. The attempts so to analyse it which we have surveyed seem manifestly to break down, and I can conceive of no other analysis which has a higher degree of plausibility.

But even if it be the case that effort of will is something unique, or *sui generis*, it does not, I think, follow that we are thereby precluded from saying anything at all about it save that it is just itself. Its uniqueness entails that we cannot define it in terms of anything other than itself, and that there is no more hope of explaining what effort of will is to anyone who has not experienced it than there is of explaining what colour sensa are to a blind man. But, given the requisite experience, there are important things that we can say about what is experienced, even if that *is* unique. For even if an experienced entity is not constituted in terms of other experienced entities, it may nevertheless have, as experienced, integral relations to other experienced entities. This, I believe, to be the case with effort of will. As I conceive it, the business of elucidating the psychological nature of effort of will can only consist in, negatively, the demarcation of it from certain other phenomena with which it might be confused, and, positively, in the ascertainment of the most fundamental of its integral relations to other elements in experience. The second of these tasks is our concern now.

Some of these relations we have already had occasion to observe in the course of our discussion of other theories. The relation of effort of will to our desires, e.g., requires little further comment. We are, I hope, agreed that effort of will is always exerted against what is felt to be the existing 'set' of our desiring nature. Not that there are *no* elements of our desiring nature directed to the end in whose service effort of will is exerted. Usually, and perhaps always, there are some so directed. All that I am interested to maintain is that the end to which effortful willing is directed is necessarily an end opposed to that to which our desiring nature at the time is felt to incline us most strongly.

Can we say anything positive about the nature of the end in whose service effort of will is made? I think that we can. If the end is opposed to that which we are conscious of most strongly desiring, why should we take an interest in its achievement at all? Only one answer seems possible, viz., that it is regarded by the agent as a *higher* end. There would appear to be two, and only two, grounds upon which we can take an interest in the achievement of an end. *Either* it must exercise an attraction for our desiring nature, *or* it must appeal to our sense of obligation. Now in the case of effort of will, the end we endeavour to achieve is felt as exercising less attractive force upon our desiring nature than the end we reject. If, then, we are taking sufficient interest in it to endeavour to achieve it, it would seem that this can only be because of the obligatory character which it wears for us. It must be regarded as the higher end, the end which has the greater authority for us though it has not the greater power. In a wide sense of the word 'moral', a sense which admittedly begs certain large questions not directly relevant here, it seems true to say that effort of will has always a *moral* orientation.

Let us turn next to the relationship, for our experience, between effort of will and the *self*.

It is evident at once that this relationship is very different from the relationship between, say, desires, or emotions, and the self. We speak of the self 'having' desires, or emotions: but it would be quite unnatural to speak of the self 'having' an effort of will. We speak of the self *making* an effort of will. Clearly we regard ourself as the *author*, and not merely the *owner*, of our effort of will.

But it is necessary to try to ascertain, by introspecting as carefully as we can, the precise nature of this 'authorship' with which we credit our self. What then do we find when we introspect our self making an effort of will? We find, certainly, that we regard our self as the 'source' of the effort. But clearly the self is not taken to be its 'source' merely in the sense that the effort is felt to 'emanate' from it. We do not, as it were, suddenly find ourselves thinking 'Hullo! Here I am making an effort of will!' On the contrary, we regard our self not as the blind origin of the effort, but as its *conscious originator*. For we are aware of the effort as issuing from our *conscious decision to exert it*. And we are further aware—or so at least I shall argue—that that decision of ours was a free or creative decision between genuinely open possibilities, in that we could have decided not to make the effort (or, in the appropriate circumstances,[1] to make it in less or in greater degree).

How can it be shown that these awarenesses concerning the relation of effort of will to the self are really inherent in the experience of making the effort, and that the relations in question may therefore be regarded as integral relations? It is obvious, of course, that they are not *explicitly* present, in the sense of being consciously

---

[1] It is quite obvious that there are such circumstances. But having formally noted the fact, I shall for the sake of simplicity ignore it in future references to the alternatives confronting moral decision in situations of temptation.

formulated in the agent's mind. No one would claim that. But that they are implicitly present, requiring only the stimulus of the appropriate question in order to rise to explicit consciousness, may be shown, I think, without too great difficulty, by suitable introspective experiment. All that we require to do is to imagine ourselves exerting an effort of will, and then put to ourselves certain questions. In the first place, this question, 'Can we, while making an effort of will, conceive it as even possible that the making of the effort does *not* issue from a decision on our part to make it?' I take it that anyone who carries out this not very complicated experiment will find, as I do, that one *cannot* conceive this as even possible. But if so, if the experience of making an effort of will compels a negative answer to this question once it is asked, the situation seems not unfairly expressed by saying that implicit in the experience of making the effort is the consciousness that the effort issues from a decision on our part to make it.

Exactly the same procedure may be followed to elicit the presence of the second of the awarenesses mentioned above. We must ask ourselves in this case 'Can we, while making an effort of will, conceive it as even possible that we could not have decided to refrain from making the effort?' And again, I take it, the only possible answer which the experiment can yield is the negative one. Wherefore, I submit, we are entitled to say that implicit in the experience of making the effort is the consciousness that we could have decided to refrain from making it.

The phrase 'could have decided to refrain' has, however, an ambiguity which has been repeatedly pointed out. It might mean 'could have decided to refrain if certain elements in the situation, and particularly the agent's desires, had been different from what they were'. Or it might mean 'could have decided to refrain in the actual situation precisely as it was, with the agent's desires precisely as they were'. Determinists have often suggested— usually without chapter and verse—that Libertarians fail to distinguish between these two meanings; that in consequence they allege as evidence in favour of Libertarianism the existence of a subjective certainty that one 'could have decided to refrain *absolutely*', whereas in fact the only subjective certainty that exists is that one 'could have decided to refrain *conditionally*'—which subjective certainty does not support Libertarianism at all. It becomes particularly important to point out, therefore, that the agent in the experience we are analysing is certain that he 'could have decided to refrain' in its absolute or unconditional meaning. To show that this is so, we must employ again our old technique. We must ask ourselves 'Can we, while making the effort, conceive it as even possible that we could not have refrained from making it unless some factor or factors in the situation had been different?' For myself, I find that I cannot entertain this even as a possibility. Once the question is put to me, I find myself completely certain, while making the effort of will, that I could have decided to refrain from making it even if the situation had been different in no particular whatsoever. It is open to anyone, of course, to contend that my subjective certainty during the experience, and yours likewise (if, as I venture to presume, the results of our introspective experiments coincide) are illusory; that there are imperative metaphysical reasons—and perhaps reasons of other sorts also—for holding that an agent could not have decided otherwise than he did decide save in the weak, or conditional, sense of these words. This contention I should, in another context, vigorously dispute. But in the present context it is wholly beside the point. We are concerned here with the *psychology* of effort of will, and with that alone. And I maintain that, whether the belief be a true one or a false one, the agent in exerting effort of will does necessarily *believe* that he could have refrained from exerting it, in the strong, or unconditional, sense of these words.

In view of the paramount importance of the question of the relationship between effort of will and the self, even when the question be dealt with from a purely psychological standpoint, it will not be amiss if we dwell on this matter a little longer. It seems worth while to observe, for instance, that the agent's attribution of freedom to his moral decision, which we have argued is implicit in his experience of effort of will, is precisely matched by the agent's view of his moral decision prior to that decision being taken. Let anyone construct for himself in imagination a situation of moral temptation and then ask himself 'Is it even possible for me in this situation to conceive that I have not an unconditional freedom to decide whether I shall make the effort to rise to duty, or take the easy, effortless course of following the dictates of my desiring nature?' I think he will certainly not find it possible. And once again it is quite vital to be clear about the unconditional nature of the freedom which (rightly or wrongly)

c*

the experiencing agent claims. It is a freedom even from the self's *character* as so far formed. That will be to many a hard saying. But if we mean by 'character' what is customarily meant—the more or less organized system of our emotional and conative dispositions (for evil as well as for good)—it is not difficult to show that the freedom claimed is indeed a freedom even from character. For the very essence of the decision we have to make, as this presents itself to us in the actual experience of moral temptation, is as to whether or not we shall make the effort required to choose a course contrary to that which we most strongly desire; contrary, that is, to the course towards which our character as so far formed most strongly inclines us. And how could we possibly regard a decision between *these* alternatives as determined by our formed character? We cannot, surely regard our formed character as determining a decision as to whether or not we shall *combat* our formed character! Surely, on the contrary, the very essence of the freedom we ascribe to ourselves in the situation of moral temptation consists in the capacity, through effort of will, to *cut loose* from and transcend a formed character which has revealed itself as being, in this situation, inadequate to the demands of our moral consciousness.

It can hardly be over-emphasized—though I have no space here to develop the theme—that the moral agent's disbelief in the influence of his character upon this particular kind of decision does not in the very least entail a disbelief in the influence of his character upon his conduct generally. It is perfectly compatible, for example, with the recognition that it is character which (in contact with circumstances) determines the range and nature of the alternative courses which suggest themselves to us, and determines also the relative strength of the various desires for the various alternatives; and again, that it is character which directly determines our choices in those situations in which there is no felt conflict between a weaker but higher desire and a stronger but lower desire, i.e., in the huge majority of practical situations in life. No Libertarian who rejects the influence of character upon conduct can find a foundation for that doctrine in the psychology of moral experience.[1]

---

[1] But I ought to add that I do not in fact know of any Libertarian who does hold such a doctrine. The nameless Libertarians whose follies are rebuked in the pages of many Determinist writers seem to me to be sheer figures of fantasy.

'Nevertheless', the critic may retort, 'your moral agent is still left, on your view, alleging something that is surely quite incredible. So far as the specific moral decision you are discussing is concerned, he believes, according to your account, that it is *not* his *character* that determines it, but yet that it *is* his *self*. And this we find frankly nonsensical—so nonsensical that it must cast doubt on the accuracy even of your psychological analysis. The self apart from its character is the most barren of abstractions, and it is hard to believe that the agent in moral experience can really attach any significance to it.'

As I remarked earlier in the paper, I have said what I have to say about this widely favoured criticism in other and more suitable places. I allude to the criticism here only because it seems to me that there is a genuine danger of our being deterred from taking the psychological facts as we find them on account of what is at bottom no better than a metaphysical prejudice. I call the view that there is no meaning in speaking of a self divorced from its character a 'prejudice' because subscription to it depends, I believe, upon making an uncritical and unwarrantable abstraction from an important part of the evidence; the evidence, namely, which is provided by the self's experience of its own acts. If we insist upon confining ourselves to the standpoint of the external observer, the standpoint from which we can alone directly apprehend the non-ego, certainly we shall find nothing that suggests an action determined by a thing's (or person's) 'self' but not determined by its (or his) 'character'. But why *should* we so confine ourselves? There is an *internal* standpoint possible in the case of the self's awareness of its self, if in no other case, and we have no right whatever, so far as I can see, to ignore the evidence that that standpoint affords in determining what can, and what can not, have meaning for us.

If we do *not* ignore the internal standpoint, it seems to me to become clear that we *can* attach a meaning to action determined by the self but not by the self's character. We do in fact attach a meaning to it, I have tried to show above, every time we, as moral agents, are confronted by a moral temptation; for the moral agent, I argued, cannot regard his character as determining his decision as to whether or not he will oppose his character, and yet he does regard his decision as determined by his *self*. Even more obviously do we attach meaning to it in the actual experience of making an effort of will. For in such cases we are equally certain *both* that it is our self that makes the effort *and* that the effort is made in opposition to the line of action to which our desiring nature as it stands, or our character as so far formed, inclines us. In view of these plain evidences that we *do* attach meaning to a determination by the self which is not a determination by its character, it is a little difficult to take seriously the allegation that we *can't*.

It is more than time, however, to bring this paper to a close; though there are obviously a number of other questions, still within the strictly psychological ambit, which it might be profitable to discuss. I cannot attempt to consider here even the question of the bearing of the psychological analysis of effort of will upon the problem of free will. Everyone, I suppose, would grant that it has some bearing, and that it is therefore worth while trying to get at the actual psychological facts. The foregoing attempt is, without doubt, defective at many points. But I venture to hope that it may do a little to stimulate interest in a problem which seems to me to have received in the past far too casual a treatment from most philosophers and psychologists. At that I must leave it; adding only, for the sake of reference, a formal list of the main contentions which the paper has sought to make good.

On the *negative* side we have maintained that effort of will, as experienced, cannot be accounted for—

(*a*) by the reinforcement of desire by other desires, from whatever quarter the latter proceed, and whether they be conscious or unconscious; nor

(*b*) by the persistence of opposing tendencies, e.g., organic cravings, during and after the taking of the moral decision; nor

(*c*) by the experience of activity involved in volition as such; nor

(*d*) by the experience of muscular activity involved in some volitions; nor

(*e*) by the experience of intellectual activity involved in some volitions.

On the *positive* side we have maintained—

(*a*) that in the apparent absence of any satisfactory way of explaining effort of will, as experienced, in terms of anything other than itself, it is reasonable to hold that it is unique;

(*b*) that this uniqueness does not destroy all possibility of elucidatory analysis, since we can still elicit, by introspection, the apprehended relationship of effort of will to other elements in experience;

(c) that, in relation to desire, effort of will is always experienced as exerted against the existing 'set' of our desiring nature, and in the service of an end which (though probably also an object of desire) possesses at least a relative moral authority for the agent;

(d) that, in relation to the self, it is always apprehended as something of which the self is not the mere passive owner but the active author;

(e) that the self's awareness of 'authorship' is implicitly the awareness that the effort issues from the self's decision to make it, and that this decision was a free decision between the genuinely open possibilities of making or withholding the effort;

(f) that the 'freedom' thus claimed by the self for its decision is an absolute freedom, unconditioned even by the self's character as so far formed;

(g) that the repeated declaration that 'we cannot attach meaning to a determination by the self which is not a determination by its character' is directly disproved by the facts which introspective analysis of our moral experience discloses.

IV

MORAL AND NON-MORAL VALUES: A STUDY IN THE FIRST PRINCIPLES OF AXIOLOGY

I

It would, I suppose, be pretty generally agreed that the fundamental cleavage within value-philosophy at the present day is between those who hold that goodness (or value) is a simple unanalysable—and hence indefinable—*quality* which certain things possess, and those who hold that it consists in a *relation* of some kind between the things of which value is predicated and some mind or minds. As labels will be convenient for views of which we shall have much to say in the sequel, let us call these two schools of thought the 'Objectivist' and the 'Subjectivist' respectively.

Of these schools, the Objectivist is, of couse, by far the more recent—dating virtually from the publication of *Principia Ethica* some thirty years ago. And I do not think it unfair to suggest that its considerable authority has been due much less to its own positive merits than to certain apparently irremediable defects in the Subjectivist theories which seem to offer the only plausible alternatives. Its authority can hardly be accounted for by the logical arguments which appeared to Dr Moore in 1903 to prove irresistibly that goodness could only be a simple quality: for these arguments have not, as a rule, been found satisfactory even by those who are most sympathetic with the general trend of the theory, and they are not now, one learns,[1] acceptable to Dr Moore himself. Nor is the doctrine qualified to attract adherents by any power of affording an intelligent comprehension of the vast and varied panorama of value-judgments disclosed to us by the student of comparative cultures: for this is just what any view of value which denies the relevance of subjective interests is singularly incompetent to do. Indeed, the advantage of Subjectivism with respect to this important requirement of a sound value-theory is at once so great and so evident that only the presence of very

[1] *Proceedings of the Aristotelian Society*, Supplementary Vol. XI, p. 127.

grave counter-balancing disabilities seems able to explain the preference accorded in so many quarters to the claims of the Objectivist type of theory.

It must be admitted, however, that very grave difficulties do beset the path of the Subjectivist. Two, I think, are outstanding, and are constantly being adduced by critics as manifestly fatal to the pretensions of Subjectivism. Let me state them very briefly.

(1) If what we mean when we predicate goodness of X is that X is liked (or desired, approved, etc.) by some mind or minds, then goodness must be something of a highly contingent character. It must, apparently, be something that comes into being and passes away not only (as is natural enough) through changes in the nature of X, but also on account merely of changes in certain conscious states. And it is very difficult to believe that this is what we do in fact mean, at least in our more considered and unqualified value-judgments. When we assert that knowledge is good, or that beauty is good, surely we do not mean that knowledge and beauty own this character only if and when certain conscious states are directed towards them? Is it not evident that we regard the goodness of each of these 'goods' as possessed of the same kind of permanence as the nature of the thing itself, and not as something which fluctuates with the fluctuation of any person's, or group of persons', feelings towards the thing?

(2) Among conventionally accepted good things there is one whose goodness we feel it quite peculiarly repugnant to identify with any relation to subjective interests. I refer to moral virtue. In the case of other good things—such as knowledge—we at least do not feel that there is anything inherently absurd in enquiring whether the goodness we attribute to the thing may not be derivable from its being an object of interest to some subject or subjects (or from its being a means to the attainment of some such object of interest). However difficult it may be to devise a formula which avoids the difficulty alluded to under (1), we at least recognize nothing crassly incongruous in undertaking the attempt. But the case of moral virtue appears to fall into quite a different category. When a man in defiance of strong temptations rises to what he recognizes to be his duty, it seems merely inept to suggest that his dutiful act derives the value which we all regard it as possessing from any subjective feelings that are entertained towards it by any one. We seem to see quite clearly that we need pay no

attention to the presence or absence of any subjective feelings whatsoever in order to know that the act has value. Whether or not the act may have some *further* value in virtue of a relation to subjective feelings, we may here be content to leave as an open question. But it can only be by confusion that we fail to distinguish the 'supplementary' value which the act may possess on *this* account from the value which it possesses simply and solely in virtue of its being the kind of act that it is, i.e., an act of duty.

Now I do not believe, for reasons which I shall later explain, that the former of these difficulties is really insuperable. But I confess that the latter difficulty does seem to me fatal to any purely Subjectivist theory of value. It is, I think, quite hopeless to seek to identify the value we attribute to moral virtue with any relation to anything that can legitimately be called a subjective interest. Indeed, the simple appeal to reflect upon our own value-responses to moral virtue seems to me to be by far the most effective weapon in the whole armoury of the critics of Subjectivism, and it has probably been responsible for making more converts to the general Objectivist standpoint than all other arguments put together. It is very noticeable—and, as I shall attempt to show, highly significant—how frequently it recurs at critical junctures in the pages of Dr W. D. Ross's recent important work.[1] I cite here only a single typical passage, from the chapter on 'the Nature of Goodness'. 'We may claim', writes Dr Ross, 'that we are directly aware that conscientious action, for example, has a value of its own, not identical with or even dependent upon our or any one else's taking an interest in it. Our reason informs us of this as surely as it informs us of anything, and to distrust reason here is in principle to distrust its power of ever knowing reality.'[2] It is a claim, I think, whose cogency will strike home to almost every reader. But note how immeasurably it would be weakened in its effect if, instead of the *moral* value of 'conscientiousness', we were to insert some non-moral value—even one of the so-called 'intrinsic' values like 'knowledge'. It is possible that, if we were to substitute 'knowledge', we should still feel an *inclination* to assert that this good 'has a value of its own, not identical with or even dependent upon our or any one else's taking an interest in it'. But I doubt if there is one of us who would go so far as to contend that 'our reason informs us of this as surely as it informs us of any-

---

[1] *The Right and the Good.*   [2] *Ibid.*, p. 82.

thing, and to distrust reason here is in principle to distrust its power of ever knowing reality'. The strength of the case against Subjectivism depends, I think, far more than is generally recognized upon the special instance of the value we apprehend in moral virtue.

Still, a single argument, if it be sound, is enough to establish any position: and I am willing to admit, on the strength of the argument we have been considering, that an adequate theory of value is not possible on purely Subjectivist lines. But before we acquiesce in a thoroughgoing and general rejection of Subjectivism, there is one alternative which, as it seems to me, we ought to explore with a great deal of care. Is it absolutely necessary, I want to ask, that we should extend to the meaning of value or goodness generally those characteristics which we find ourselves forced to apply to it in the case of moral virtue? Is it quite certain that we mean the same thing by 'good' when we judge that moral virtue is good as we do when we judge that knowledge is good— or indeed as we do in any other of those instances (the crucial ones, of course, for the determination of the ultimate nature of value) in which we predicate goodness in an apparently 'absolute' sense? If this is *not* so, then it may remain possible to give a Subjectivist account of value in respect of non-moral values, even while we recognize that such an account is definitely false in respect of moral values: a consummation which would deliver us from the embarrassment, which presses so sorely upon the Objectivist school, of holding a theory of value which leaves in outer darkness by far the larger proportion of the value-judgments of mankind.

I hope that the reader will not dismiss this alternative too hastily as savouring of mere convenient eclecticism. It has, I believe, a much more solid basis. Indeed it is, in my opinion (which I shall endeavour to substantiate in this paper), the one view capable of introducing coherence into the general theory of value. I believe that the chief source of the confusion which envelops current value philosophy lies precisely in the failure to recognize that there is an absolutely vital distinction of kind between our value-reaction to the value of moral virtue and our value-reaction to any other value whatsoever.

To explain my thesis in more formal terms, what I am going to argue is that a subjectivist definition of value is valid, *save only* in the single case of the value which inheres in moral virtue. How exactly we are to understand the meaning of value in the latter connection, and what is the nature of the identity or analogy between it and value in the former connection which leads us to employ the same term 'value', or 'goodness', in respect of both, are questions which must engage our attention at some later stage. But our chief preoccupation will be with the meaning of value in the former connection; and our chief problem in the effort to vindicate a subjectivist interpretation of 'non-moral' values will be to devise a formula in terms of subjective feelings which will escape, along with other difficulties, the major difficulty alluded to at the outset of this paper.

II

It is perhaps desirable, before we settle to the task of constructing a subjectivist formula for non-moral values, to say something more of a general character in support of the uniqueness of the value which we attribute to moral virtue. Let us begin by trying to give to the difference in kind which we allege, at least the status of an initial probability: for the reader who is already persuaded that this alleged difference at least *may* have a foundation in fact, is likely to explore with considerably greater sympathy the hypothesis that a subjectivist interpretation is valid for non-moral values.

One piece of evidence in support of the validity of the distinction has already been referred to, and I shall develop it only briefly. I quoted a passage from Dr Ross which purported to show that the value which we accord to conscientious action cannot be given a subjectivist interpretation, and I invited the reader to observe the effect upon the argument of substituting for conscientious action some non-moral value. If we carefully examine our value-reactions in the two cases, it seems to me that the difference between them is very marked, and highly important. We feel, so Dr Ross contends, completely certain that conscientious action has value irrespective of any subjective interest in it— a value to which subjective liking and disliking are merely irrelevant. I think that very few persons, if any, would maintain that a value like beauty (or, as I should prefer to express it, aesthetic experience) evokes a corresponding assurance. The habit of mind, engendered by a long tradition, which tempts us to take it as established verity that Truth, Beauty and Goodness are a sort of holy trinity of 'intrinsic' values may, and only too probably will, predispose us to believe in objectivity in this value-realm also. But we surely cannot pretend that we here enjoy anything even approximating to *certitude*. We should not stake the very validity of our reason upon the objectivity of this value. The difference in our attitudes is very easy to understand if the distinction I am contending for is *bene fundatum*. It is not easy to explain on any other hypothesis.

Further evidence may be derived from considering a problem which has evidently very much exercised the author of *The Right and the Good*—the problem of the commensurability of values. If we suppose that the goodness possessed by moral virtue on the one hand, and by non-moral good on the other hand, is goodness in the same sense of goodness, then presumably it should be possible, since goodness admits of a more and less, to measure the goodness of virtue against the goodness of the other goods in at least a rough and ready, approximate fashion. Yet in actual truth it seems impossible to dissent from Dr Ross's own considered judgment that the goodness of virtue is really incommensurable with the goodness of any of the other 'intrinsic goods'. Critical examination of our own value-responses strongly suggests that we decline to accept any amount, however large, of a good like knowledge as exceeding in value the very smallest amount of moral virtue. 'When I ask myself', says Dr Ross, 'whether any increase in knowledge, however great, is worth having at the cost of a wilful failure to do my duty or of a deterioration of character. I can only answer in the negative.'[1] And this is surely a correct answer. For my own part, I should say that the very question has about it an unreal, artificial flavour. It is the kind of question which no one could seriously put to himself save in a mood of half-conscious sophistry, or else—as here—under the influence of a philosophical motive which demands the explicit examination of even the most remotely possible alternatives. I am not myself aware of any philosopher, with the possible exception of Dr Moore—who in theory assigns to moral virtue a very modest degree of value—likely to return an affirmative answer to the

[1] *The Right and the Good*, p. 152.

question, and it seems fair to take the negative answer as possessing a pretty high measure of certainty.

Now if the goodness of virtue is really felt to be incommensurable with the goodness of other good things, can we still hold that we are meaning by 'goodness' the same thing in both cases? Dr Ross tries to evade the difficulty, which his own candour has so clearly exposed, by suggesting that 'virtue belongs to a higher order of value, beginning at a point higher on the scale of value than that which (the others) ever reach'.[1] But I feel very doubtful whether this supposed relationship will bear examination. If it is really the *same scale* to which they belong—and this condition seems to be necessary if they are to be defended as 'good' in the same sense—two difficulties emerge. In the first place, since it does not seem possible to set any assignable limit to the amount imaginable of goods like knowledge and pleasure, must we not say that at *some* point the goodness possessed by these goods equals the goodness possessed by the minimal amount of virtue? And, in the second place, ought we not to feel that with increasing amounts of knowledge and pleasure we are continuously *getting nearer to* the degree of goodness which the minimal amount of virtue possesses? I think that if the values do indeed belong, as Dr Ross says they do, to the *same scale of value*, an affirmative answer to both of these questions is logically entailed. Yet it seems to me in the last degree doubtful whether an affirmative answer can be supported by the actual responses of our value-consciousness, and I imagine that Dr Ross's own recognition of the peculiar claims of moral value must make him extremely reluctant to accept that answer himself.

Now the difficulties, it should be noticed, which beset the attempt to measure the value of virtue against the value of other goods, are precisely what one would expect if the thesis that I am to defend in this paper is a sound one. If virtue is a value not just of a *higher order* but in a *different category*, if it is, in fact, the one thing which has a value independent of all relation to subjective interests, then little wonder that we are aware of an inherent impropriety in seeking to apply a common yard-stick to it and other goods.

---

[1] *The Right and the Good*, p. 150. In the context the statement relates only to the non-moral value of 'pleasure', but the sequel makes it clear that Dr Ross intends his view to apply to other non-moral values also.

III

It is rather more than time, however, that we passed on to our main task. Our real problem still awaits us, viz., to justify the contention that all value-judgments other than those referring to moral virtue involve an essential reference to human liking.[1] Let me say a word or two, first of all, about the method I propose to adopt.

Naturally, I shall not attempt to deal explicitly with every variety of value-judgment. Our main concern must be with those judgments which are especially appealed to by the Objectivists as furnishing indubitable instances of the apprehension of a value which is not reducible to subjectivist terms. There is, indeed, no list common to all the Objectivists; but the claims of knowledge and aesthetic experience (Truth and Beauty, in popular parlance) have received such wide-spread acknowledgment that it is certain that no Subjectivist theory has any hope of acceptance which cannot make clear the disguised relationship to human liking which obtains in their case. If we can find a formula in terms of human liking which can be regarded as representing fairly what is really meant by goodness or value in the value-judgments directed upon these crucial instances, it will probably be agreed that we have surmounted by far the greatest obstacle to the vindication of our general thesis.

Now the formula which I shall venture to put forward is, as might be expected from the nature of the case, of a somewhat intricate character. The one thing abundantly certain is that no simple formula—such as 'liked by the person judging', or 'liked by the majority of the community'—has the faintest chance of withstanding criticism. But, because of its complexity, our formula, if stated baldly at this juncture, would convey very little meaning indeed. I propose, therefore, to lead up to it gradually by undertaking a systematic examination of the nature and growth of our value-consciousness in so far forth as that value-consciousness *is* rooted in human liking.

For the sake of clearness, let me outline very briefly in advance the main stages through which we shall pass on the way to our goal.

---

[1] I shall explain shortly why, in my judgment, 'liking' is to be preferred in this connection to 'interest' or 'desire', or any other term that Subjectivist axiologists have proposed.

I shall start from what appears to me to be the most rudimentary expression of 'subjective value-consciousness'—if I may so entitle the value-consciousness that is rooted in human liking— viz., that which is ingredient in simple private liking and which manifests itself in the concept 'good-for-self'. I shall then endeavour to show how, by an entirely natural development, incited by the growing recognition of certain distinctions which force themselves upon an intelligent subject of experience, that value-consciousness comes eventually to identify with 'good for self' only objects of its liking *which are qualified in a highly specific way*. I next turn to consider the reaction of our value-consciousness to the recognition (in practice, of course, present from the start) that other persons also have likes and dislikes, and that there are also likes and dislikes which may be said to be inherent in our common human nature as such. This leads us to see that our value-consciousness (still operating on the basis solely of human likes and dislikes) will naturally take a vital interest not only in the concept 'good for self', but also in the concept 'good for man', and that what it means by 'good for man' is an object of liking to human nature qualified in a specific way parallel to that which we found to be involved in the developed concept 'good for self'. We then observe that the formula to which we have been led in considering the true meaning of 'good for man' is one which, if applied to the matter of experience, must issue in a list of goods which bears a remarkable resemblance to that which is currently supposed to represent goods that are intrinsic and objective, goods without any relational qualification. This discovery suggests the possibility that the concept which controls our recognition of the so-called intrinsic goods, is really the concept 'good for man'. An explanation will, of course, require to be given of how it is that the relational qualification—good *for man*—if it controls our thoughts, does not appear in our speech. If we really mean 'good for man', why do we say just 'good'? This difficulty, however, proves to be superficial. Further difficulties are also considered and rejected, and the final conclusion come to that our real meaning when we seem to be asserting intrinsic goodness of such goods as knowledge, aesthetic emotion, etc., is that they are specifically qualified objects of liking to human nature.

IV

We start, then, from the experience of simple private liking. That which we like, we 'put a value upon', as the common phrase has it. It is, to be sure, only a value-*for-self*, not a value *in itself*. For the value which we attach to the thing merely in so far forth as it is an object of our liking is certainly not regarded by us as a value 'in the nature of things', nor even as a value for anyone besides the person liking. But it certainly *is* regarded as a *value*. It is possible to dispute the relevance of the term 'value' here, only if we quite arbitrarily, and indeed perversely, decide that the term 'value' is to be used as the equivalent of the term 'objective value'. There seems no excuse whatever for such a usage, which can hardly be so much as intelligibly formulated to oneself without drawing a distinction in thought between objective and subjective value; a distinction which, if admitted, at once makes nonsense of the proposed identification of 'value' with 'objective value'.

I take it, then, to be indisputable that there is a fundamental manifestation of value-consciousness which is the consciousness of 'value-for-self'. But before we go any further, a word must be said about the choice of 'liking' as the basis of that consciousness. That the interruption may be as brief as possible, I shall do little more than tabulate the chief grounds (as I see them) for preferring 'liking' to certain other terms that have from time to time been suggested in a subjectivist interest.

If we compare 'liking' first of all with 'desire', the advantage of the former term is two-fold.

(1) We often ascribe value to an object (or state, activity, etc.) understood to be already in existence, and which we therefore—since desire is always for something conceived as not yet existing—cannot be said to desire. Perhaps it will be said that desire *is* present in such cases, in that we desire the continuance in existence of the object. But clearly that desire is posterior to the consciousness of the value of the object. It is because we value the object, 'like' its existence, that we desire the continuance of its existence. 'Liking' is to be preferred, then, in that, unlike 'desire', it applies indifferently to the existent and the non-existent, just as valuing does.

(2) Desire, as ordinarily understood, is always an *actual* state of mind, whereas there are certainly value-*dispositions*. It is awkward,

if not impossible, to say that a person desires an object if he does not have a present conscious attitude towards it. Yet he may certainly be said to value an object under these conditions. We may legitimately say that X values exercise, even if we know that while we say it X is in bed asleep. In this respect too, then, 'liking' shows its superiority to 'desire'. For 'likes and dislikes' signify conative dispositions quite as much as they do present mental states.

The claims of 'pleasure' to be the basis of value-consciousness have some prima facie strength. But a fatal objection is that we can certainly feel pleasure without being conscious of an object which we are pleased with, or at, whereas value-consciousness is essentially transitive, implying an object which is evaluated. Our chosen term, liking, obviously possesses the same transitive implication. It might be suggested, perhaps, that 'being pleased with' is the basic state. But 'being pleased with' seems to be just a longer way of saying 'liking'.

Mr Perry's term 'interest'—to take note of one further possibility—does not lie open to any of the above objections. It is transitive, it can refer to dispositions, and it is applicable both to the existent and the non-existent. On the other hand, the use to which this term has been put in the science of Psychology has left it with associations misleading in the present connection, and it has not the natural power, which the term 'liking' possesses, to suggest that favouring attitude of the subject mind which is absolutely fundamental. Moreover, it is a disadvantage that the term 'interest' is applied indifferently to the psychical state and to the object of the psychical state. And, finally, it would be inconvenient to be precluded from using the term 'interest' when we wished to signify that cognitive attentiveness which the term is commonly used to signify.

'Liking', then, seems on the whole to be the best term to express the basic element in the consciousness of value-for-self. We must now take up our task of tracing the manner in which the concept of value-for-self acquires for the reflective consciousness a much more specific meaning than mere 'object of self's liking', owing to the recognition of certain distinctions within objects of liking. I shall set out these distinctions in logical rather than historical order, beginning with the most simple and working towards the more complex.

The first distinction is the very elementary one between objects liked *more* and objects liked *less*. This distinction need not detain us. It introduces, in its crudest form, the distinction between major and minor values-for-self, corresponding to objects of major and minor liking respectively. It ought not, in strictness, to have any effect in modifying the meaning of the concept 'value-for-self'; although I shall have to point out later that it is not altogether certain that it does not in fact have some slight modifying influence.

The next distinction has greater importance. There are some objects that we like for themselves, others that we like only because they help in the attainment of objects liked for themselves. Recognition of this distinction leads us to make a distinction between *end* values-for-self and *instrumental* values-for-self, corresponding to objects of independent and dependent liking respectively. And with the emergence of this distinction the meaning of 'value-for-self' does begin to undergo definite modification. Since it is from end values that instrumental values derive all the value that they possess for us, it will be natural to recognize that it is only end values that have a direct claim to the title 'value'. In so far as this distinction is active in the mind, therefore, there will be a tendency to identify value-for-self not with object of *any* liking of the self, but with object of an *independent* liking of the self.

Our next distinction, one which has very important consequences, arises within the field of end values. It rests upon recognition of the fact that some end values have *also* instrumental value, being conducive to the attainment of certain other things liked for themselves, while other end values have from the same point of view a definite *dis*value. Thus ends like health and knowledge may be liked for themselves, but liked *further* because seen to contribute usefully to the attainment of many other liked things, whereas a good many things liked for themselves, e.g., idleness and gluttony, have quite obviously an opposite tendency. We may perhaps express the situation that arises by saying that end values fall roughly into two classes, according as their main tendency is to co-operate with or to obstruct the end values of the self as a whole.

Now the 'co-operative' end values, if we may so christen them, will certainly be accorded a much higher status as values-for-self than the 'obstructive' end values. But the precise nature of this 'higher status' is something which we must determine with a good deal of care, for in truth we meet here with a very important development in the meaning of the concept 'value-for-self'. There is no question, indeed, of any modification in principle of the original equation 'value-for-self'='liked by self'. But a complexity now reveals itself within the meaning of 'liked by *self*' which reacts profoundly upon the meaning of 'value-for-self'. For it now appears that 'liked by self' may mean either, on the one hand, to be an object of liking to the self as a whole, to the self as the unitary centre of its several likings—as in varying degrees is the case with what we have called the 'co-operative' end values—or it may mean, on the other hand, to be an object of liking to the self only in some very partial aspect of its being, and so inimical to the self's other likings as to be more properly called an object of *disliking* to the self as a whole—as in the case of the 'obstructive' end values. Now it can hardly be denied, I think, that it is in the former of these two conceptions of itself, i.e., in its being as the unitary centre of manifold likings, that the self recognizes its essential selfhood to consist. Accordingly, it will be only those objects of liking which are harmonious, if not positively at least negatively, with the self's likings as a whole, objects which belong to the class of co-operative end values, or, at the least, of neutral end values, which will now be accepted by the self as genuinely representing what is 'liked by *self*'; and it is they alone which will now be recognized as 'values-for-self'. It is evident that when this distinction has become operative in the mind many things previously regarded as values-for-self will present themselves quite definitely in the light of *dis*values: because, though in one sense still 'liked by self', in a more profound sense of 'self' they are in antagonism to what is 'liked by self'.

The distinction which is now engaging us concerns our ultimate purpose so closely that I may be excused if, in spite of the limited space at my disposal, I dwell for a little upon its general principle. The general principle is, I think, neither obscure nor seriously debatable. The essence of the matter is just this, that as self-consciousness develops, and the self becomes conscious of itself as the unitary centre of manifold likings, the meaning of 'object of liking to self', and consequently of 'value to self', becomes deepened, and in a manner transformed. Whatever is now re-garded as good or valuable for the self has got to be something that respects the systematic manifoldness that belongs to the nature of a self. 'Good-for-self' will now mean object not merely of an independent liking, but of an independent and *integral* liking of the self—an 'integral' liking being definable as one which is substantially consistent with the likings of the self as a whole.

We must note now, but more briefly, a further modification of the meaning of value-for-self which arises at the same level of reflective self-consciousness as that which we have just considered. At this same level, the self will become explicitly conscious of its perduring identity, conscious of itself as a relatively *abiding* subject. For a self which so understands its self-hood, an object of liking will tend to be regarded as fully deserving the title of object of the *self's* liking only in so far as the liking in question is of a relatively permanent and not a merely ephemeral character. It would appear, therefore, that the epithet 'relatively permanent' ought to be added to the epithets 'integral' and 'independent' in order to denote accurately the kind of object of liking which is on this developed plane of experience identified with 'value-for-self'.

There is just one other distinction which must, I think, add its quota of meaning to the concept 'value-for-self'. The immediately preceding determinations rested upon the self's consciousness of a distinction between a relatively real and a relatively unreal expression of self-hood. But self-consciousness leads to the recognition of a further distinction within self-hood, the distinction of the self as it is from the self as it is capable of becoming. We become aware of the self containing within itself possibilities of desirable development in a multitude of directions. Now when we consider the significance of this manifestation of our self-consciousness in its relation to the self's likings, we can see that the self will recognize (1) that there are many things which it does not now like, but which it is in principle possible for it to *come* to like; and (2) that among these things there are some which there is good reason to suppose that it is *worth while* coming to like, since we can even now see their nature to be such that the liking of them is in a high degree integral, and relatively permanent, as well as independent. Thus a person might very well have no present liking for scientific pursuits, or for music, but at the same time, because fully realizing their fulfilment of the conditions required for a high degree of value-for-self to any self which does like them, he might *want* to like them. What will be the attitude of the value-consciousness towards such objects of prospective but unawakened liking, objects which it does not now like but would only, as it were, *like* to like? On the whole, it seems probable that their relation to the likings of the ideally developed self will bring them recognition as values-for-self in some sense. Just how much the concept of value-for-self must be modified thereby it is not easy to determine, and it is fortunate that, as will become apparent later, this particular modification has not the importance of its predecessors for the fulfilment of our ultimate purpose.

Now we have so far been studying only that branch of our value-consciousness which is connected with the self's consciousness of its *own* likes and dislikes. But man's life is lived in a social medium, and it is very certain that every self is aware that the other selves with whom it is in contact have their likes and dislikes also. To be conscious of a value-for-self relative to one's own likings is thus in principle to be conscious also of a value-for-others relative to others' likings. It must further become apparent at no very advanced level of reflection that likes and dislikes show a considerable amount of variation as between different persons, and that accordingly things which are values for A and B may very well be disvalues for the differently constituted persons C and D. But what must especially engage the attention of man as a member of a social group, of a body organized for a substantially common purpose, is not the values which are private to the individuals A and B and C and D, but the values that are *common* to all of them; the values which are values for *man*, rather than for this man or that man. Doubtless the 'manhood' or 'common human nature' to which reference is thus made will in early communities be interpreted exclusively in terms of the common human nature of the members of that community. But it is clear that this is a stage destined to be superseded with the advance of civilization. The growing sense of an universal human kinship can hardly fail to bring in its train a conscious interest in a human nature common to all men, and a consequent interest in the concept of a good which is good relatively not merely to the likings of this or that man, nor even to the likings of the typical man of this or that community, but rather good relatively to the likings of man as such, to the likings inherent in the common constitution of human nature.

It is, I think, altogether to be expected that when men have become '*kind*-conscious' the concept of 'value for man as such' should evoke a very particular interest. Unlike the concept of value-for-self, it is conspicuously a concept of common interest, and thus an appropriate subject for the mutual interchange of ideas. What is good for the individual A is of great interest to A, but not as a rule of very much interest to individuals B, C and D. But what is good for man as man, in virtue of the common human nature shared by A, B, C and D alike, is a topic of interest to them all, a topic upon which they may pool their powers and their knowledge to mutual advantage. We might perhaps put it in this way, that mankind will have little interest in 'subjective' goods *except* where the 'subject' in question is the human self as such.

I think we may regard it as natural, then, that just as our value-consciousness is interested in value-for-self, conceived on the basis of the self's likes and dislikes, so also it should be interested in value-for-man, conceived on the basis of the likes and dislikes inherent in human nature as such. And it seems fairly obvious that substantially the same distinctions whose recognition sharpens, and at the same time gives depth to, the meaning of good-for-self are equally applicable to the conception of good-for-man. The distinctions of major from minor likings, of independent from dependent likings, of integral from partial likings, and of relatively permanent from sporadic likings, all retain their significance when it is the conative constitution of the human self as such, rather than of the individual historic self, that is under consideration: and in a way strictly analogous to that already discussed in the case of good-for-self, the appreciation of these distinctions must issue in the recognition of good-for-man as equivalent not to *any* object of liking to human nature, but rather to 'object of an independent, integral, and relatively permanent liking of human nature'. Thus—to take a simple illustration which may help to elucidate the somewhat arid formula—knowledge would naturally come to be regarded as a good-for-man on the ground that man is so constituted that he has a liking for it which is entertained towards the object for itself, is compatible with his liking nature as a whole, and is relatively enduring.

One distinction appealed to in the determination of the meaning of good-for-self is, however, not here in point, viz., the distinction of present from prospective likings. It is not in point, because the meaning which human nature has for us at any time defines itself, as a matter of course, in terms of all that human nature has ever revealed itself to be, in its most ideally advanced quite as much as in its elementary manifestations. Accordingly, since the most developed human likings of which we have any conception will enter into what we mean by human nature, there will be no room here for a contrast between present and unawakened likings, appropriate as that distinction is to the case of a developing historic self.

As to the distinction of major from minor liking, it is not at first sight obvious whether the epithet 'major' ought not to be added to the qualifications of liking necessary to make an object of liking equivalent to 'good', both in the case of good-for-self and in the case of good-for-man. Strictly, I do not think it ought to appear. On the other hand, it seems clear that if anyone were attempting to draw up a list of 'goods-for-man' (to confine ourselves to this issue), he would probably not be satisfied to include in the list an object liked for itself, liked integrally, and liked in a relatively permanent way, if it should happen that it was not *also* liked *much*. Perhaps, however, the explanation is really a very simple one, just the fact that any attempt to draw up a list of goods will tend naturally to limit is field to the major representatives of the class. On the whole, I think we should say that the question of major or minor liking has no bearing on the *meaning* of goodness, but has a good deal of influence in determining what things we select as typical examples of 'goods'.

We have reached the point, then, of seeing the meaning of good-for-man, for a developed consciousness, to be an 'object of an independent, integral, and relatively permanent liking of human nature'. I do not mean, of course, that these several determining characters are explicitly present in the minds of all persons who use, even significantly use, the concept 'good-for-man'. But I do maintain that this formula expresses the meaning of the concept which we must suppose to have been operative in men's minds throughout the gradual process of determining what things are good for man, if that process has been a work of intelligence at all. This is the meaning, I believe, which has underlain and guided, whether explicitly recognized or not, the unsystematic reflections of the value-consciousness of generations of men, reflections which have resulted in the now traditional acceptance by the civilized world of a more or less definite set of things as pre-eminently 'goods-for-man'.

But *are* there certain things that have received this public and traditional endorsement? The phrase 'good-for-man' is not a common phrase in ordinary discourse, and the critic may very reasonably ask what kind of value-judgment I have in mind when I speak of the value-consciousness of mankind having found expression in the endorsement of a definitive set of things as good-for-man. I answer—and here we come to the kernel of the matter—that the kind of judgment I have in mind is precisely the kind of judgment which is commonly supposed by the Objectivist to assert a good simple and unqualified, an 'intrinsic' good. When goodness is predicated of such things as knowledge or aesthetic experience, the Objectivist holds that we are using, or may be using, the term goodness in an absolutely simple, unrelational, unanalysable sense. I contend against this that the apparent simplicity is never a real simplicity; that actually there underlies the predication of goodness in all such cases the conception of a certain relationship between the things and the emotional nature of man as we know it, a relationship which is indispensable to the recognition of the things as good; and that this relationship is precisely expressed by saying that the things are objects of independent, integral, and relatively permanent liking to human nature.

This then is our hypothesis. And before considering the evidence in its favour it will be well to deal at once with an obvious objection. If people really mean 'good-for-man' in these judgments, why do they say just 'good'? The objection is, I think, less formidable than it appears. It seems appropriate, on reflection, that the relational qualification should tend to drop out where the relativity in question is to our common human nature. In the case of a quality which (as we claim to be the case with goodness) is naturally thought of as relative to persons in some sense, it will be necessary to add a relational phrase only where a *special* relativity to some *special* person or persons is intended. If *no* relativity is indicated, the natural presumption will be that the quality is relative not to any special party, but just to our common human nature. Hence the *omission* of the relational qualification may be said in such cases to serve exactly the same purpose as would be served by its *inclusion*. We might perhaps imagine a parallel case, to illustrate our point, in respect of colour-judgments. Even if we all believed, as many people do believe, that red is red only for man, we should continue to say 'this is red', not 'this is red-for-man'. We should only feel the need of appending a relational qualification if the relativity was to an *individual*; as, e.g., a colour-blind person who was aware of his peculiarity might say 'this is red *to me*'. The omission of a relational qualification would imply that the relativity was merely to our common sensitive organization.

Passing from this difficulty which meets us at the threshold, let us now consider the positive evidence that the formula I have reiterated does represent, in the sense of making fully explicit, what is really meant by good when that term is predicated in an ostensibly unqualified sense. The first and the chief point to which I wish to call attention is that the so-called 'intrinsic' goods of the Objectivist are precisely the kind of things that would come to be called just 'good' if our theory of the meaning given to goodness is correct. If goodness means the quality of being an object of independent, integral and relatively permanent liking to human nature, then the particular group of things which tradition has called just 'good', and which the Objectivist declares therefore to be intrinsically good, is exactly the group of things that we should expect. Truth and Beauty, for example, in their more philosophical dress as knowledge and aesthetic experience, fall into line at once. Each has in a pre-eminent degree the characteristic of being an object of independent, integral, relatively permanent—and we may properly add here, major—liking of human nature. And the same thing may be said of such goods as health and friendship, on whose behalf the common value-consciousness of mankind has also made high, though less high, claims. Pleasure, I agree, occupies a somewhat equivocal position for our formula. It is an object of human liking, of major liking, of independent liking, and of relatively permanent liking. But whether or not it is an object of *integral* liking, a liking consistent with the liking nature as a whole, depends entirely upon what *kind* of pleasure it is. But then is not this equivocal position of pleasure for our formula precisely the kind of position it occupies for the value-consciousness of mankind also? The general attitude towards pleasure would probably be expressed fairly enough by saying that it is regarded as good in so far as it is not seriously obstructive of other values. But if so, that would admirably fit in with our formula. For it would mean that wherever the pleasure was of such a kind that it could be an object of integral liking to man it would be a good; and if not of such a kind, not good. But that is just what would be maintained if our formula were operative.

Now this applicability of our formula to the so-called intrinsic goods is not, indeed, conclusive *proof* that our formula expresses what is really meant in these contexts by goodness. Nevertheless, I think we may say that if this is *not* what is meant by goodness, then the applicability of the formula is a very odd coincidence indeed. Actually, I think we are entitled to go further. I think we are entitled to say that the onus of proof now lies upon the Objectivist. For consider just where we stand. Our account started from a value-experience, admittedly subjectivist, which all must concede to be actual, and it proceeded from that basis to show, without any appeal to other than well-recognized psychical and other factors, how man would eventually come to pronounce as 'good', without explicit relational qualification, whatever was an object of independent, integral, and relatively permanent liking to human nature. We then found that the very things which are in *fact* pronounced to be good in this way—the so-called 'intrinsic goods'—possess all the characteristics of our formula. The Objectivist, on the other hand, has to appeal to an unique kind of perception whose claim to be something real is still, at best, *sub judice*, and whose strangely erratic behaviour even among its best friends is something of a scandal. Moreover, as was hinted earlier, the Objectivist is powerless to explain why so many mutually contradictory things have been called good in the same apparently unqualified way by different peoples in different ages—a phenomenon which is easily explicable on our view, since we can recognize the vast difference which different conditions of life and different levels of mental development must make to the things that are conceived to be objects of integral, independent and relatively permanent liking to human nature. It seems to me, therefore, that the onus of proof now lies upon the Objectivist, our present theory being one of greater prima facie probability. And I propose to devote most of what time remains to repelling objections to our theory, rather than to seeking for further positive support.

V

It will not, I think, present itself as a very serious objection to anyone that our formula is certainly not explicitly present in the

D

minds of most of those who predicate goodness (in the context we have been considering). It seems fairly clear that a formula can accurately represent what persons really mean by good even although they have no recognizable version of the formula before them. In ordinary discourse we are very seldom indeed conscious of the full definitory meaning of the complex terms that we use; and yet, in so far as we are using the terms intelligently, that meaning is operative in and controlling our usage. I am glad here to be able to enlist the authority of Dr Ross. 'It appears', he writes, 'as if we cannot avoid recognizing that there is such a thing as using a term which implicitly refers to a certain complex, while yet the complex is not explicitly present to our minds. And in principle this might, it seems, be true of good.'[1] After all, even in philosophical discourse, the valuable maxim 'define your terms' has to be applied with something less than absolute rigour if the argument is to advance at a tolerable pace at all.

But by what test, it may fairly be asked, are we to determine whether any particular complex, not explicitly before our minds when we use a term, is in fact implicitly present? Again I am well content with Dr Ross's answer. 'If it is the correct definition,' he holds, 'what should happen is that after a certain amount of attention to it we should be able to say "Yes, that is what I meant by 'good' all along, though I was not clearly conscious till now that it *was* what I meant".'[1] The process of criticizing proposed definitions, he adds, has two moments. A definition of a term must be rejected if (*a*) we are able to point to things of which the term is predicable and the definition not, or vice versa: or if (*b*) even when the denotations of the term and of the definition coincide (or when we cannot be sure that they do not), we can 'see that a proposed definition does not express what we *mean* by the term to be defined'.[2] This seems to me to be a valid and valuable statement of the situation, and I should make no objection whatever to the application of such a test to the formula I have put forward as representing the meaning of 'good' in the value-judgments which 'at the first look' predicate intrinsic goodness. I am well aware, of course, that in Dr Ross's judgment the application of the test proves fatal to *all* relational definitions of the nature of goodness. But while fully agreeing that it is fatal to the relational definitions which Dr Ross actually cites, and which he

[1] *The Right and the Good*, p. 93.   [2] *ibid.*, p. 93.

appears to have alone before his mind, I must point out that our particular variety of relational definition does not appear in Dr Ross's list at all—either explicitly or implicitly.

It will be worth our while, however, to consider with some care Dr Ross's criticism of relational definitions of goodness, or at least of the subjectivist group of relational definitions. For, while we are claiming exemption for our own particular formula, it is evident that Dr Ross intends his criticism to have an exhaustive reference. On pages 80–83 he furnishes what, I take it, he regards as a systematic classification of those theories of the nature of goodness which make goodness depend upon a relation to subjective or psychological factors. He arranges them under two main heads, A and B. A consists of those theories which hold that a thing's being good means that some person has, or some persons have, some kind of *feeling* towards it, B of those theories which hold that what is meant is rather that some person *thinks*, or some persons *think*, the thing to be good. Upon the second group, B, Dr Ross wastes few words; and, being in perfect accord with all that he says, I propose to waste even fewer by making no further reference to this type of theory. But we must follow Dr Ross into his sub-division of group A, to which our own theory would most naturally belong, and which Dr Ross allows to possess a much greater prima facie plausibility than the other group. The sub-division adopted will be best explained in its author's own words. 'Theories of this type', he says, 'are divisible into those which identify goodness with the presence of some feeling (1) in at least one person, no matter who he is, (2) in the person who judges an object to be good, (3) in a majority of persons of some class or other—say persons belonging to a particular stage in the history of civilization, (4) in a majority of mankind, or (5) in all mankind.'[1]

Now of course the most conspicuous feature of Dr Ross's classification from our point of view is that it omits altogether the particular variety of type A which seems to ourselves to offer the true definition. For it need scarcely be pointed out that being an object of liking to human nature is by no means identical with being an object of liking either to all mankind or to a majority of all mankind—while much less is it identical with any of the other suggested formulae. Yet there is surely nothing unintelligible, or

[1] *The Right and the Good*, pp. 82–83.

even strained, about the concept 'object of liking to *human nature*'. There are appropriate objects of liking to human nature just as there are appropriate objects to cat nature or dog nature. Cat nature is so constituted as to like stalking its prey and to dislike immersion in water. What is the difficulty about saying that human nature is so constituted as to like and dislike certain specific things also? Indeed, aren't we saying that kind of thing almost every day of our lives? And aren't our psychologists busily engaged at this very time in trying to ascertain just what the basic likes and dislikes of human nature are? And wasn't it the chief aim of the Greek moralist to determine what mode of life human nature was so constituted as in the end, and on the whole, to like best?

I hope, then, that no one will retort against me that while Tom, Dick or Harry can have likings, it is not possible to assign likings to what is not a person but an abstraction, viz., human nature. If we are to take that view in earnest, then we ought likewise to insist, I presume, that *instincts* cannot intelligibly be assigned to human nature either, since, strictly speaking, it is only an actual living creature that can have an instinct. But I fancy that the critic would wish neither to forbid other people to speak, nor himself to refrain from speaking, of 'the instincts of human nature'. In neither case is there any real difficulty about the meaning that is intended. Just as there are instincts which men have in virtue of their common human nature, so too there are likings which men have, or tend to come to have, in virtue of their common human nature.

But perhaps the best analogy for our usage is provided by the usage of the Greek philosophers in their search after man's *summum bonum*. Who is the 'man' whose *summum bonum* is sought? Not surely any particular man, but just 'man as such', the exemplar of our common human nature. The Greek moralist works with a *type man*, constituted by the conative, emotional, and intellectual proclivities believed to be common to human nature, sets him in a natural and social environment which, though inevitably relative to the age and place of the moralist, is made as little specific as possible, and seeks to determine what mode of life will afford the fullest satisfaction to a being so constituted and so conditioned. It is not anything essentially dissimilar, in my judgment, that mass opinion has been doing in the long process of constructing its list of 'goods for man'. The chief difference is due to the simple fact that in the one case the process is undertaken with scientific thoroughness and method, and in the other case not. That is why mass opinion is content with a set of preeminent *goods*, and does not concern itself with the deeper, and to ethical science vitally important, question of the relation of these goods to one another within the unity of *the good*. But so far as the concept of 'human nature' is concerned, the procedure seems fundamentally the same; and there seems no more difficulty in applying the concept in one case than in the other.

I must claim, then, that the subjectivist definition of good which I have placed before you is not to be put out of court on the score of being unintelligible, and I must insist that Dr Ross's criticism of subjectivist theories is not exhaustive of the type so long as the classification upon which it is based ignores this particular variety. It *might* be the case, indeed, that the exclusion of it was only formal. That is, it might be the case that some of Dr Ross's criticisms of the theories on his list are capable of being adapted, with more or less trifling modifications, to the destruction of our theory too. It is therefore of first-rate importance to observe that this is not even remotely the case—as anyone may assure himself by even a cursory inspection of the relevant pages of Dr Ross's book.[1] His criticisms simply do not touch our theory at all. And this is not really surprising. For in spite of superficial resemblances, there is one highly important difference between our theory and any of those which Dr Ross considers. Each of Dr Ross's theories makes the goodness of a thing depend upon the feelings (we may say, for convenience, the 'likings') of *some definitive existing person or persons*. Now it is extremely easy to show, as Dr Ross does clearly show, that when we say 'X is good' we are not, as these theories would imply, meaning to assign to X a quality so impermanent that its coming to belong to X, and its ceasing to belong to X, are contingent upon the mere shift of favour on the part of some particular person or persons. There is undoubtedly an implication of permanence and 'objectivity' about our more 'absolute' value-judgments which belies any such description. But if goodness is made relative, as we make it, to the likings not of definitive persons but of human nature as such, this implication is saved. If what we mean when (in these value-judgments) we say 'X is good' is that X is related in a certain way to the liking nature of

[1] *The Right and the Good*, pp. 83–84.

man, we are not implying, nor indeed even allowing, that X's possession of goodness is at the mercy of the changing likes and dislikes of any persons whatsoever.

I want to turn next—and, I may add, finally—to a difficulty of quite a different kind. It would, naturally, be a crushing objection to our theory, as to any other relational theory of the nature of goodness, if the Objectivist were able to exhibit to us *just one thing* (other, of course, than moral virtue) whose goodness is beyond question underived from relationship to subjective liking or to anything else. Has this ever been achieved? I am going to argue here that no Objectivist has even come near to achieving it. There are, of course, in the writings of all Objectivist axiologists chapters ostensibly directed to 'proving' some selected list of 'intrinsic' values. But close inspection will, I think, reveal a fatal flaw in these arguments. What we find in them is, as a rule, a very cogent demonstration that certain things are good irrespective of any relation to other *goods*, but it is merely *taken for granted*, on the basis of a prior attempted refutation in principle of subjectivist accounts of the nature of goodness, that these things are good irrespective of any relation to subjective feelings *also*. Hence if the prior 'refutation' be itself fallacious (as we have seen reason to believe must be maintained in Dr Ross's case), the proof of the intrinsic value of particular good things will be fundamentally defective.

I shall illustrate once again by a reference to Dr Ross's stimulating book. In his short chapter upon 'What things are good' Dr Ross claims to be offering considerations which will assist the reader to apprehend virtue and knowledge and certain other things as each having a value absolutely in and for itself. What the reader in fact finds is that his arguments are one and all designed to demonstrate that the goodness of each of these goods is independent of any relationship to other goods, but that nothing whatsoever is done to show that the goodness in question is independent of a relationship to subjective feelings. The latter question is not, I think, affected one way or the other by a single word in the whole chapter. We may take the thoroughly typical argument whereby Dr Ross seeks to persuade us of the intrinsic value of knowledge. He asks us to 'suppose two states of the universe equal in respect of virtue and of pleasure and of the allocation of pleasure to the virtuous, but such that the persons in the one have a far greater understanding of the nature and laws of the universe than those in the other. Can any one doubt', he goes on, 'that the first would be a *better* state of the universe?'[1] Dr Ross expects, and rightly expects, that this question will receive an affirmative answer. But I must point out that an affirmative answer does not carry with it a recognition of *intrinsic* value in knowledge. Dr Ross has so constructed his hypothetical situation that an affirmative answer certainly entails the recognition that knowledge has a value which is not dependent upon a relationship to other *goods*. But, so far as his argument here is concerned, it must remain an entirely open question whether the value recognized is an 'objective' quality, or whether, on the other hand, it is dependent upon a relationship to subjective factors—such as, e.g., the likings of human nature. The terms of Dr Ross's argument are such that no light at all can be shed upon this crucial issue.

How, one might ask, would Dr Ross's argument require to be supplemented in order to become relevant to the question of the *objectivity* of the value of knowledge? It would, I think, be formally satisfactory if, in being invited to appraise the relative value of these two states of the universe, we were at the same time instructed to rule out from our minds all considerations arising from our familiarity with human likes and dislikes. Thus we should be obliged to suppose, for the sake of the argument, that there is no native impulse of curiosity in man which makes him come to like knowing for its own sake. If, fulfilling these conditions, we were to proceed to put to ourselves Dr Ross's question, an affirmative answer *would*, I think, imply the recognition of a strictly 'intrinsic' value in knowledge.

But *should* we then be able to return an affirmative answer? It is a matter which each must decide for himself by personal experiment, but I feel convinced that, if the experiment be performed with due observance of the conditions, only a negative answer will be found possible. No legitimate ground remains, I believe, for judging the first state of the universe to be the better. Old emotional habits, like old cognitive habits, die hard, and there is undoubtedly a great mass of prepossessions to be broken through before one can hope to return a fair answer. But I must leave the experiment with the reader, pausing only to draw attention to two pit-falls which seem especially liable to engulf the

[1] *The Right and the Good*, p. 139.

unwary. (1) We know that knowledge, even if it were not itself liked, would still be instrumental to a host of things that are liked, and this makes it difficult for us not to think of the state of the universe with knowledge as the 'better' state. But it is clear that the terms of the hypothesis make this consideration irrelevant. Reference to other goods, whether as 'objects of liking' or in any other sense, is definitely ruled out. (2) A good many of us are more deeply influenced than we are apt to realize by an inherited religious tradition which leads us to think of our faculties as given to us by God for use and development, so that it is in accord with the Will of God, and so far 'good', that they should be exercised to the full. On this ground alone there is a powerful disposition in most of us to regard a state of the universe in which the faculty of knowledge finds active expression as better than a state in which it does not. Evidently, however, we are not, in making this judgment, recognizing knowledge to be something 'good in itself'. We are merely recognizing respect for the gifts of God, or obedience to the Divine Will, to be a duty.[1]

It appears to me, then, that Dr Ross totally fails to demonstrate the objective goodness of his 'intrinsic goods', and I am not able to conceive any other method likely to yield a different result. Dr Moore's attempt fails for exactly the same reason as Dr Ross's. His argument in Chapter VI of *Principia Ethica* depends essentially upon a prior supposed refutation of relational theories of the meaning of good in Chapter I; and, as we noted earlier, Dr Moore is himself the latest recruit to the ranks of those who find the reasoning of Chapter I fallacious. I do not find, therefore, in Dr Moore's attempted demonstration of intrinsic goods anything which places in serious jeopardy the central contention of this paper—the contention that there is nothing whatsoever, with the single exception of moral virtue, which does not derive its goodness from a relationship to subjective liking.

[1] It must be admitted that it is extremely difficult, in an ideal experiment such as that which we are here called upon to perform, to prevent one's value-judgments from being affected by the cross-currents of moral and religious duty. Many, perhaps most, educated persons, even apart from religious considerations, believe it to be their duty to develop their capacity for knowledge. On that account the conception of 'knowledge' is closely associated in their minds with the conception of 'goodness'. But clearly the effort has got to be made to abstract from the influence of this connection, if we are seeking to discover, by the device of experiment upon our value-responses, whether knowledge is good simply *as such*, in and by itself, as the Objectivist claims that it is.

VI

It is more than time that this paper drew to its belated close. Nevertheless, I must add just a very few brief words upon a matter alluded to at an early stage of the paper, if I am to round off my theory with any pretence of completeness at all. It has been an implication of my argument that when we predicate value of morally virtuous conduct we mean something rather radically different by the term value from what we mean when we predicate value of anything else whatsoever. In the latter applications the meaning always involves an essential relation to human liking. In the former application no such reference is involved. Yet there clearly must be some common factor in the two meanings. Otherwise, why use the same term 'good' or 'valuable' in both cases? What is this common factor? What is the analogy between the usages which justifies us in employing common terms?

The correct answer, I think, is that all usages of the term 'good' signify at least this common feature in that to which goodness is attributed, viz., that it is the object of what may perhaps least misleadingly be called a *pro*-attitude: just as that to which badness is attributed is always the object of a *contra*-attitude. An object of liking is quite obviously the object of a *pro*-attitude. But it is equally obvious, when we reflect upon it, that morally virtuous conduct is likewise the object of a *pro*-attitude. The latter *pro*-attitude is certainly not the same kind of *pro*-attitude as is entertained towards an object of mere liking. But a *pro*-attitude it undoubtedly is. The identity and the difference can probably be made most plainly apparent by reflecting upon the value-judgments ingredient in any simple case of so-called 'moral temptation', in which the course we believe that we ought to follow is recognized to be incompatible with the course that we like best. Our mental attitudes towards the two courses are conspicuously different, but both of them are beyond question *pro*-attitudes. Indeed, if they were not, there could be no consciousness of inner conflict. It is equally certain, on the one hand, that the morally right course does not appeal to our mere 'liking', and, on the other hand, that it does *appeal* to us. Its appeal is such, indeed, that it may be made by us the motive of our act, and thus be adopted as our 'end' in preference to that which we 'like best'.

If this is true, it appears that what we mean ultimately when
D*

we predicate goodness of moral virtue is that it is an object of approval or favour to the moral consciousness. Does this then imply, it may perhaps be asked, that even the goodness of moral virtue is in the last resort 'subjective', consisting in a certain relationship to a state of consciousness? It is, I think, partly a question of the use of words. Most people, however, would probably agree that the moral consciousness, though it must be *in* a subject, is yet not 'subjective' in the same sense as desires and likings are 'subjective'. But I cannot now embark upon the long and arduous task of defining the true status within the self—much less within the whole scheme of things—of the moral consciousness. A fully adequate theory of value could not, I am sure, be dispensed from this obligation. But the pretensions of the present paper are more modest. I am content if I have established a prima facie case for the view that the meaning of value as applied to all the so-called intrinsic values with the exception of moral virtue involves an essential relationship to human liking.

MORAL INTUITION AND THE
PRINCIPLE OF SELF-REALIZATION

This address will fall into two parts. In the first part, after pointing out that every non-sceptical ethical theory necessarily accepts the authenticity of moral intuition at least in respect of its own ultimate principle or principles, I shall go on to consider the conditions that must be fulfilled by an ethical principle in order that it may be established as a genuine object of intuition: and I shall argue that there is *one* of these conditions which almost all of the ethical principles most commonly offered for our acceptance fail to satisfy. I then observe that the particular disability which is fatal to the ethical principles so far noticed does not, or does not obviously, attach to a certain principle once popular but now very seldom heard of—the principle of 'self-realization'. This suggests that it may be worth while to re-examine the claims of this principle to be an object of moral intuition. Part II will be wholly occupied with this task. The principle of self-realization will be expounded, defended against common misconceptions and common criticisms, and tested, so far as limitations of time permit, in the light of the conditions required of a valid moral intuition as these were laid down in Part I. The conclusion which will (I hope) emerge is that the forgotten ethics of self-realization has merits which the serious student of morals can ill afford to ignore.

Let me admit at once that what I have to say will rest upon certain assumptions which are to-day called in question in important quarters. But this procedure, reprehensible in a treatise, is, I fear, inescapable in a discourse of the present modest dimensions. Thus it will be found that I accept what may be called the traditional, as against a positivist or a subjectivist, analysis of the general import of moral judgments: but if I were obliged to justify this framework of ideas before being permitted to discuss my specific problem, it is pretty clear that the specific problem could never, within the prescribed limits, be reached at all. It is true, of course, that in cases where a framework of ideas has been abandoned by almost all reputable investigators, it would be foolish to conduct an elaborate argument within that framework without preliminary justification of the framework itself. The assumptions I shall make, however, whatever their future fate may be, are certainly not now to be placed in that category. I venture to hope, therefore, that at least the majority of moralists will still find the issues raised in this lecture worthy of their consideration.

PART I

It hardly seems open to doubt that every ethical theory—though not, of course, every theory *about* ethics—accepts either explicitly or implicitly the existence of moral intuition. So-called 'Anti-Intuitionist' theories do not reject moral intuition. They merely deny a *plurality* of moral intuitions. According to Intuitionist ethics, there are a number of acts (or kinds of act) each of which is morally obligatory in its own right; i.e., for no reason save that it is the act (or kind of act) that it is. In each case the obligation is self-evident, unmediated, and the act of discerning it is thus an intuition. According to Anti-Intuitionist ethics, on the other hand, the obligatoriness of particular acts (or kinds of act) is never ultimate or self-evident. It is derivable from the obligatoriness of some supreme principle, e.g., the general happiness, the perfection of man, or the maximization of good, under which the act (or kind of act) is conceived to fall. But it is obvious that for this type of theory the *supreme* principle must be obligatory in its own right, and discernible only by direct insight, by 'moral intuition'. In respect of epistemological status there is no difference between the ultimate obligations of Intuitionist and Anti-Intuitionist ethics.

The intuitive character of ultimate obligations does not entail, of course, that no considerations can be adduced in support of the obligatoriness that is claimed for them. On the contrary, to exhibit such considerations in the most persuasive light is the main task confronting the expositor of an ethical theory. But it does entail that the considerations adduced can never be of the nature of reasons why the obligation is obligatory.[1] This is manifestly

---

[1] The fact that one can, in the nature of the case, offer no 'reason' for the obligatoriness of ultimate obligations has, I think, been misconstrued in some quarters as a ground for supposing that, in the last resort, ethical theories are forced back upon mere personal 'preferences'—or, in the language now so fashionable, personal 'decisions'. Understandably enough, the alternative that ultimate obligations are self-evident objects of moral intuition is not

impossible where the obligation is *ex hypothesi* ultimate—unless, indeed, one takes the view, which perhaps no one with a clear conception of what is involved is likely to take, that what 'ought to be' can be deduced from what 'is'.

Belief in moral intuition, then, may be said to be a basis of agreement (not always recognized) underlying all the differences of different ethical theories. In that respect a classification of ethical theories into Intuitionist and Anti-Intuitionist is somewhat misleading. The opposition is better described as between Pluralistic Intuitionism and Monistic Intuitionism. And the ultimate problem of the moralist, no matter to what school he belongs, is to establish the authenticity of the basic intuition or intuitions which he favours.

By what general methods, let us ask, may the moralist hope to accomplish his task of persuasion?

On the positive side, the chief requirement must be a formulation in precise and unambiguous terms of the content of the obligation which he claims to know as an object of intuition. The final court of appeal is the moral consciousness of those to whom the argument is addressed; and we cannot expect that consciousness to respond properly unless we give it a fair chance by presenting in clear terms the material we are submitting to its judgment. But, as everyone knows, adequate formulation is here a much more troublesome matter than appears on the surface. Those philosophers may be right who hold that many of our familiar everyday 'moral rules' have a solid basis in intuition; but it is certain that in their familiar everyday formulation these moral rules are far too vague for us to know whether there is an intuition of them or not. 'You ought to keep your promises.' Is there a moral intuition here? Perhaps, but one must first know what exactly is meant by a 'promise'. When I make a promise, do I undertake to do or refrain from doing something subject only to

regarded as a real alternative by those philosophers who deny outright that synthetic *a priori* propositions are even possible. Less easy to understand is the logic whereby the synthetic *a priori* proposition that there can be no synthetic *a priori* propositions has gained acceptance. If, on the other hand, the logical basis of the belief that there can be no synthetic *a priori* propositions is the empirical evidence, it is legitimate to ask that the case of ethics should not be prejudged, and that the empirical evidence from the field of moral experience should be examined on its merits.

such conditions as I expressly state, or are there also certain *implied* conditions the non-fulfilment of which negates the promise in just the same way as non-fulfilment of the *stated* conditions? Is there, for example, as seems fairly obvious, an implied condition that the promisee does not himself release me from my promise prior to its discharge? Or again—a more debatable question—is there an implied condition that no drastic change occurs in the circumstances anticipated by promiser and promisee when the promise was made? And if that condition *is* implied, just how drastic must the change be in order to negate the promise? We cannot know whether or not we have an intuition of an obligation to keep promises until the answers to these and other questions are set clearly before us in the formulation and interpretation of the alleged obligation. And, of course, the case of promise-keeping is not exceptional in this regard. We must be equally ignorant of whether or not we have an intuition that we ought, for example, to act 'justly', or again that we ought to 'maximize good', until we are clearly informed as to what exactly is being meant here by the terms 'just' and 'good'.

Looking now to the negative side, it will be proper for our moralist to take a good deal of pains to destroy the credentials of rival claimants to the title of 'moral intuition'. This may seem, indeed, to be a work of supererogation where the rival claimants are incompatible with the intuition he aims at establishing—and if they are not incompatible they need not be feared as rivals. It *will*, in fact, be a work of supererogation, in so far as he is successful in the *positive* side of his task. Still, however convinced a moralist may be of the existence of a given intuition, he can hardly be equally confident that he has succeeded in bringing home its existence to others. The independent disproof of rival intuitions is therefore by no means without value, if only as a means of inducing in others a greater readiness to accept the intuition one is advocating.

The technique for disproving rival intuitions is almost always the same. It consists in the citation of relevant practical situations in regard to which an impartial mind feels bound to concede that it is at least doubtful whether the alleged obligation holds: in which case it can scarcely be maintained that the obligation is *self-evident*, an object of *intuition*.

It is in the course of exercising this technique that one is most readily made aware of a difficulty in the traditional Intuitionism which has had an important bearing upon recent developments in ethical theory. Provided that the obligations in question are held to be *absolute* obligations, it would seem that not more than *one* intuition, with its corresponding obligation, can be retained. When Pluralistic Intuitionism of the older type presents us with a set of allegedly absolute obligations, it seems always possible in principle to use *one* of the set to disprove all the rest. Let A, B, C, D be four allegedly absolute obligations. If A's absoluteness be taken as established, then B's obligatoriness cannot also be absolute if it is possible to conceive a situation in which B obliges to a course of action incompatible with the course to which A obliges. For the admission of B's obligatoriness in this situation would entail the denial of A's obligatoriness. The same holds, of course, if we substitute C or D for B. But it would appear that it is in fact possible in the case of *any* two alleged obligations to devise situations in which the courses they prescribe will be mutually exclusive. If so, there can be only *one* absolute obligation. Largely on account of this predicament the practice of most contemporary Intuitionists has been (following Ross) to regard the object of moral intuition as not an *absolute*, but only a prima facie, obligation. A prima facie obligation does not bind to action irrespective of all other considerations. In a particular situation promise-keeping (for example) binds to action only in so far as it is not outweighed by such contrary prima facie obligations as are also relevant to the situation. Conflict of prima facie obligations thus does not involve us in the theoretical contradiction and practical impasse that beset the conflict of absolute obligations. There is no doubt that Intuitionism has taken on a new lease of life since Ross's ingenuity provided it with this device for turning the edge of what was perhaps the critic's deadliest weapon.

But there is a third procedure which the advocate of an ethical theory cannot afford to neglect, and to which I wish to direct rather special attention in this first part of my lecture. He must be prepared to show his intuitive principle or principles to be compatible with the moral judgments of mankind. Moreover, 'mankind' here must mean mankind not merely as represented in his own particular age and civilization, but mankind *everywhere* and *always*. For the data of ethics consist in the moral judgments of mankind without restriction of time or place. One may, of course, be able on occasion to deny the relevance of moral judgments awkward for one's theory on the ground that they are not what they seem to be—not *really* 'moral' judgments. But in so far as ostensible moral judgments do remain accredited as moral judgments, i.e., as authentic manifestations of man's moral consciousness, *all* of them are relevant to ethical theory, and no alleged principle of obligation can be allowed to be a genuine object of moral intuition if it is demonstrably discordant with any of them.

This proposition does not, of course, carry with it the absurd consequence that the moralist should expect to find, if his principle is a valid principle, that the particular moral rules of other times and other places coincide with the particular moral rules which, in the context of his own civilization, appear to him to follow from the principle. Quite obviously, where there are substantial differences of physical and social environment, and still more obviously where there are substantially different factual beliefs about animate and inanimate Nature (not to speak of the 'supernatural' world), there cannot fail to be notable differences of view concerning the modes of conduct by which man can best fulfil the demands of a given moral principle. Identity of ultimate principle is consistent with the widest diversity of particular moral rules. But the important point which remains is this. The moralist must be prepared to show that the particular moral rules of other communities, where different, are yet differentiations of the same basic principle or principles, deriving their differences quite naturally from a different contextual conditioning.

Now it seems to me that in 'compatibility with the moral judgments of mankind' we have a test of the validity of ethical principles, and of the intuitions on which they are based, which deserves much more attention than it is accustomed to get. It is a test, I believe, which the intuitions of Pluralistic Intuitionism, even in their modern form, are unable to survive. Nay, more. It can, I think, be shown that when we apply the test to the basic intuitions which are, as we saw, implicit even in Anti-Intuitionist theories, these show themselves, almost without exception, to be no less vulnerable. But if we are to see that this is so, we must first spend some little time in securing the test itself against criticism and in clarifying its nature.

The truth (as I conceive it to be) that a valid ethical principle must be compatible with the moral judgments of mankind has been obscured, I think, by a somewhat facile reliance upon the notion of *development* as applied to man's moral consciousness. No doubt the moral consciousness of man does develop. But it by no means follows that this 'development' is of such a kind as to justify a suggestion that there can be incompatibility in the ultimate principles animating the moral judgments of different communities.

To one possible meaning of 'development' of the moral consciousness we have already alluded in a slightly different connection. The increase and improvement of factual knowledge naturally brings in its train more enlightened views about the kinds of behaviour best calculated to implement a given moral principle. It is not unreasonable, though it may be a little misleading, to speak of the more enlightened rules which result as signifying 'moral development', or even 'development of man's moral consciousness'. Clearly, however, the fact of moral development in *this* meaning lends no support to the view that there might be differences of ultimate principle in the moral judgments of mankind.

A second valid meaning, and a much more important one for our present issue, is based on the fact that even an ultimate moral principle, a genuine object of intuition, may fail to be apprehended by a given mind. There may not be present in that mind certain conditions which are in fact indispensable to the intuiting. No one, I fancy, denies that there can be development of the moral consciousness in *this* sense also: in the sense that the mind may earlier lack, and later come to enjoy, conditions that are indispensable to a given intuiting. Nor can we doubt that this kind of development is relevant to the testing of an ethical theory by its compatibility with the moral judgments of mankind. The precise extent and manner of its relevance, however, will depend upon the answer to the question, 'what *are* the indispensable conditions for the intuiting of an intuition?'—in particular, for the intuiting of a moral intuition?

To this question Sir David Ross's answer seems to me to be in principle the correct one, though his account stands, I think, in need of some elaboration. Ross points out that when he claims that the rightness of a certain type of action is 'self-evident' he does not mean that 'it is evident from the beginning of our lives, or as soon as we attend to the proposition for the first time, but . . . that when we have reached sufficient mental maturity, and have given sufficient attention to the proposition, it is evident without any need of proof, or of evidence beyond itself'.[1]

So far as it goes, this account is one with which I have no quarrel. But we may be permitted to wish that Ross had developed his argument at greater length, and had left us rather less in the dark as to what constitutes 'sufficient mental maturity'. What *kind* of mental maturity is required of a man in order that he may reasonably be expected to intuit a 'self-evident' obligation? The question seems vital, and the answer by no means obvious, but I cannot find that Ross has anywhere much to say on the matter. It seems to me pretty certain, however, what is the answer that *ought* to be given to the question. As I have argued elsewhere, *neither* the sort of mental maturity which consists in ability to sustain a complicated train of reasoning, *nor* the sort of mental maturity which consists in the possession of an ample stock of factual information (e.g., about possible consequences of a particular type of act), has any bearing upon the kind of apprehension here at issue. So far as I can see, the only sort of mental maturity which can legitimately be demanded of the subject mind is (if I may be allowed to quote words of my own) 'such as enables it to understand the meaning of the different terms in the proposition and . . . to make the effort of abstract thought required to hold together the different "terms" in their propositional relationship'.[2] This is, I think, precisely the same sort of mental maturity as would be needed for the apprehension of self-evident logical or mathematical 'axioms'; a function of the mind which Ross himself regards as analogous to the apprehension of self-evident moral obligations.

We have now reviewed two senses in which it is possible to speak of 'development' of the moral faculty. In the second sense we agree that an appropriate 'development' *is* a precondition of intuitions being evoked in the moral consciousness: and of this fact we must take careful account in any application of the test 'compatibility with the moral judgments of mankind'. But there

[1] *The Right and the Good*, p. 29.   [2] *Scepticism and Construction*, pp. 239-40.

is, I think, no further sense in which 'lack of development' can be appealed to as adequate ground for failure to intuit an allegedly self-evident obligation. If a person or community fulfils the preconditions of intuiting noted above and yet fails to apprehend the supposed obligation, I do not know how we are to resist the inference that the self-evidence of the obligation, and the intuition, are fictions. Otherwise, what the admitted discrepancy in moral response seems to imply is not two different states of the moral consciousness, one developed and the other undeveloped, but rather two different *sorts* of moral consciousness, one of which accepts, while the other rejects, the principle '*x* is obligatory'. But to accept *this* state of affairs is to abandon the possibility of any objective ethics whatsoever. We may amuse ourselves, if we like, by trying to ascertain what are the ultimate principles of 'our own' moral consciousness. But the result will have no more than an autobiographical interest. There will be no ground for supposing that they are *better* principles than those of someone else's moral consciousness; whether that consciousness has happened to function in a remote past, or will perhaps only come to function in some distant future. It is surely a presupposition of there being any objective ethical truth that the moral consciousness of man is *one*, functioning according to uniform ultimate principles, and that whatever conflict there may be in particular applications of the principles there can be no conflict between the principles themselves.

The position we have now reached may be said to be as follows. The test of the authenticity of a moral intuition—or of an ultimate moral principle, or of a self-evident moral obligation, which are the same thing from different points of view—that it be 'compatible with the moral judgments of mankind', remains a valid test despite the fact of 'development' in man's moral consciousness. The nature of this 'development' affects the application of the test only in the following respects: that it cannot be regarded as evidence against the authenticity of a moral intuition that it is found to be wanting in certain persons, provided there is reason to believe (*a*) that the minds of these persons are not mature enough to understand the meaning of the relevant terms or to hold them together in their propositional relationship, or (*b*) that these persons have not given sufficient attention to the relevant situation.

Let us now attempt application of the test, giving regard first to Pluralistic Intuitionism. How, for example, do such prima facie intuitions as are listed by Sir David Ross fare under the test? The crucial question will clearly be this. Is there, or is there not, compelling evidence that some persons who fulfil the required preconditions of mental maturity and attentiveness to the appropriate situations fail nevertheless to apprehend even as prima facie duties such behaviour as keeping promises, making reparation for injury, giving return for services rendered, forbearing to inflict gratuitous pain, and so on?

It seems to me that there *is* compelling evidence: indeed, that the documents of social anthropology literally abound with it. It is perfectly true, of course, that many, perhaps most, primitive communities do recognize obligations like these just enumerated, *in a certain conditional form*. But, paradoxically enough, it is just these very communities which furnish the most conclusive evidence *against* Ross's intuitions. For in the first place their actual recognition of the obligations (though in conditional form) makes it exceedingly unplausible to argue that the communities in question are either too mentally immature, or too little attentive to the relevant situations, to be capable of the appropriate intuitions. And in the second place, as we shall see, the specific nature of the limiting condition under which alone they accept the obligations as holding seems to show that, whatever intuitive basis there may be for this acceptance, it is not to be identified with Ross's intuitions.

What, then, is this 'limiting condition'? There is nothing mysterious about it. Anthropological records disclose that a large proportion of the communities which recognize these obligations recognize them as holding *only where the prospective beneficiaries are members of that community*; or, at most, members of a limited social group within which that community falls. The actual 'dimensions' of the group are, of course, subject to wide variation. The point is that in respect to persons outside the group, whatever its dimensions, no moral obligation whatever seems to be felt by members of the community. Lying, murder, robbery, rape, and torture, if practised towards an 'alien', are not merely morally condoned but even tend, often enough, to be regarded as meritorious.

The fact of this 'social limitation' of moral obligation seems incontrovertible. We need not squander any part of our time in giving examples of beliefs and practices that are reported by the score in every considerable manual of primitive life and culture. But the significance of the limitation in relation to the Intuitionists' theory appears to me to have been very inadequately appreciated. It is of the essence of the Intuitionists' view, as Ross's own statements repeatedly illustrate, that the 'self-evident obligations' are apprehended as obligatory simply because they are acts of a certain kind—the keeping of a promise made, the repairing of an injury that one has inflicted, and so on. There is no 'reason' discerned why one ought to keep the promise beyond the fact that one has made it, no 'reason' why one ought to repair the injury beyond the fact that one has inflicted it. But the aspect of 'social limitation' inherent in the obligations recognized by these primitive communities surely implies that there just is *not* this discernment of an obligation in promise-keeping *qua* promise-keeping, or in making reparation *qua* making reparation. If there were, surely there could not fail to be recognition that there is a least a prima facie obligation to behave in these ways *irrespective* of the relationship in which the prospective beneficiaries stand to the community? Yet in many communities there seems to be no vestige of awareness that the obligations are relevant towards anyone outside the community's own circle.

But is there no significance, it may be asked, in the fact that certain definite obligations such as those named are, even though under a limiting condition, all but universally accepted in savage no less than civilized communities? Must they not be credited with a rather special status in the realm of obligation? I agree that there is great significance in the fact. But if the fact be interpreted with due regard to the aspect of social limitation as well as to the aspect of universal recognition, the significance cannot be that these obligations are obligatory in their own right, simply *qua* promise-keeping, *qua* making reparation, etc. The implication of the aspect of social limitation would seem to be that in these primitive communities it is not the 'abstract' situation, but the situation *in relation to the life of the community* which is felt to create the obligation. Indeed, when one reflects upon the character of these obligations, and on the singular benefits that accrue to the community from their observance, it is difficult to resist the conviction that the true significance of the 'universality of recognition' is simply this: that there are a number of routine situations, regularly recurrent in the life of *every kind* of organized community, in respect to which certain responses by the members are readily recognized to be *vital to corporate well-being*. Corporate well-being need not be, and I shall later argue that it is not, the *ultimate* principle of obligation involved. But it must be much nearer to an ultimate principle than promise-keeping, making reparation, etc., if it be the case that these obligations are recognized by primitive communities only subject to their discharge serving the corporate well-being.

Moreover, support is lent to this reading of the situation when one considers certain of the working conceptions of the social anthropologist. It would, I think, be fairly generally agreed among anthropologists that in their endeavours to find a meaning in bizarre and apparently perverse moral customs in particular tribes (as distinct from the moral customs more or less common to primitive and civilized communities, which are apt, because not 'queer', to seem to us not to call for explanation) the key conception can only be 'supposed conduciveness to tribal well-being'. And it is a 'key' that surely works pretty well. To the investigator who has steeped himself in the lore of a tribe and has thoroughly grasped its traditional beliefs about gods and men and the processes of Nature, the use of this key permits all kinds of grotesque moral customs to become intelligible. Given the tribe's esoteric beliefs, many of these customs present themselves as no longer unaccountable aberrations, but as reasonable prescriptions for ensuring tribal security and prosperity. But if conduciveness to communal well-being is the principle underlying the moral obligations *peculiar* to particular communities, there is at least a presumption that this principle underlies also the moral obligations which these communities *share* with other communities: i.e., obligations like promise-keeping, repairing injuries, etc.

It is unnecessary for my present purpose, however, to press any positive theory about the principle which may underlie the limited acceptance by primitive communities of the Rossian obligations. I shall venture to outline a positive theory in Part II. All that at the moment I am concerned to urge is that the aspect of social limitation shows that these communities do not intuit the obligations in question as obligatory in their own right: whereas they *should* so intuit them if that is in fact their nature. For even without making appeal to general considerations drawn from recent anthropological research, which suggest that primitive man approximates much more closely to civilized man in intellectual powers than was earlier supposed,[1] the requisite degree of mental maturity for intuiting these obligations, and of attentiveness to the relevant practical situations, seem sufficiently established, as we noted above, by the fact that the obligations do in their conditional form occupy a prominent place in the moral codes of primitive communities. It seems to me very hard to believe that the Rossian intuitions are really intrinsic to man's moral consciousness when they fail to manifest themselves in the moral consciousness of these communities. It is perfectly true, of course, that the member of a primitive tribe is very unlikely ever to have given attention to the relevant situations *in their full abstractness*. He has given his attention to the situation of making a promise to a 'clansman', and to the situation of making a promise to an 'alien', but he has not, presumably, isolated for separate consideration the situation of making a promise *as such*. Still, it would be most unplausible to suggest that an intuition intrinsic to the moral consciousness comes into play only when the situation supposed to evoke it has become present to the mind in its full abstractness. No such suggestion is likely to be made by Ross himself, who tells us that 'what comes first in time is the apprehension of the self-evident prima facie rightness of an individual act of a particular type. From this we come by reflection to apprehend the self-evident general principle of prima facie duty.'[2] Presumably the general principle is operative from the beginning, and moral intuitions take place *in accordance with it* long before the principle is attended to *per se* and become itself an *object* of intuition. But in that event, how could the general principle of promise-keeping, if it really is an intuitive principle intrinsic to the moral consciousness, fail to make itself felt in the moral response of primitive man to so many individual cases of promise-keeping where the promisee is a member of an alien group?

It seems to me, then, that the aspect of social limitation in the moral obligations recognized by primitive communities is enough

[1] An interesting account will be found in Professor A. Macbeath's contribution to the symposium on 'Is Anthropology relevant to Ethics?' in the *Aristotelian Society Supplementary Volume* xx. See especially pp. 116 ff.

[2] *The Right and the Good*, p. 33.

in itself to show that Pluralistic Intuitionism is not in harmony with the moral judgments of mankind, and therefore fails to pass one of the tests of a valid ethical theory. Its supposedly self-evident rules of behaviour are in fact repudiated, even as prima facie obligations, by large numbers of persons who are well able to appreciate them. But what now of Monistic Intuitionism, of the so-called 'Anti-Intuitionist' theories? Is the (implied) self-evidence of their respective ultimate principles any easier to reconcile with the social limitation of primitive morality?

It certainly looks as though it would not be any easier in the case of *most* theories of this type. In most cases the ultimate principle is no more limited in its range of prospective beneficiaries than are the special rules of the Pluralist. Indeed, for many Monistic theories the transcendence of the group is explicitly proclaimed, and is of the very essence of the doctrine—the greatest happiness of the *greatest number*, the *Common* Good, the full realization of *human* capacities, the efficiency of the *race*, and so on. In other Monistic theories, such as Ideal Utilitarianism with its ultimate principle the 'maximization of good', social 'universality' is not explicit but is clearly implicit. The command to maximize good permits of no discrimination in favour of one social group against another. In principle, if an act which benefits Hottentots at the expense of one's own nearest and dearest is the act which adds most to the sum of good in the world, it is the act which ought to be done. Must it not be concluded, then, that these Monistic theories too are discordant with the moral judgments of mankind, in that the basic intuitions they imply are also inoperative in the moral judgments of primitive communities?

I cannot for myself see any good reason for refusing to accept this conclusion. I cannot see how we can hold that the ultimate principle of obligation informing the moral consciousness really has the aspect of social universality intrinsic in it when the moral consciousness of so many actual communities so sharply restricts the range of beneficiaries. The factors which, by common consent, can impede or prevent the proper functioning of an intuition do not seem to be in point here. It can scarcely be pleaded that the primitive communities are too mentally immature to appreciate that there *are* human beings outside their own social group; or again that their attention has not been sufficiently called to this fact. It seems to me, therefore, that whatever the ultimate principle of man's moral consciousness may be, it cannot be one in which the aspect of social universality is intrinsic.

But it is time now that the work of destruction began to give way to some attempt at construction. Having eliminated almost all of the ethical theories that compete for contemporary approval, on the ground that the basic intuitions asserted or implied by them fail in each case to pass the test of harmony with the moral judgments of mankind, we must now face the question: 'what is the alternative?' Is there *any* basic intuition one can think of that might pass the test? If there is, it must (we have seen) be of an obligation which is not in its intrinsic nature socially *universal*. Equally evidently, however, the obligation must not be, in its intrinsic nature, socially *limited* either: for the moral judgments of civilized communities are at least as important a part of the data of ethics as those of savage communities, and a 'socially limited' principle of obligation (in the sense in which we have been using that term) is emphatically irreconcilable with most moral judgment in most civilized communities. It looks, therefore, as though, if there is an authentic moral intuition at all, it has got to be of a principle of obligation which is, in its primary or intrinsic nature, *neither* socially universal *nor* socially limited, but socially *neutral*. At the same time, since the 'social reference' of the vast majority of the obligations recognized by primitive and civilized communities alike is simple matter of fact, it is absolutely necessary that the principle should be one such that, in its actual application in the context of human living, it takes on a social reference as a matter of course: a social reference, moreover, which tends to be limited to the group in the case of primitive communities, and to be universal in the case of civilized communities.

Is there any hope of finding such a basic intuition? The omens are certainly not very propitious. Not many candidates are left in the field. There is, indeed, one ethical principle which does not seem to suffer from the specific defect on account of which we have condemned so many others, a principle which might with some plausibility be regarded as socially neutral in its intrinsic nature and as assuming naturally a social orientation in actual practice. I refer to the principle underlying those theories which fall under the general rubric of 'self-realization ethics'. But 'self-realization', we shall be told, has not less serious defects of its own, and has long been discredited as an ethical principle.

Nevertheless, I propose to take my courage in both hands and to see what can be done with 'self-realization': not in any spirit of mere bravado, but because it really does seem to me that the case for it is strong—immeasurably stronger than one would be likely to gather from references to it in current ethical writings. Obviously, within the limits of this lecture, I can deal usefully with no more than certain very fundamental points. Nevertheless, I shall hope to say enough to persuade you that the 'standard' criticisms of self-realization ethics are based on grave misunderstanding of its essential purport, and that this type of ethical theory, whether finally tenable or not, cannot be dismissed without a far more careful study than moralists have for long been disposed to give to it.

PART II

At the root of by far the greater part of the criticisms of the ethics of self-realization is the belief that self-realization is essentially an *egoistic* conception. According to the most usual interpretation, self-realization as a moral principle implies that the end at which man ought to aim, the ultimate goal of moral aspiration, is a completely satisfying state of his self; all particular obligations deriving their obligatoriness, in the last resort, from conduciveness to the attainment of this egoistic end.

Let me say at once that if I believed this charge of egoism to be well founded I should range myself unhesitatingly on the side of the critics. There may very well be, I think, *a* duty relating to a prospective state of the self, e.g., a prima facie duty of 'self-improvement' to whose claims a moral agent may legitimately give consideration, though only in relation to the competing claims of other prima facie duties. This much egoism, perhaps, most of the critics would themselves be prepared to admit into the body of morals. But that our *ultimate* and *sole* duty is to promote some future state of our self is a proposition so violently at variance with the actual moral judgments of mankind that one cannot wonder if contemporary moralists deem it hardly worth their powder and shot. It is certainly not of an obligation to realize the self in any such sense that I shall venture to urge that there is a basic intuition.

One must also, in fairness, concede to the critic that he has a good deal of excuse for his egoistic interpretation of this theory. Not only does the term 'self-realization' itself carry with it a strong suggestion of egoism, but, in addition, the initial impression thus created tends to be confirmed by the phraseology which leading members of the school, like Green and Bradley, use for the formulation of the central propositions of their moral psychology. Thus we are told that the object of desire is always a 'conceived personal good', and that in all morally responsible conduct, good or bad, the agent is seeking some form of 'self-satisfaction'. These typical expressions can, in my opinion, when carefully related to their contexts, generally be seen to have no necessary connection with egoism: but it must be admitted that they can very easily put the unwary or the unsympathetic reader on the wrong track. And one would be hard put to it to deny that still more must be conceded to the critic. At times self-realization moralists have fallen into forms of expression which, even in their context, cannot easily bear any but an egoistic interpretation. Where these occur, however, they should, in my opinion, be regarded not as betraying the inherent egoism of self-realization theory, but rather as momentary lapses from grace on the part of certain self-realization theorists. For—or so I shall endeavour to prove—there is, in the fundamental and distinctive thesis of self-realization ethics, no necessary implication of egoism whatsoever.

What, then, *is* this 'fundamental and distinctive thesis'? No short answer can be more than a 'pointer': but by way of a preliminary formula, to be explained and developed in the sequel, one might venture the statement that the essence of self-realization ethics is a certain integration of the moral consciousness with the desiring consciousness. There is no question, of course, of *identifying* the two, or of reducing the moral consciousness to some form of the desiring consciousness. But it is central to this doctrine that the moral consciousness gets all its content from the ends of desire, and is thus capable of being understood only in the light of its positive relationship to the desiring consciousness. What that positive relationship is and entails remains to be seen: but we should be clear at the outset that the 'self' whose realization is for this ethical school the moral norm is a self which is essentially a unity of desires and interests.

So far as this very general description is concerned, there is plainly nothing to warrant the suggestion that the doctrine is egoistic. Such a doctrine may, of course, very well appear obnoxious on *other* grounds. Where the content of the moral consciousness is alleged to be drawn from the ends of desire, there is at least a prima facie difficulty about showing how such content can present itself to the agent with all the authority of morality's categorical imperative. But, waiving this difficulty for the moment, it is clear that the derivation of the content of morality from the ends of desire does not—apart from some special theory of the nature of desire—entail the further difficulty that the theory is 'egoistic'. For desire, as ordinarily understood, can as readily be for non-egoistic as for egoistic ends. Indeed, most people would probably agree that a desire which has for its object a prospective state of the self is a comparatively rare event. There seems, then, no reason to suspect the ethics of self-realization of being egoistic simply on the ground that its moral content is derived from the desires.

'Apart', we said, 'from some special theory of desire.' That, however, is just where the trouble arises. As a result of his analysis of desire, the self-realization moralist pronounces, as we saw, that all desire is for a 'conceived personal good'. Does he mean by this that the object of desire is always a prospective state of the self? If he does, the charge of egoism is justified. If he does not, then what *does* he mean and why does he choose to express that meaning in a phrase so perilous in its suggestions?

Actually, the point which these moralists wish to make when they identify the object of desire with a conceived personal good is, I believe, in essence extremely simple. It is also extremely important and extremely easy to miss. It emerges best when one attempts to make clear to one's self what precisely it is which distinguishes 'desire' from 'instinctive impulse'. We do all in fact recognize a distinction between these phenomena of our inner life. Just what is the basis of the distinction? It seems, on reflection, to be as follows. Both in impulse and in desire we are conscious of an inner 'urge'; and, normally, we are conscious also of the 'object' of the urge. But in impulse, by contrast with desire, the *self-referent* activity characteristic of a self-conscious subject has not, or not yet, occurred: so that the object is, so far as I am aware of it, merely object of an *impulse in me* and not, as yet, object of my *self*. Impulse becomes desire when, and only when, through the operation of self-conscious thought, I become aware of the object as *my* object, as something which *I* want. But to be aware of an object as something which *I* want is, in a perfectly legitimate sense of the words, to be aware of it as a 'good for me', i.e., as a 'personal good'. Thus the point of the proposition that desire is always for a personal good is not in the least to advocate psychological egoism. Plainly an object which I am conscious that I want need not be (and seldom is) 'a state of my self'. The point of the proposition is to draw attention to a function which is distinctive of the conative experience of *persons*, and which is of paramount importance in determining the coherent development of that experience, viz., the self-referent activity of the self-conscious subject.

It is essentially this point which Green is making when he argues that in all strictly motived action the object aimed at is conceived as a personal good.[1] Green bases his discussion throughout on the contrast between 'motive' and 'animal want', and the whole burden of his thought is that an operation of self-consciousness upon animal want is the indispensable precondition of the want becoming a 'motive'. If we view that operation of self-consciousness upon animal want (as Green does) in the manner described above, there is, I submit, no difficulty in understanding why Green judged it proper to conclude that all motived conduct aims at a 'personal good': and no difficulty, I should have thought, in seeing that this conclusion has nothing whatever to do with 'egoism'.

Nevertheless, it is, I think, radical misunderstanding on this point, more than any other factor, which is responsible for the present-day disrepute of self-realization ethics. Even so exceptionally accurate and scrupulous a thinker as Mr Prichard has, in my opinion, fallen victim to the common error: and unhappily, in virtue of the authority so justly accorded to his writings, his account of the matter has done much to consolidate and perpetuate the error in the minds of contemporary students of morals. It is of such crucial importance to gain a true view on this issue that, even at the risk of some repetition, I must dwell

[1] *Prolegomena to Ethics*, §§ 88 ff.

for a space on Mr Prichard's interpretation of Green's moral psychology.

Mr Prichard's most explicit statement of his view occurs, I think, in his *Duty and Interest*, pp. 25 ff. He begins with a quotation from the *Prolegomena to Ethics* which, for reasons that will appear, I must transcribe in full:

'The motive in every imputable act for which the agent is conscious on reflection that he is answerable is a desire for personal good in some form or other. . . . It is superfluous to add, good to *himself*; for anything conceived as good in such a way that the agent acts for the sake of it, must be conceived as *his own* good, though he may conceive it as his own good only on account of his interest in others, and in spite of any amount of suffering on his own part incidental to its attainment.'[1]

The most significant thing about this quotation is, if I may so put it, the bit that isn't there. Mr Prichard has omitted—and this can only be because it seems to him to contribute nothing of consequence to the elucidation of Green's position—the very part of the text which, as I interpret Green, is absolutely indispensable if one is to grasp the point of his formula for motives. No one could guess from Mr Prichard's quotation that Green has been asking himself on what principle we can distinguish *motived* action from *instinctive* action. Yet the half-dozen sentences which Mr Prichard has omitted are largely concerned with just that point. If Green's formula for motives is not interpreted in *this* context, it is, I think, virtually bound to be misunderstood. We need feel no surprise, therefore, that Mr Prichard, having missed the significance of Green's contrast of motived with instinctive action, should go on to take an egoistic interpretation for granted, and to urge that the doctrine which emerges cannot 'stand the test of instances'.

'It seems impossible to allow that in what would usually be called disinterested actions, whether they be good or bad, there is not at least some element of disinterestedness. It strikes us as absurd to think that in what would be called a benevolent action, we are not moved at least in part by the desire that someone shall be better off and also by the desire to *make* him better off, even though

[1] *Prolegomena to Ethics*, §§ 91-2.

we may also necessarily have, and be influenced by, the desire to have the satisfaction of thinking that he is better off and that we have made him so.'[1]

Mr Prichard adds other instances to the same effect, but the case of benevolence will suffice. It seems plain that Mr Prichard thinks that to say that a benevolent desire has for its object a 'personal good' is equivalent to saying that it has for its object a future state of the self—'the satisfaction of thinking that he [the beneficiary] is better off and that we have made him so'. And this analysis of benevolent desire he not unnaturally denounces as absurd. But so too would Green. In fact Green *has* denounced it, in almost so many words, as anyone may find for himself by turning to § 161 of the *Prolegomena*, where Green cites with approval Butler's view that 'benevolent desires terminate upon their objects, upon the benefits done to others'. And Green can take this line with perfect consistency because for him, as I have been urging, to hold that a benevolent desire is for a personal good is *not* to hold that it is for a future state of the self. It is to hold that, just in so far as it really is a *desire* and not a mere *impulse*, the well-being of the prospective beneficiary must be consciously apprehended by the agent as something which *he* wants, therefore as a *good for him*, therefore as a *personal good*.

If, then, we must agree that the psychology of the self-realization school is not, after all, egoistic, there is a pretty strong presumption that its notion of the moral end, derived as it is from the ends of desire, will not be egoistic either. This presumption will, I think, be amply borne out when we consider, as I propose to do now, the nature and basis of the doctrine that the moral end is 'self-realization'. As I am concerned primarily not with historical interpretation but with the doctrine's validity, I shall take leave to develop the argument in my own way.

The key to the doctrine lies in the contrast and conflict which tend to occur in the life of a self-conscious self between the conceived good of the self *as a whole* and the conceived good of *partial aspects* of the self. Let us trace the emergence of this contrast and conflict.

[1] *Duty and Interest*, p. 26.

Every self is, and knows itself to be, the owner of many and diverse desires and interests.[1] And the end of each desire, in as much as it is apprehended as something which the self wants, is, as we have seen, legitimately describable as a 'personal good'. But clearly these desires—and their corresponding 'goods'—are not necessarily in any sort of pre-established harmony with one another. The course of action in which the self might satisfy one desire is a course which may either impede or facilitate or be neutral towards the fulfilment of other desires of the same self. Now a self-conscious subject of desires, aware of its self as the common subject of many desires and interests and not merely as the being who now desires this or that, cannot be indifferent to the bearing which the fulfilment of any one of its desires has upon the fulfilment of others. It will be natural for a self to consider, in the case of a given felt desire, whether its fulfilment, which *ex hypothesi* is a good for the self in a partial aspect of its being, is also a good for the self as a whole, for the self as the common subject of *this* desire and of *many other* desires and interests besides. Often the verdict of such reflection will be that it is not: and where this is so, some degree of aversion to the object of the given desire must needs be engendered in the self from the side of those desires whose fulfilment is seen to be frustrated by satisfying the given desire. It does not follow, however, that the aversion thus begotten by reflection will be felt as 'stronger' than the original desire.[2] Sometimes that does happen, and there is then coincidence between what the agent conceives

[1] Those 'potential desires' or 'dispositions to desire' which we call 'interests' can, of course, no more be ignored than 'actual' desires in any theory which professes to give an intelligible account of the conative experience of a self.

[2] The language of 'stronger' and 'weaker' desires used in the text, which is the language of ordinary persons, is challenged by the doctrine held by some psychologists that the relative strength of competing desires can only be measured 'after the event', by observing which of them finds expression in action. This doctrine seems to me patently false. In most cases we surely know very well which of two competing desires *would* find expression in action if we were called upon to act at once under determination by nothing save desire. It is the same thing as knowing which of two ends of desire is in 'the line of least resistance' in regard to our desiring nature. I can see no ground whatever for supposing that our confidence is misplaced, and that we are not in such cases validly appraising the relative strengths of the two desires. Sometimes, of course, we do find it difficult to say which of two competing desires is the stronger. But the correct inference from that situation is surely not that we lack the ability to measure the relative strength of desires in advance of action, but just that in such cases the competing desires are approximately equal in strength.

to be the good of his self as a whole and the object of his felt strongest desire. But common experience at least *seems* to show many occasions on which there is not *coincidence* but *conflict*: where desire for a course clearly recognized by the agent as inimical to the good of the self as a whole, of the self as the common subject of manifold desires and interests, still continues to be felt by him as the strongest desire. Now it is just here that we come to the crucial moral situation from the point of view of self-realization ethics. The agent regards course A (which may simply be 'abstaining from a course B') as that which is in the given circumstances for the good of the self as a whole. At the same time he feels his desire for the contrary course B to be stronger than his desire for A. Have the relevant emotional 'constants' in the situation been exhausted when we have noted merely the comparative strengths of the competing desires? The self-realization moralist would answer, most emphatically, that they have not. There supervenes in such situations, he would insist, a further experience, unique in character, and of supreme importance. This is the consciousness on the part of the agent that he *ought* to choose course A: that there is an *obligation* laid upon him to override his stronger desire, in as much as that prescribes a course contrary to the good of his self as a whole. And what can this consciousness of obligation be but a *moral* consciousness?—a moral consciousness distinct from, and indeed sharply opposing itself to, the desiring consciousness, yet at the same time drawing its content solely from the ends of desire.

So much for what we may perhaps call the abstract basis of self-realization ethics. Central to it is the thesis that conduct conceived to be for the good of the self as a whole is intuited as morally obligatory or dutiful, as against conduct which, though for the conceived good of some partial aspect of the self, is recognized to be opposed to the good of the self as a whole. It is easy to see why the moral end, thus understood, should be described as 'self-realization'. In one sense, no doubt, achievement of the end of a mere desire, no matter what, is a case of self-realization. Unsatisfied desire is a state of tension in which the self feels blocked, bottled up. With fulfilment of the desire comes release from the felt tension and a consequent feeling of 'self-realizedness'. But achievement of the *moral* end, the good of the self as a whole, is, and is recognized to be, self-realization in a peculiarly signifi-

E

cant sense. For the 'end' here is the objective counterpart not just of a particular *aspect* of the desiring self, but of the desiring self as a *whole*, in its *unity*. Now a self-conscious subject, conscious as such of its own unity, cannot but regard its self-hood as finding authentic expression in conduct which respects that unity rather than in conduct which flouts it. Hence where the ends in question are apprehended as in conflict with one another, it is natural for the self to look upon the end representing the good of the self as a whole as alone affording *true* self-realization, realization of the *true* self: and upon the contrary end, though affording a *form* of self-realization as explained above, as hostile to true self-realization. Critics of self-realization ethics are, I am well aware, fond of deriding all talk of a 'true' or 'real' self, as though it were mere obscurantist mumbo-jumbo. I suggest that, in the simple sense I have just indicated, it is a notion with which no adequate analysis of our practical experience can afford to dispense.

Now if the above account of the relation between the moral consciousness and desires fairly represents the view of the self-realization school, no further argument is needed to show that self-realization as an ethical principle is devoid of egoistic implications. The conceived good of the self as a whole is constructed out of the ends of desire ('partial' goods for the self); and if, as we have seen, the ends of desire are not necessarily egoistic, no more is the 'moral' end—the good of the self as a whole. It is, perhaps, unfortunate that self-realization moralists, in their anxiety to stress, in particular against the older Naturalism, the all-important activity of self-reference characteristic of *human* experience, should have been guilty of some very dubious forms of expression. To say, as Green does, that 'the quest of self-satisfaction is the form of all moral activity',[1] is almost to invite misunderstanding. Nevertheless, such verbal suggestions of egoism should, I think, mislead no one who has once grasped the essential purport of his analysis of human desire and its relation to animal impulse.

But to rebut the charge of egoism so constantly levelled against the self-realization theory is not, of course, to establish the theory as in itself tenable. It is only to remove the most potent obstacle

[1] *Prolegomena to Ethics*, § 160.

to its sympathetic consideration. In order to establish the theory upon firm foundations it would be necessary to pursue systematically some such programme as that prescribed for projects of the kind in the early part of the address. Roughly speaking, we should require to elucidate and defend in detail (*a*) the proposition that rational beings do in fact intuit action for the good of the self as a whole as morally obligatory; (*b*) the proposition that rational beings have no *other* moral intuitions; and (*c*) the proposition that the self-realization principle is in harmony with the moral judgments of mankind—of primitive and civilized mankind alike. To try to implement such a programme in the short time left to us would clearly be absurd. The most useful course will be, I think, to concentrate attention upon certain considerations which seem to me of special importance for the just appraisal of propositions (*a*) and (*c*). Proposition (*b*) I must regard as, for the purposes of this lecture, sufficiently discussed in Part I.

First, then, concerning the actual existence of the alleged moral intuition. As already indicated, 'proof' here can be only a matter of inducing the sceptic to see what he has hitherto failed to see, by presenting to him as precisely as possible the situation which evokes the intuition, and by removing certain hampering pre-possessions which are apt to prejudice the issue. The sceptic's good will must, of course, be taken for granted. We also take for granted, as any ethical theory must, that the moral consciousness of all men functions according to the same ultimate principles. Let us begin by inviting our sceptic, then, to think himself into a practical situation in which he is confronted with mutually exclusive courses of action A and B, and in which A is the course which he clearly recognizes to be most conducive to the good of his self as a whole, whereas B is the course towards which he is well aware that he entertains the strongest desire Given that situation, our submission is that *whatever* be the respective contents of A and B, *whatever* be the nature of the desires which serve to determine them, the sceptic will find that he *cannot but* feel that he ought to follow A and eschew B; and that if (prolonging his 'ideal experiment') he further supposes himself to have yielded to the stronger desire, he will find that, in so far as he is conscious of so yielding, he *cannot but* feel the characteristic moral emotion of self-reproach for what he recognizes to be an act of 'self-indulgence' inimical to 'self-realization'.

But there are many 'hampering prepossessions', as we called them, which militate against the return of a fair verdict in such situations. On one of them, the stubborn 'egoistic fallacy', we have said more than enough already. But there are others. And there is one in particular which we must attack without delay; for despite the force which accrues to it from the very respectable reasons on which it is based, it has received most inadequate attention from the self-realization school. I refer to the belief that the psychological situation of conflict we have just declared to be evocative of moral intuition *does not and cannot ever occur*; that it is just not psychologically possible for the end towards which one feels the strongest desire to be *other than* the end which one conceives to be for the good of the self as a whole, *so long as the good of the self as a whole is interpreted in terms of objects of desire.*

There is a very real problem here. Suppose I reflect upon two conflicting desired ends A and B, with a view to assessing their respective claims to represent the good of my self as a whole. In virtue of such reflection, I bring before my mind the bearing of A and B respectively upon the fulfilment of my many other desires and interests. Evidently these other desires and interests will now play a part in determining the actual desiring situation, some doubtless reinforcing desire for A, others desire for B; and the original balance of desire may, or again it may not, be disturbed. Now the troublesome point is this: how can I have any other basis for deciding, as a result of my reflection, which course is the more conducive to the good of myself as a whole, save that I find the balance of my actual felt desires tipped in one direction rather than in the other? In other words, can the good of my self as a whole, if construed in terms of ends of desire, ever be for me anything but that end towards which, after due reflection upon implications and consequences, I feel the strongest desire?

Certainly it is by no means obvious in what other way one can decide. And yet presumably there *must* be some other way. For it seems plain matter of psychological fact that one does on occasion feel one's strongest desire to be for an end which one realizes well is obstructive of the good of the self as a whole. The stock example of the habitual toper will serve as well as another. It is very difficult to gainsay the evidence that the toper may be acutely conscious, even in the very midst of his potations, that what he most strongly desires, viz., to continue drinking, is clean contrary to the good of his self as a whole. If one may trust his own account of the matter, he is at times well aware that so to act means frustration of a self which owns not merely this desire to drink, but also an interest in maintaining health, in holding his job, in providing for his family, in being respected by his neighbours, and so on. Yet his recognition that to continue drinking is contrary to the good of his self as a whole, though it inevitably involves rousing into overt action many desires which oppose themselves to the desire to drink, does *somehow* fail to manifest itself in a desire to desist comparable in strength with the desire to continue. The question is, *how?*

The solution in principle lies, I suggest, in the fact that the particular desires which are brought into play by reflection upon the situation vary for the self not merely in felt *strength* but also in felt *status*. For some desires, in virtue of definitely assignable characteristics, are regarded by the self as representing, more authentically than other desires, the self's *real* nature. What are these assignable characteristics? They flow from the self's awareness of itself as essentially a *unity*—the awareness which gives point and meaning to the self's concern for its good as a whole. From this source there arise two connected but distinct criteria for appraising the 'status' of desires, corresponding to the two main aspects of the self's essential unity. The unity of which the self is conscious in itself is, in the first place, a perduring unity. The self is aware of itself as a being which persists as a relatively permanent identity throughout all the successive changes of life. It is natural, therefore, that the self should regard an interest or desire of a relatively permanent nature as being, *ceteris paribus*, more authentically representative of itself than one which is relatively transient. In the second place, the unity of which the self is conscious in itself is, as it were, a 'lateral' as well as a 'longitudinal' unity, a unity comprehending contemporaneous, as well as successive, differences. It is natural, therefore, that the self should regard interests or desires of a relatively comprehensive nature—'broad' interests, like those in raising a family or propagating a religion, which spread over a wide span of experience, informing wellnigh the whole content of personality— as being, *ceteris paribus*, more authentically representative of the self than interests or desires of a relatively narrow compass. My contention is, then, that in reaching a decision as to which of two or more ends of desire is for the good of the self as a whole, the agent will naturally take account of the relevant desires not merely in respect of their felt strength, but also in respect of these twin aspects of relative permanence and comprehensiveness, in virtue of which desires are recognized as more truly representative of the self in its real or unitary nature.

If I am right in this contention, there need clearly be no coincidence between the end deemed to be for the good of the self as a whole (even though that end be construed in terms of desire) and the end towards which the strongest desire is felt. To apply our principle to the case of the habitual toper. It is not difficult to see how the several desires which, according to our hypothesis, oppose themselves in his mind to the desire to drink will be regarded by him as superior both in relative permanence and in comprehensiveness to the desire to drink, and as thus of higher status, more truly representative of his essential self. And if this be so, there is no mystery after all in his conceiving the good of his self as a whole to prescribe abstention, at the same time as he is aware that his strongest desire continues to urge him in the opposite direction.

I submit, then, that we are fully entitled to accept as actually, and indeed frequently, occurrent the psychological situation which, according to our view, evokes the basic intuition of obligation. But an objection of another sort now calls for some remark. Are we also entitled to identify, as we have done, this 'obligation' with *moral* obligation? Some people who would be willing enough to grant that the psychological situation in question does occur, and that in it we do feel that we *ought* to pursue the course which we believe to be for the good of the self as a whole, would nevertheless wish to insist that the 'ought' here is not a *moral* but a merely *prudential* 'ought'? This objection seems to me to be based upon a confusion, but it is, I think, too widely felt for us to ignore it wholly.

It seems likely that most of those who regard the obligation as merely prudential are guilty of the old error of interpreting 'the good of the self as a whole' as an egoistic principle. It is, at any rate, very much less plausible to regard the obligation as prudential if, as is in fact the case, 'the good of the self as a whole' can oblige to action which, so far from being egoistic, or even selfish, would normally be called altruistic. Still the difficulty, such as it is, remains, since we cannot deny that our principle *could* find expression in a purely self-regarding end. Suppose, to take a trivial but topical example, one is tempted to exceed one's self-imposed tobacco ration, and that, purely from egoistic considerations of long-term health, wealth, and happiness, one judges that the good of the self as a whole prescribes resistance to the craving. There arises, the critic may allow, a consciousness that one 'ought' to resist the craving. But should we on our part concede to the critic that an obligation thus to pursue what is, after all, the path of self-interest is not a moral but merely a prudential obligation?

It seems to me that such a view has force only so long as the notion of 'prudential obligation' is left conveniently vague. For what, after all, *is* a prudential obligation? So far as I can see, it can only mean one of two things: either a *moral* obligation to be prudent, in which case *cadit quaestio*; or else the sort of thing that Kant meant by his 'counsels of prudence'. Now the 'ought' in Kant's counsels of prudence is admittedly not a moral ought. It is expressed in merely hypothetical imperatives: '*if* you want happiness, you ought to adopt such and such appropriate means'. It is proper enough to call this sort of obligation 'prudential', for its appeal is merely to good sense, not to the moral consciousness. But then this is surely *not in the least* the form in which the obligation presents itself in the type of situation with which we are here concerned, a situation in which the agent is conscious that he ought to resist rather than indulge his craving because the former is the course prescribed by the good of the self as a whole? In cases of *this* sort 'prudent' action is *the expression, in the given situation, of the categorical imperative* to aim at the good of the self as a whole. There is nothing hypothetical about it. In most situations in life, of course, the conceived good of the self as a whole will find expression in content of a less trivial and more conventionally 'moral' nature. But the *formal* character of the obligation must be identical, whether the principle finds expression in the risking of one's life for a friend or merely in the resolute pushing aside of the tobacco jar.

And after all is there anything so very paradoxical in the view that a genuinely moral obligation may be felt even within the ambit of purely private ends? Certainly it is opposed to the common opinion that 'all morality is social'. But it has, I suggest, an ally much more philosophically respectable than common *opinion* in common *experience*. For it is hard to deny that we do all in fact experience emotions indistinguishable from the characteristic moral emotions in situations where we are 'tempted', as we say, to an imprudent act of self-indulgence. No doubt it is abstractly possible to hold that we experience these emotions (such as shame and remorse if we succumb to the temptation) *only* where we see that self-indulgence has bad *social* effects. But I think we cannot hold this without doing quite conspicuous violence to the actual facts. It is, I suggest, one of the merits of the self-realization theory of ethics that it has no difficulty in accepting the facts at their face value. As we shall see presently, self-realization ethics is at one with most other ethical theories in according to the idea of social well-being a place of peculiar centrality in man's moral apprehensions. But it is able to do this without prejudice to the apparent fact that we do at times experience the authentic moral emotions where there is no thought whatsoever of the social implications of our conduct.

We must now, however abruptly, pass from proposition (*a*), taking some comfort against the inadequacy of our treatment of it from the thought that indirect support will be lent to it in so far as we are successful in establishing the proposition to which we now address ourselves, proposition (*c*). Proposition (*c*), it will be remembered, was to the effect that the moral judgments of mankind, as manifested in the vast variety of primitive and civilized moral codes, are consistent with the basic intuition of self-realization ethics. If, then, we can meet the main difficulties in the way of accepting this proposition, the former proposition that there is in fact a basic moral intuition of 'self-realization' must enjoy at least some measure of confirmation.

Our special problem, as I see it, is as follows: we have sufficiently shown, it is to be hoped, that there is nothing in the principle of the conceived good of the self as a whole which entails that its content must be egoistic. But we have not as yet given any reason at all why its content should have a predominantly *social* reference. This it is clearly incumbent upon us to do, if we are to make good our claim that our principle accords with the moral judgments of mankind. For it will be agreed that, if there is any identity amid the almost limitless diversity of actual moral codes, it lies precisely in their predominant regard for communal well-being. And there is a further duty incumbent upon us. We noted earlier an important difference between primitive and civilized morality, viz., that in the former the 'community' whose well-being was of concern tended to be narrowly limited, whereas in the latter it tended to be universal. Our principle must be shown capable of accommodating this difference.

Now in view of the relationship which the self-realization principle was interpreted as bearing to the self's desires—as the objective counterpart of the *unity* of the desiring self—it is fairly plain what our plan of campaign should be. We must try to show that there are factors common to the constitution of man, and factors common to his development within a community, which make it natural that he should regard his *social* desires as desires especially representative of his unitary self. In so far as they do assume for him this higher status, the conceived good of his self as a whole will perforce find predominant expression in 'social' ways of behaviour.

Two relatively distinct sets of factors fall to be considered in this connection: first, those relating to man's natural equipment in the way of social desires, and secondly, those relating to the influences brought to bear upon man by his community with the aim of exciting, encouraging, and fortifying the social desires.

To begin, then, with man's natural equipment.

It is often said that man is by nature a 'social' animal. What is meant by the phrase, however, is by no means always the same thing. The reference may be (1) to man's essential 'gregariousness'. It seems true that the normal man takes pleasure in being in the company of his fellows; and that this applies not merely to physical proximity but also to 'mental' proximity—as is only to be expected, since for rational beings physical proximity is consistent with a strong sense of *isolation* from one's fellows if there is not in addition some real community of thought and emotion. Or again, the reference may simply be (2) to the fact that man needs, and is normally conscious of needing, the co-operation of his fellow men for the most effective achievement even of his more 'private' ends. But although in both of the above meanings man's 'essential sociality' has some bearing upon the social orientation of his moral codes, there is a third meaning

E*

which, I think, has much more importance in this connection. We may mean by man's essential sociality (3) that man has *a natural tendency to wish well to his fellow men*. In this meaning, however, by no means everyone would assent to the proposition; and it must be admitted that appearances provide ample excuse for scepticism. Nevertheless, I believe the proposition to be true, and I shall endeavour to defend it.

Let me begin by reminding you of a homely but telling illustration which David Hume uses to recommend the principle of 'disinterested benevolence'. 'Would any man', he asks, 'who is walking along, tread as willingly on another's gouty toes, whom he has no quarrel with, as on the hard flint and pavement?'[1] Hume takes for granted that to this question the answer must be 'No'. And if he is entitled to make this answer, he seems entitled also to draw the inference, far-reaching as it must seem by contrast with the simplicity of the premiss, that man is so framed by nature as to take a sympathetic interest in the well-being of his fellows, that he has a 'natural tendency' to wish them well.

But *is* Hume justified in taking for granted a negative answer? I think he is not in fact *quite* justified; because, although he has been careful to include in his hypothetical situation *one* condition which must be fulfilled if a negative answer is to be plausible, he has failed to notice another equally important but less obvious condition. The condition he has recognized is expressed in the words 'with whom he has no quarrel'. And it is clear that where there is specific cause, real or imaginary, for hostility to our neighbour, our natural tendency to wish him well *qua* fellow man may be overborne by our inclination to wish him ill *qua* personal enemy. But, quite certainly, this condition will not suffice of itself. The simplest observation of men and communities reveals that in a host of instances they behave with callous indifference towards fellow beings who neither are, nor are imagined to be, their 'enemies'. How are we to reconcile these obvious facts with the thesis that man has a natural tendency to wish well to his fellows?

That brings us to the second condition that must be fulfilled if Hume's negative answer to his own question is to be justified. It is not enough merely that other men should not be regarded

---

[1] *An Enquiry concerning the Principles of Morals*, p. 226 (Selby-Bigge's edition).

as our enemies. Their actual 'kinship' with ourselves as *fellow men* must be appreciated. The natural tendency to wish well to our fellows can hardly be expected to operate where we do not recognize that they *are* our fellows. There must be some measure of imaginative realization of that identity of human nature which binds men into a single family; at the very least, of a common identity as sentient beings.

It is the non-fulfilment of this condition, I think, that accounts for most of the phenomena which at first sight seem to contradict the principle of man's inherent sociality. Imaginative realization of another as an *alter ego* is often dim and feeble, and not seldom totally absent. It is absent, for example, in the very young child, and the lack of it is the obvious explanation of much of the so-called 'cruelty' of young children. It is significant that the accepted method of curing a child of 'cruelty' is to induce in it an imaginative realization of its victim as a subject of pains and pleasures like itself. In principle it is not otherwise with the adult person. There is, normally, a vivid enough appreciation of the kinship with one's self of a specific group—a family, a clan, or a class—but with this there often goes, at best, only a vague and abstract recognition of kinship with wider groups, let alone of kinship with all mankind. Such failure in imaginative realization is particularly easy where other persons, or other communities, differ conspicuously from one's self in the superficial features which force themselves first upon one's attention—differences of colour, of dress, of language, of manners, of customs, and the like. The striking character of the differences is apt to obscure the underlying identity of human nature, and any recognition of kinship there may be is likely to be merely formal and not imaginatively actual. It is probably true to say that the 'inhumane' man is, more often than not, simply the 'unimaginative' man. Stimulate in him imaginative appreciation of the other's essential kinship and, in the absence of strong counteracting factors, some concern for his interests follows almost as a matter of course. Even in the hardest of men, it has often been observed, indifference to others' well-being cannot easily survive the experience of actual intimate personal intercourse: and the reason is simply that in intimate personal intercourse it is almost impossible not to be vividly aware of the human identity underlying the superficial differences between man and man.

It seems to me, then, that Hume is right, despite appearances, in claiming that 'disinterested benevolence' belongs to 'the original frame of our temper'.[1] We do tend to wish well to our fellow men, provided that we realize that they *are* our fellow men, and provided that we have no specific cause for enmity towards them. The earliest manifestations of the tendency will doubtless be in relation to persons with whom we are in close and regular contact. But the process cannot end there. With the growth of reflection (aided, of course, by education, formal and informal), the range widens of those whom we recognize to be akin to ourselves, and there is in principle nothing, though there is in practice much, to prevent the range from extending to include all mankind. Thus in most men there gradually develop social sentiment, settled dispositions to well-wishing of comparatively wide scope, and these find overt expression in appropriate emotions and conations wherever it appears that the interests of the relevant persons are at stake.

So much for man's social *nature* as distinct from his social *nurture*. Of the latter, of the influences brought to bear upon the individual by the community with a view to developing and strengthening his social sentiments, much less need be said. It would be agreed that there has perhaps never been an organized community which failed to appreciate how vital it is to its safety, stability, and prosperity that its citizens should have a lively concern for the interests of their fellows. Obviously a good deal can be done to ensure from citizens the more indispensable kinds of social behaviour by enlisting the sanctions of law and custom. A good deal more can be done if social behaviour can be successfully represented as being backed by the authority of a moral imperative. But it requires little subtlety of statesmanship to realize that the sanctions of law and custom are of limited efficacy, and that appeals to a 'sense of duty' towards others reap but a slender harvest, unless there dwells in the citizens a direct desire for the well-being of their fellows. 'If citizens be friends', says Aristotle, 'there is no need of justice: whereas if they be just they still need friendship as well.'[2] It is not surprising, therefore, to find that in organized communities everywhere the agencies whose business it is to mould the character of the young citizen

---

[1] *Loc. cit.*, p. 302.
[2] *Nicomachean Ethics*, 1155ª.

should seek with rather special care to stimulate and foster the growth of strong social sentiments.

We are now in a position to show what we set out to show: viz., that the good of the self as a whole will naturally be, for the ordinary man, predominantly social in character. We have seen that there is in man a powerful natural tendency to the formation of social sentiments, and that it is an obvious requirement of wise policy, everywhere implemented, for organized communities to encourage in all possible ways the development of such sentiments. We have also seen, in an earlier discussion, that certain desires or interests, in virtue of assignable characteristics, are recognized by the self as representing more authentically than others the real nature of the self, and accordingly have especial influence in determining for the agent the content of the 'good of the self as a whole'. Now these assignable characteristics were, it will be recalled, 'relative permanence' and 'relative comprehensiveness'. But it seems clear that these characteristics are both present in notable degree in the average citizen's interest in others' well-being. Such an interest is relatively permanent, for it is rooted in a *sentiment*, a settled disposition of the mind. And again, as an interest which has a relevance for all or almost all the normal concerns of human life, comprehensiveness pertains to its nature no less than permanence. One may doubt, indeed, whether there is any other interest so intimately interwoven into the whole fabric of the average citizen's personality. It follows that the object of this interest—the well-being of others (though the 'others' may consist of a narrowly limited group)—must enter vitally into the constitution of that end or system of ends which, as the objective counterpart of the unity of the desiring self, is accepted by the agent as the good of his self as a whole. In short, the ultimate principle of moral obligation proclaimed by self-realization ethics not only need not manifest itself in egoistic content, but in actual fact must strongly tend to manifest itself in content that is predominantly social.

The fact that the moral codes established in, inherited by, and freely accepted by the most various communities are predominantly social in orientation is, then, I suggest, entirely compatible with the thesis that the basic moral intuition is of 'self-realization'. It only remains to show—what perhaps at this stage hardly needs the showing—how natural it is that this social reference of moral codes should be so much narrower in primitive than in civilized communities. In the first place, primitive communities enjoy far fewer opportunities for entering into personal relationships with other communities. It is normally only with the expansion of trade and commerce and the accompanying development of communications that any substantial degree of community 'mixing' is practicable. Primitive conditions of life are thus much less favourable to the extension towards other peoples of that imaginative realization of a common human nature underlying superficial differences which we saw to be indispensable to the actualization of man's potential social sentiments. In the second place, education of the young in most primitive communities, is, for solid reasons, normally directed to a narrowing rather than a broadening of social sympathies. Where a tribe is struggling to extract from a niggardly Nature the means of bare survival, its neighbours are apt to be its rivals. The most important aim of tribal 'education for citizenship' becomes, not unnaturally, the inculcation of so powerful a sense of unity with the group that all members of adult status can be securely counted upon to think and feel and act as one in whatever crises arise to threaten the tribal welfare. It is only to be expected, then, that a social sentiment of exceptional strength, but at the same time of exceptional narrowness, should be engendered in the mind of primitive man; and only to be expected, on the self-realizationist view of the intimate relationship between the content of the moral consciousness and the content of desires, that the moral codes of primitive peoples, while directed almost exclusively to social well-being, should normally exhibit no concern at all for the well-being of members of communities other than their own.

I submit, therefore, that there are good grounds for the assertion that the self-realization principle, properly understood, is in harmony with the moral judgments of mankind—primitive and civilized mankind alike.

And with this we complete the programme—or the skeleton programme, as perhaps I ought to call it—which we set before ourselves. It has not been possible to deal with more than certain very central considerations relevant to a just appraisal of self-realization ethics. No absurd claim is made to have *established* our principle. But I should be happy to believe that what has been said may help in some measure to revive interest in a type of ethical theory which seems to me to be ignored at the present day only because its essential nature has been largely misconceived.

VI

ETHICS WITHOUT PROPOSITIONS

I want in what follows to comment upon two central points in Professor Barnes's stimulating Presidential Address to the 1948 Mind-Aristotelian Conference at Durham. The first is his contention that there is something queer or paradoxical about the notion of 'normative assertions'. The second is his admission that 'a peculiarly moral feeling' must be recognized as a component of those 'attitudes' which—according to his own theory—it is the function of ethical statements to 'express'.

I. NORMATIVE ASSERTIONS

Barnes's criticism of 'normative assertions' is presented with a brevity which is a little surprising in view of the weight which he apparently attaches to it. I do not doubt that he has other grounds for finding the traditional analysis of ethical statements objectionable, but as a matter of fact it is to this ground alone that appeal is made in his address. I give the relevant passage in full.

'Ethical statements are traditionally held to be normative assertions. But how can a statement both assert a fact and prescribe a norm? There seems an obvious difference between telling someone that something is the case and telling him to do something; between deciding that something is so and deciding to do something: between stating that someone is acting in a certain way and recommending approval of his so acting.'[1]

I submit that this argument depends for any plausibility it may have upon a misleading suggestion as to the manner in which ethical statements are, on the traditional analysis, concerned with norms. If the traditionalist does suppose that an ethical statement *prescribes* a norm, admittedly he ought to be more embarrassed than he is by his inclination to say that it is also an assertion. But does he in fact suppose this? Surely not. It is important to distinguish statements which *prescribe* norms (and are of the nature of imperatives) from statements which *affirm the existence of norms*

---

[1] *Arist. Soc. Supp.*, Vol. XXII, p. 2.

(and are of the nature of assertions). If, as seems to me clear, ethical statements on the traditional analysis fall into the latter category, the alleged difficulty vanishes.

The distinction just noted tends to be blurred by the fact that, in non-ethical fields, the same form of words can be used for either function—prescribing a norm or affirming its existence. 'Candidates must write on one side of the paper only.' As spoken (or written) by the appropriate examination authority, this sentence 'prescribes a rule'. But suppose that (the instruction being given orally) one of the candidates fails to hear clearly what has been said, and asks a fellow-candidate if any rules have been laid down. He is told 'candidates must write on one side of the paper only'. As now uttered, the sentence does not prescibe, but states the existence of, a rule. In the former case the speaker is, and knows himself to be, the imponent of the rule: in the latter case the speaker is, and knows himself to be, not the imponent of the rule but a mere 'reporter' of the fact that the rule exists. Indeed, we might quite well point the difference between these two kinds of normative reference by using the very language which Barnes uses to distinguish between normative and assertive. In the former case the sentence 'tells him (the candidate) to do something', and in the latter case it is 'telling someone (the candidate) that something is the case' (viz., that there is a rule that candidates must write on one side of the paper only).

It does not appear to me doubtful into which category ethical statements, on the traditional analysis, must be deemed to fall. 'You ought to pay back that money you borrowed.' A rule or norm is referred to, but the speaker does not conceive himself to be the imponent of it. If he did, he would not suppose himself to be making an *ethical* statement. He is asserting the existence of a rule which has application to a given situation.

I conclude, therefore, that whatever valid objections there may be to the traditional analysis of ethical statements, this analysis cannot be ruled out of court *ab initio* on the charge that the very notion of 'normative assertions' is formally absurd. I can understand, indeed, that many philosophers to-day may be predisposed to scepticism about the notion of 'normative assertions' by reason of a prior scepticism about what normative assertions, in the field of ethics at any rate, seem to assert; viz., the 'existence' of 'objective' moral laws. One's general philosophical principles may very well lead one to regard assertions which assert anything of this sort as extremely paradoxical. But in that case the 'paradox' will derive from the content, not from the form, of the assertion. Scepticism about 'objective moral laws' will not justify scepticism about normative assertions as such; about, e.g., the particular normative assertion that rules exist for the conduct of examinations.

But are ethical statements as a matter of fact normative assertions? We shall be better able to give an answer to that question when we have considered what Barnes has to say on the second (and, I think, more interesting) topic of the 'peculiarly moral feeling'.

II. THE PECULIARLY MORAL FEELING

Barnes's positive theory is, it will be recalled, that 'ethical statements express attitudes'. 'Attitudes', pro or contra, are normally directed to *kinds* of action, and they have three components.

'If there is a kind of action which a man has a disposition to do himself, to encourage others to do, and to feel pleased at, when done by others, then he has a pro-attitude to that kind of action. An anti-attitude can be defined similarly.'[1]

But Barnes is clear that not all attitudes, so defined, are 'moral' attitudes. A man may, e.g., have a favourable (or unfavourable) attitude towards smoking or drinking which is not what we recognize as a *moral* attitude.

'I think we must admit that if there is to be a moral attitude, it must contain at least one peculiarly ethical component, viz., the pro- or anti-emotion which I feel when I contemplate actions of the kind in question.'[2]

It is in virtue of his recognition of this peculiarly ethical component, or 'peculiarly moral feeling' as he later calls it, that Barnes is able to claim that his ethical theory, although subjectivist, is not naturalistic.

On Barnes's view, this moral feeling is a recognizable constituent of our moral attitudes which distinguishes them from non-moral attitudes. Of its positive character as experienced, however, he has nothing to say. And it may be that there *is* nothing to say. It may be that it is a 'simple nature', ultimate and unanalysable; definable, if definable at all, only by reference to the kind of actions

[1] *Arist. Soc. Supp.*, p. 19.   [2] *Ibid.*, p. 22.

to which it is most habitually directed. It may be, on the other hand, that it is not simple, but complex, and that its analysis yields consequences of capital importance for ethics. In any event, it is a matter to be settled not by assumption, but, in the last resort, by interrogation of one's own experience. We must evoke in imagination what seem to us unquestionably authentic representatives of moral and non-moral attitudes respectively, and see whether attentive scrutiny will not enable us to give some account of the difference between their feeling-components.

As an example of a non-moral attitude we may, with Barnes, take an attitude to smoking: though I shall prefer, unlike him, to consider the case where this is a favourable, rather than an unfavourable, attitude—if only for the reason that the votaries of smoking are less apt than its critics to invoke moral sanctions for their attitude. As an example of a moral attitude, that towards promise-keeping will do as well as another.

Suppose, then, we ask an ordinary unsophisticated person, who happens to have a moral pro-attitude towards keeping promises and a non-moral pro-attitude towards smoking, how he would describe the distinction between his specifically moral feeling towards the former and his non-moral feeling towards the latter. I suggest that he would by no means find himself at a loss for an answer. He would almost certainly describe the distinction in terms which, however objectionable in point of strict psychology, are yet surely not uninstructive. He would almost certainly say, I think, that towards promise-keeping, but not towards smoking, he has a feeling of 'oughtness' or 'obligation', a feeling that he and others 'ought' so to behave.

Now so long as it is conceded (as by Barnes) that there *is* a peculiarly moral emotion, and so long as no rival account is offered of its nature as experienced, it seems to me that we are bound to take seriously the account which the plain man offers of it. His description, such as it is, holds the field until such time as it is shown to be untenable. It just will not do to say simply that the emotion is unanalysable, when we find that ordinary moral beings are perfectly ready with a description of it, and, what is more, with the *same* description of it.

As a matter of strict psychology, of course, the plain man's description *is* untenable. A feeling *that* . . . is not a mere 'feeling' at all. But this technical offence does not invalidate, but rather throws into relief, the essential point of the description offered. What the plain man is trying to tell us when he says that his feeling is a feeling of 'oughtness', a feeling that one 'ought' so to behave, is, I think, that the so-called 'feeling' has an aspect of *assertion*, or *judgment*, as well as of feeling; that his moral feeling towards promise-keeping includes the *judgment* that promises ought to be kept.

The specific manner in which this judgment aspect is integrated within moral feeling clearly calls for further elucidation. A point has now been reached, however, at which it becomes reasonable to ask the reader whether, when he appeals to the testimony of his own introspection, he is really able to escape giving the same sort of answer as the plain man gives. If one is careful to prevent a preconceived theory about ethics—or perhaps about knowledge in general—from colouring one's report, can one really avoid recognizing that what is distinctive about moral feeling is precisely that it is inseparably united with a judgment of 'oughtness'? If that is *not* its distinguishing mark, then what *is* its distinguishing mark? And if it has no *describable* distinguishing mark, for the reason that what distinguishes it is some simple unanalysable quality, then what explanation is to be given of the apparent unanimity with which ordinary moral beings *do* offer a definite description of it?

Let us, then, look more closely at the manner of integration of judgment with moral feeling. My contention is that the peculiarly moral feeling towards keeping promises involves the judgment that promises ought to be kept. The moral feeling, I am suggesting, is not *itself* without the judgment—it requires the judgment for the completion of its own nature. Two opposite, but equally ruinous, errors of analysis must be carefully avoided. We must not say that our moral feeling towards promise-keeping *generates* the judgment that promises ought to be kept: for (we have urged) it is not the distinctively *moral* feeling at all unless the judgment of oughtness is already present. But neither must we say that the moral feeling is *generated by* the judgment of oughtness: for if this judgment is a moral judgment proper, and not the mere mechanical repetition of a conventional formula (if, in other words, the 'ought' of the judgment is before our minds in its intrinsic moral meaning) then the distinctively moral feeling towards promise-keeping is already present. Most of the moralists who have held that the moral feeling is prior, and the moral judgment sequent upon it, have held this, I think, largely because it appeared to them that the only alternative was to suppose that the moral judgment *precedes* the moral feeling; an alternative which they rightly reject. Similarly, most of the moralists who have held that the moral judgment is prior, and the moral feeling sequent, have held this largely because it appeared to them that the only alternative was to suppose that the moral feeling precedes the moral judgment; an alternative which they, too, are right to reject. The possibility which is missed by both parties is that feeling and judgment are twin *aspects* of a *single* experience, neither of which has precedence over the other. This I believe to represent the true state of the case.

If this view is sound, then the Rationalist school and the Sentimentalist school of moralists are equally right in what they affirm and equally wrong in what they deny. The 'peculiarly moral feeling' shows itself on analysis to be something which may be called, indifferently, either a feeling with a judgment aspect, or a judgment with a feeling aspect. Neither can be excluded from the description of the essential moral apprehension. But it is quite crucial that the two should not be thought of as merely *conjoined*—'judgment *plus* feeling'. The aspects are *aspects*, not *entities*; analytically distinguishable, but only as abstractions from the unity of a single experience.

The 'double-aspect theory' (as we may call it) of moral apprehension is not, of course, something new in ethical thought. What else but this was in Bishop Butler's mind when he spoke of the moral faculty as alike 'a sentiment of the understanding' and 'a perception of the heart'? In Butler, it must be admitted, such expressions are little more than *obiter dicta*, and they are not followed up either by himself or by his immediate successors. But there is exceedingly interesting evidence supplied by Hastings Rashdall that the double-aspect theory had authoritative currency in Oxford in the early years of this century. Rashdall quotes a clear instance from the letter of a friend who takes exception to his own account of the relationship between reason and feeling; and in apologizing for the publication of a private correspondence he observes that he 'cannot call to mind any printed expression of this doctrine, though it is taught by high authorities in Oxford'. The passage from the letter is worth transcribing in full:—

'I think that the "reason" and "feeling" which are to be found in moral judgements, though no doubt distinguishable, are not only always found together, but each is unintelligible and empty apart from the other. The judgement "this is right" is not a moral judgement unless one has, more or less, the moral emotion (for in the judgement "this is right", when the ground is any authority, the moral emotion and the judgement proper fall upon the authority, not strictly upon the particular point), nor is it a moral emotion unless it claims universality. This, I think, is the same view as yours, but perhaps you might more carefully avoid the use of language which suggests juxtaposition (reason *plus* feeling); which is surely unsatisfactory, and leads to what one finds inadequate in the language of Hume on one side and Kant on another.'[1]

This is *not*, in fact, the same view as Rashdall's. Rashdall is fundamentally a Rationalist, as his reply immediately makes clear. But it *is* the double-aspect theory. Had the writer, or some other of the 'high authorities' alluded to, found an opportunity to develop the theory at length, and in print, it is not inconceivable that the later course of ethical thinking in this country might have been markedly different.

The conclusion to which we are forced is, I submit, this. It is only when the 'peculiarly moral feeling' is allowed to remain unanalysed that a subjectivist can at once recognize its existence and retain his subjectivism, even a subjectivism on such relatively conservative lines as that so ingeniously developed by Professor Barnes. Barnes's suggestion is that the ethical statement 'X ought to be done' can be interpreted as an expression of a moral pro-attitude towards X. But if a moral pro-attitude towards X admittedly contains 'a peculiarly moral feeling' towards X, and if, as I have argued, this peculiarly moral feeling itself involves the assertion or judgment that X ought to be done, the interpretation is circular. The ostensible assertion with which we started, and of which we had hoped to rid ourselves by analysis, remains on our hands, as 'objective' and as 'normative' as ever it was.

[1] Rashdall, *Theory of Good and Evil*, Vol. I, pp. 168–169.

VII

ARE THERE 'DEGREES' OF THE MORAL EMOTION?

It is generally agreed that the apprehension of the moral 'ought', of duty, is accompanied by a specific kind of emotion. This emotion it is customary, following Kant, to designate by such terms as 'reverence' or 'respect'. We speak of action from the purely moral motive as inspired by 'respect for duty', or 'reverence for the moral law'. These terms, indeed, are not altogether satisfactory. Nothing is more evident about the emotion felt towards the moral ought than its qualitative uniqueness; and terms like respect and reverence, which have a fairly extensive non-moral employment, hardly do justice to that uniqueness. But a more suitable name does not seem available: and so long as it is understood that the relationship between moral respect and all varieties of non-moral respect is one of analogy rather than of species within a genus, the common usage need not mislead us.

So much, I think, is common ground amongst almost all ethical writers. It also appears to be common ground that this moral emotion is susceptible of degrees of intensity. This has been not so much explicitly maintained as tacitly assumed. That 'respect for duty' is an emotion which may be felt more or less strongly as between different persons, or as between different generations of persons, or as between different phases in the mental history of a single person—all this has seemed too obvious to call in question. And it certainly finds abundant support in the psychological implications of our common speech.

Yet I am inclined to believe that, if the question *is* raised, it will yield rather surprising results. There seems to me to be good reason for holding that the moral emotion cannot vary intensively at all, that it is quantitatively as well as qualitatively a 'constant'. In what follows I propose to argue the case for this view.

We shall best begin, I think, by considering some emotion which is beyond question capable of varying in degree, and enquiring as to the grounds of its variation. Let us take pity. Pity is an emotion evoked by the apprehension of calamity occurring to other beings in whose welfare we feel a sympathetic interest. Its stimulus is a complex situation, the constituents of which are subject to wide variation. And it seems evident at once that at least the primary cause of the variation of intensity in the emotion of pity is the variation of the constituents of its stimulus. The calamity may be great or slight, its victims may be close friends or casual acquaintances, and in accordance with these and other like variations in the stimulus our pity is strong or mild.

The same holds good, I think, for all our ordinary human emotions. If we are asked why, in a given situation, we feel so very angry, or so very fearful, the natural reply is to point to certain characteristics in the constituents of the stimulus which explain the high intensity of the emotion we feel.

But let us turn now to the moral emotion. The moral emotion is evoked by apprehension of the moral ought. But the moral ought is a 'simple'. It is not resolvable into constituents, much less into 'variable' constituents. Nor can there be variations of degree in 'oughtness' itself. Moral oughtness cannot be more or less of a moral oughtness, but just either is or is not moral oughtness. And if this is so (I shall defend the view later against one possible line of attack) it would seem that the emotion evoked by apprehension of the moral ought cannot vary in intensity by reason of its external stimulus at any rate.

Our ordinary emotions may, however, vary in intensity in response to *internal* conditions as well as to *external* stimuli. What are we to say of this possible source of variation in the moral emotion?

These internal conditions may be classified sufficiently for our purpose under two heads. (1) Conditions which vary within a single person—such as the condition of one's liver or 'nerves', which may induce variations in the intensity of anger or fear in spite of identical external stimuli. (2) Conditions which vary as between persons, but are substantially invariable in the life of a single person. Under this head come any 'constitutional' tendencies to feel particular emotions with unusual strength or unusual weakness.

As regards (1), I do not find that any evidence has ever been advanced for the view—nor even that anyone has ever held the view—that the moral emotion can vary with varying conditions of body or mind, as such emotions as fear and anger obviously can. It hardly seems worth while, therefore, to discuss this abstract possibility. But it would be, I think, more plausible to assert variant internal conditions of the *second* class—if only because such an assertion is much less amenable to either proof or disproof by experiential evidence. The natural argument in its favour would be one based on analogy. If the intensity of the emotion of fear, or anger, or sex may vary according to the congenital constitution of the subject, why should not the congenital constitution of the subject induce variation in the moral emotion likewise?

I think there is a very good reason why not, a reason which becomes apparent when we appreciate the vital difference in the relationship between emotion and idea in the respective cases. In the case of fear (and the same seems true of all our ordinary human emotions) that relationship is relatively external. It is in principle possible to conceive the idea without conceiving the emotion: even if (as is by no means certain) the two are inseparable in fact. We can in principle think of the awareness of danger existing without there existing also the emotion of fear. We do, of course, *expect* the awareness of danger to generate the emotion of fear as a matter of *fact*, on account of the empirically known constitution of the normal human subject. But my point is that this expectation is not guaranteed by *the idea itself*. Now in the case of the moral emotion it is quite otherwise. Here idea and emotion are intrinsically inseparable. Here it is *not* in principle possible to conceive the idea without conceiving the emotion. We cannot think of an *awareness* of the moral ought which is not at the same time the *feeling* of the appropriate *emotion* towards the moral ought. The relationship between the two is indeed far too intimate to be described in the language of stimulus and response, which we were hitherto content to use. In this case the idea involves the emotion by its intrinsic nature.

This, I think, was a large part of what Kant meant when he urged that respect for duty, though a feeling, differed from other feelings in that it was 'self-wrought by a rational concept'.[1] We may not agree with all that is implied for Kant by this phrase. But its main point, I think, is sound, viz., that the moral emotion is

[1] *Grundlegung zur Metaphysik der Sitten*, p. 22, footnote 2. (Rosenkranz' edition.)

intrinsically bound up with the moral idea itself, and does not imply for its explanation, as ordinary human emotions do, an additional reference to the particular constitution of the experiencing subject.

This seems to me an adequate reason for rejecting the argument based on the analogy between moral emotion and other human emotions. The uniquely intimate dependence of the moral emotion upon the moral idea, and its consequent independence of the particular constitution of the experiencing subject, causes the analogy to break down just at the point at which it would be serviceable for the argument. The conclusion to which our analysis points is that if the moral idea, the idea of the moral ought, does not vary, the moral feeling, since it is just the emotional aspect of that idea, cannot vary either.

But is it really the case, it may be asked, that the moral ought, as apprehended, is not capable of variation in intensity? This brings us to a new set of considerations. I have so far done no more than appeal to the reader's own moral experience to support the contention that it is strictly meaningless to speak of *more* or *less* of moral oughtness. But it is undeniable that we do all of us use forms of speech which seem to imply that we find meaning in that phrase. When we say, as we often do, that we apprehend act A to be a 'stronger obligation' than act B, what do we mean if we do not mean that the 'ought' which we apprehend in A presents itself with a greater degree of oughtness than the 'ought' that we apprehend in B?

These expressions are entitled to careful consideration. Any theory which hopes to establish the view that the moral emotion cannot vary in intensity is obliged to try to 'explain them away' satisfactorily. It must try to show that the kind of experiences to which these expressions refer are not really the kind of experiences of which they are a strict verbal description: that the expressions are, in fact, loose and misleading forms of speech.

This I shall attempt now. I shall endeavour to show what it is that people really mean when they speak of apprehending a 'stronger' obligation to act A than to act B.

We may consider first the case in which A and B are mutually exclusive acts in a particular given situation. I may, for example, in a given situation, intelligibly say that I apprehend a stronger obligation to tell a lie, and thus prevent great mental distress in a critically ill patient, than to tell the truth. Here it is, I think, pretty clear what is really meant by 'stronger obligation'. Strictly speaking, I apprehend in this situation only *one* moral obligation, viz., to tell the lie—for obviously we cannot believe that we ought to do two mutually exclusive acts: as Butler long ago pointed out, to be under two contrary obligations is equivalent to being under none at all—but I speak of it as the 'stronger' obligation (and thus seem to imply that telling the truth is *also* an obligation, though a weaker one) because I recognize that in all *ordinary* circumstances telling the truth is *also* a moral obligation. In the given situation, it is perfectly clear, telling the truth is not apprehended as having *less* moral oughtness than telling the lie, but just as having *no* moral oughtness at all.

We may also, however, speak of stronger and weaker obligations when A and B are not particular acts contemplated in a given situation, but general *types* of acts. We may say, perhaps, that we recognize justice as a 'stronger' obligation than charity. What do we mean when we speak thus? I suggest that our meaning is as follows. We recognize that both justice and charity ought, as a rule, to be ensued: but we recognize also that, since justice on the whole conduces more powerfully than charity does to the ultimate end or ends from which both derive their moral authority, we ought, should conflict ever occur between these 'virtues', to be 'just' rather than 'charitable'. In other words, we do not really, when we use this form of speech, apprehend a greater degree of oughtness intrinsically inhering in justice. What we apprehend is a greater degree of conduciveness to the ultimate end or ends from whose moral authority both justice and charity derive the moral authority they may have.

This interpretation would, of course, be denied by the Intuitionalist. He would say that both justice and charity are apprehended as possessing 'oughtness' in their own right: and some Intuitionalists, alive to the problem of conflicting obligations, would go on to say that one of them is recognized—presumably as a result of direct comparison—to possess a more 'stringent' oughtness than the other. I am not able, for many reasons, to accept the Intuitionalist account of our moral experience. But in the present connection it will perhaps suffice to say this. The above doctrine implies that, when I bring charity into comparison with justice, I recognize that charity must sometimes 'defer' to justice, i.e., that charity is not *always* right. This can only mean that, whatever I may have previously believed to be the case, I now recognize that charity is not an unconditional obligation. I do not now apprehend moral oughtness as an inherent characteristic of the class of acts we call 'charitable'. But if so, there is no question of the apprehended oughtness of the one class of acts having 'more oughtness' than the apprehended oughtness of the other class. For only one of the two classes *has* apprehended oughtness.

I venture to cite one further illustration which, while it raises no new point of principle, may help to confirm what may still seem a somewhat paradoxical thesis. We should probably all say that we recognize a stronger obligation to attempt, at personal risk, to save the lives of 100 men than to save the life of a single man. Our real meaning, I have been suggesting, is that while we recognize that normally both are things that we ought to do, we also recognize that saving the group is more conducive to the ultimate moral end than saving the single man, and that, accordingly, if a situation arose in which the two lines of action were mutually exclusive, we ought in preference to try to save the group. If that is our meaning, it is quite intelligible to express it by saying that we recognize the obligation to try to save the group as the 'stronger' obligation. It would even be intelligible to say that we recognize it as 'a hundred times stronger'. But it would be quite unintelligible, I submit, to speak of the obligation as a hundred times stronger, if we mean by that that it presents itself with a hundred times the intrinsic oughtness of the obligation to try to save the life of the single man.

There are, of course, other forms of speech that are prima facie indicative of degrees of the moral emotion, or of degrees of moral oughtness. But there are none, so far as I can see, which are not capable of fairly easy resolution along lines similar to those set out above. Kant himself has given countenance to the view against which I am arguing in more than one passage, notably in the passage where he urges us to the 'cultivation' of the moral feeling 'and the strengthening of it even by admiration of its inscrutable origin'.[1] But his mistake is, I think, obvious. The 'admiration' of

---

[1] Preface to the *Metaphysische Anfangsgründe der Tugendlehre*, p. 247. (Rosenkranz' edition.)

the 'inscrutable origin' of the moral feeling will, no doubt, enhance the emotional colouring of our apprehension of duty. But it will do so not by intensifying the specifically moral emotion but by adding a new emotion. The reason why it seems plausible to speak of this new emotional factor as 'strengthening' the moral feeling is just that there is a natural disposition to identify 'inscrutable origin' with 'Divine origin', and the new emotional factor therefore tends to *support* the moral emotion by lending something in the nature of a religious sanction to moral conduct. The 'strengthening' of the moral feeling is, it is clear, a strengthening by external support, not by inherent intensification.

In conclusion, it seems proper to add a word or two about the philosophical significance of the issue we have been considering: for at first glance the matter may appear a somewhat minor one, hardly worthy of so prolonged an investigation. As I see it, however, our problem has a vital bearing upon the interpretation of what is perhaps the crucial situation in the Libertarian-Determinist controversy—the situation in which the agent seems to himself to be 'rising to duty' in defiance of his strongest felt desires. The Determinist holds that this act is fully explainable in terms of antecedent emotions and conations; but he has considerable difficulty in working out his explanation in detail. McDougall's explanation is well known, that the 'weaker' desire is reinforced by a new impulse excited from within the self-regarding sentiment. But apart from certain other grave difficulties (which I have pointed out elsewhere), this solution is defective by reason of its limited application: since we certainly *sometimes* have the experience we call 'rising to duty' in 'the line of greater resistance' when the most careful introspection reveals no trace whatsoever of impulses from the self-regarding sentiment. It then occurs to one to ask, may we not, perhaps, in those cases where the self-regarding sentiment is inoperative, appeal to the moral emotion of 'respect for duty' to furnish the new reinforcing impulse? It is in this connection that the question of the capacity of the moral emotion (and its corresponding 'impulse') to vary in intensity will be found to be of great moment. A decision one way or the other will not solve the free will problem. But it will contribute very substantially, I think, to its more profitable discussion.

VIII

DOES RELIGION CHALLENGE
ETHICAL AUTONOMY?

I

I propose in what follows to consider the challenge to the autonomy of ethics that comes from the side of religion. This challenge, I think, expresses itself in three main ways. The *first* is concerned with the nature of moral obligation. If religion is right here, ethics loses its autonomy by becoming a branch of theology. The *second* is concerned with the possibility of 'revealed' moral truth. If religion is right here, ethics is relegated to the rôle of, at best, junior partner in the business of elucidating moral law. The *third* is concerned with the place of 'sin' in human nature. If religion is right here, ethics, inasmuch as it is based upon a 'moral experience' which turns out to be riddled with illusion, becomes so trivial an affair that the question whether it is in any sense 'autonomous' ceases to be worth discussing.

On the first of these challenges I shall say almost nothing. What requires to be said about it from the side of ethics has been already said admirably and often.[1] On the second I shall limit myself to a very few observations: though the issues here would repay a much closer examination if space were to spare. It is the third challenge which seems to me especially to call for a reply from the moralist at the present day, and upon it the larger part of this brief paper will be concentrated.

I must begin by giving some account of what I shall be meaning by the term 'religion'. Without raising ultimate questions of definition, and purely for the purposes of this paper, I ask leave to identify 'religion' with 'theism': for it is theism that people have in mind when they talk of a challenge to ethical autonomy from 'religion'. And, indeed, the common essence of theistic religions is such, I think, that the threefold challenge outlined above does spring from it very naturally—though not, I shall suggest, with impeccable logic.

[1] Never better, perhaps, than by Dr A. C. Ewing in his article 'Ethics and Belief in God' (*The Hibbert Journal*, July 1941, pp. 375 ff.).

The central affirmation of (theistic) religion I take to be of the reality of a Supreme Being infinite in power and goodness. And it will be agreed that the ultimate basis of this affirmation is not 'rational' evidence (though rational evidence may support it), but the evidence of 'direct experience'. The characteristic content of this direct experience is perhaps best formulated in Otto's famous phrase, *mysterium tremendum et fascinans*. *Tremendum* may be said to denote, roughly speaking, the aspect of Divine *power*; *fascinans* the aspect of Divine *value or goodness*; *mysterium* the aspect of *infinitude* which qualifies both the power and the value and raises them to a new, and more-than-human, dimension. This last aspect, implying God's transcendance of all finite measures and modes of representation, though it presents obvious difficulties for 'rational' theology, seems indisputably integral to the religious experience which is theology's primary datum. Its clear recognition has important bearings upon the whole question of the relation between ethics and religion. For it means that the 'goodness' ascribed to God on the basis of religious experience, though it has identity with, is also different—and different not merely in degree—from 'goodness' as we know it in the moral life. The element of identity which justifies us in applying the term 'good' in both cases lies, I think, in the recognizably analogous feelings evoked in man by the 'object' of religious experience on the one hand, and manifestations of finite goodness on the other.

II

Now if God's power is infinite, presumably all that is must be ultimately dependent upon him. It is natural, therefore, that 'the moral law', apprehended by our moral consciousness, should be regarded by religion as having its source in God. And if the moral law is regarded as having its source in God, it is tempting to think of it in terms of the metaphor of 'Divine command'. The next step is fatally easy; the identification of 'moral obligatoriness' with 'being commanded by God'.

This first challenge to ethical autonomy seems to me, as already remarked, to have been very effectively repelled in recent ethical writings. The 'ought' of morals is demonstrably not susceptible of analysis into 'being commanded by God'. I am content here, therefore, to point out that religion does not *need* to quarrel with ethics on this issue. Doubtless the fundamental religious affirmation (as we agreed to understand it) does entail the proposition that the moral law is, like everything else, ultimately dependent upon God. But that proposition is not equivalent to, nor does it entail, the proposition that 'being under moral obligation' means 'being commanded by God'.

III

The second challenge involves a collision in which injury to one party is less easily avoidable.

It is usual for religion, having interpreted moral laws in terms of Divine command (or will), to go on to insist that there are certain privileged historic persons to whom God has directly revealed his will for man. The typical method of ethics for the elucidation of moral law is systematic reflection upon the products of man's moral consciousness. The typical method of religion is the consultation of sacred writings in which are enshrined the moral precepts which God has revealed to his prophets. Religion may, indeed, concede some value to 'rational' ethics in that the 'moral consciousness' with which that science deals is, presumably, the 'voice of God' in man—however subject to distortion God's voice may be by the imperfect medium through which it is finding expression. But religion will certainly contend that rational ethics is not merely not the *only* way of discovering moral truths, but is also an *inferior* way, and that it must yield to the way of religion whenever its conclusions conflict with the deliverances of 'revealed' ethics.

On this situation it must suffice to make three brief comments:

(1) In the light of a study of the cultural contexts in which the great religions have emerged and grown, it is surely hard to gainsay that the moral utterances of the 'prophet' are coloured throughout by the moral ideas that prevail in his historic milieu. Granting the prophet's finer sensitivity to moral issues, the facts seem to suggest irresistibly that his moral precepts do little more than reflect at their highest pitch the moral ideas of his time and place. The votaries of the great religions are usually not averse from admitting this principle for the interpretation of the moral (and other) pronouncements of the prophets of all religions but their own: and even of *some* prophets of their own religion. Are there

really good objective reasons for denying that the principle applies *universally*? If not, the degree of truth in the precepts of the prophets is a matter to be assessed by straight ethical thinking and not vice versa.

(2) And, of course, that *is* what happens in the *end*. If according to some prophetic utterance it is right, e.g., to visit the sins of the fathers upon the children (a view not unnatural at a stage in cultural history prior to the emergence of a clear concept of 'personality'), whereas our ethical thinking convinces us that it is wrong, it is not our ethical thinking that yields in the long run. But in the *short* run it is: and it is bound to be, in any community conditioned to regard the precepts of its religious prophets as infallible. How grave have been the consequences in the way of retarding the natural development of enlightened moral theory and practice need hardly be emphasized.

(3) One has little hope of a *rapprochement* between ethics and religion on this issue. Belief in prophets of God divinely inspired to utter eternal moral truths is an integral part of most of the great religions. Nevertheless, it is not integral to *religion*, on any definition of religion that merits the slightest respect. If a man has a sincere personal faith in a Supreme Being of infinite power and goodness who is the ground of all that is, to say that he is 'without religion' seems a mere impertinence—no matter how one may deplore his inability to share certain *other* convictions.

IV

We turn now to meet the 'third wave'—a challenge by religion to the autonomy of ethics by comparison with which what has gone before seems almost paltry. For if this challenge be well founded, nothing that is recognizable as 'the moral life' remains standing. Naturally enough, the challengers seldom say this in so many words. But it appears to me to be the inescapable implication of what they do say.

The challenge is implicit in the doctrine of the Fall of Man, which dominates so large a part of contemporary religious thought. I cannot here, of course, attempt to give an account of even its main variants in Christian theology—much less of its analogues in the theologies of other religions. But something must be said of its common essence, in order that we may be clear both about

F

its roots in religious experience and about its bearing upon morals.

We may, I think, take the fundamental premises of the doctrine to be, on the one hand, the infinite power and goodness of God, revealed in religious experience, and, on the other hand, the sinfulness of man—also supposed to be revealed, or at least brought home to us, in religious experience. How is the sinfulness of the creature to be reconciled with the perfect goodness and power of the Creator? Note that the problem is not one of reconciling with God's perfection the fact that man *can*, and often *does*, will evil. That problem, though assuredly a hard one enough, might receive a not too paradoxical solution in the postulate that God, by an admittedly mysterious act of Self-limitation, has 'created creators'; conferring upon man thereby the free will which alone makes possible his realization of moral good, but which carries with it, of necessity, a corresponding possibility of his realizing moral evil. But the situation that sets the present problem is not that man *can* sin, but that man (so it is alleged) has a *natural bias* towards sin. We have to try to reconcile the perfection of the Creator with a human nature that is *essentially* corrupt. The solution offered is the doctrine of the Fall. Man in his original state was without taint. But by some primal act of sin he 'fell', and in falling not merely alienated *himself* from God but implicated in that corruption the whole succeeding race of man, so that 'Adam's seed' thereafter and for ever is vitiated by a congenital bias towards sin. Thanks to God's goodness, the bias is sometimes counteracted; but not by human effort, only by the operation of Divine grace. By some thinkers the human situation is so interpreted that man can of himself do nothing at all to resist his natural bias to evil. Other thinkers concede to man a measure of active co-operation, so that it lies with him, at least in part, whether he will respond to or decline God's gift of grace. But common to all versions is the insistence that man by his own effort can achieve virtually nothing in the way of goodness.

It seems to me not difficult to show that this doctrine makes nonsense of our moral experience, repudiating its most fundamental deliverances.

Let us look at a typical moral situation, and let us choose the situation of 'moral temptation', for in it the central characteristics of the moral life are conspicuously exposed. In 'moral temptation'

I am conscious of at least two possible but mutually exclusive courses of action: *A*, which I believe to be my duty, and *B*, which I am aware that I desire more strongly. I am certain that if I follow the 'set' of my purely desiring nature, I shall adopt course *B*: that is entailed in my recognition of my desire for *B* as the 'stronger'. But I also feel quite certain that I *need not* let my desiring nature take its course, that I *can*, by effort of will, 'rise to duty' and adopt course *A*. In so believing I may be right or I may be wrong; but *qua* moral agent I cannot at the moment of temptation believe otherwise than that it rests with me here and now whether I rise to duty or succumb to temptation. It remains to add that if I do succumb, I regard myself as, so far, morally bad and blameworthy, and if I make the effort and rise to duty I regard myself as, so far, morally good and worthy of respect.

Now whether the claims made by the moral agent, as above described, can or cannot be ultimately substantiated is in the present context irrelevant. I happen to believe that they can. But the present point is that they are claims *inherent in moral experience*; as anyone can verify for himself by thinking himself into the situation of moral temptation. It follows that the rejection of these claims is tantamount to the condemnation of moral experience as illusory.

But it is plain that the theology of the Fall is totally incompatible with these claims. The Fall doctrine declares that I can be good only by the grace of God. The moral consciousness declares that I can be good by my own effort. The conflict is far too sharp to leave room for compromise (though its clean-cut character can be, and often is, obscured by a dense cloud of words). Deny to the moral agent the power which he believes he has of resisting by his own effort his inclinations to evil, and you deny to him what he cannot help regarding both as a fact, and as an indispensable condition of his being a morally responsible person.[1]

It may be instructive to look for a moment from a slightly different angle at the alleged bias towards evil in human nature. What are the supposed psychical facts that are being referred to when this bias is asserted? Presumably not the fact that human desires are such that, if they are allowed to take their course, if we always obey our strongest desire or 'follow the line of least

---

[1] On the notion of 'collective responsibility' which the doctrine of the Fall implies, and with which I have no space to deal, attention may be drawn to the admirable analysis by Professor H. D. Lewis in *Philosophy*, January 1948.

resistance,' they will often (by no means always) lead us into evil. That is certainly a fact. But it is a fact which is a condition of moral goodness every bit as much as of moral badness, and no more constitutes a natural bias to evil than it constitutes a natural bias to good. If our desires conformed to duty 'of their own nature', calling for no exercise of control, there could be no such thing as a moral life at all. Moral good and evil are fundamentally a matter of the *will*, of the way in which the self deals with the situation created by desire. Hence a 'bias towards evil' should properly mean that in moral temptation there is, *apart* from the 'pull' of contrary desire, some *further* 'pull' which weights the balance against our rising to duty. What evidence is there from psychology of the operation of this malign influence? Presumably, since it may not be identified with the contrary set of desire, it must be supposed to involve some sort of tampering 'from the outside' with the will itself. I submit that not only do we in fact find nothing of the sort by the most painstaking introspection, but that we cannot even attach any clear meaning to it—doubtless because it would imply a psychical state incompatible with that freedom of will which, rightly or wrongly, the self in the moral situation cannot help thinking it enjoys.

It seems to me, then, that if the doctrine that man is by nature sinful, and can achieve goodness only by the operation of external grace, is really integral to religion, we are bound to conclude that religion and ethics are irreconcilably opposed to one another. One may accept the religious point of view, or one may accept the moral point of view, but one cannot logically accept both.

But is this doctrine really integral to religion? Are we really reduced to the dilemma of making a choice between religion and ethics? I do not for a moment believe that this is so: and I propose to use what little space remains in trying to uncover what seems to me the fallacy underlying the belief that religion obliges us to maintain a doctrine so repugnant to the ordinary moral consciousness.

V

Whatever is entailed by the essential nature of religious experience we may agree to regard as 'integral' to religion: and what I have called 'the central affirmation of religion'—the affirmation of a Supreme Being infinite in power and goodness—does seem to me to bear this character. But belief in universal human wickedness, I submit, has no such credentials. The tendency to suppose that it has arises from the fact that religious experience does carry with it a consciousness of 'estrangement from God'. But it is only by avoidable misinterpretation, I shall argue, that this estrangement is taken to imply that man is by nature corrupt.

It is important to distinguish two 'moments' in the 'estrangement' of which religious experience makes man conscious.

The basis common to both is the *mysterium* aspect of religious experience: the sense of the Divine *infinitude*, of a power and value in God that transcend all our human categories. To the man who is vouchsafed some vision, however partial, of the 'Glory of God', there must come an overwhelming awareness of the immeasurable, and humanly impassable, gulf that separates man from God.

This is the first 'moment', and it is conditioned simply by a shatteringly vivid realization of the imperfection of our finite, creaturely nature. The second and deeper moment is conditioned by a consciousness of moral wickedness. In so far as this consciousness is also present, the felt gulf between man and God must take on a new, and far more terrible, significance. Man will be aware now not merely of estrangement from God, but of *self-*estrangement from God—the estrangement that is *sin*.

Now although there seems no reason why, theoretically, the first moment of estrangement should not exist without the second, there is little doubt that in fact the two moments are normally fused in man's religious experience. For normally the 'subject' of it is aware not merely of his finite or creaturely imperfection, but aware also that he is a morally imperfect being, in that he certainly does *sometimes* will what is evil.

But it is surely clear that it is only by confusion—though an easily understood confusion—that man takes this estrangement to imply that he is *by nature* corrupt, that his will is *essentially* sinful? That conclusion does not at all follow from the actual data which engender his consciousness of estrangement from God. The error can arise, I think, in two main ways. Failing to grasp the implications of 'free will' as the condition of the moral life, he may suppose that a sinful *act* implies a sinful *nature*; not seeing that the fact that *sometimes* he wills what is evil no more implies that he is by nature sinful than the fact that *sometimes* he wills what is good implies that he is by nature sinless. Or he may confuse the conditions of the one moment of estrangement with the conditions of the other, and ascribe to the imperfection of 'sin' the universality and necessity which rightly belong only to the imperfection of 'finitude'. But however one chooses to explain the confusion, the one thing that seems certain is that the data upon which the consciousness of estrangement is based do not justify an interpretation of that estrangement in terms of a human nature *essentially* corrupt.

If this account of the matter be in principle correct, the doctrine in dispute is not 'integral' to religion at all. It is in no sense a necessary implication of religious experience. And as for allegedly 'independent' arguments for a natural bias towards sin, these seem to me wholly without force save for those who are already persuaded on religious grounds; or perhaps for those who have failed to see that the fact that human desires do not 'naturally' conform to duty is simply a pre-condition of there being a 'moral life' at all.

VI

Is there then no ultimate conflict between the affirmations implicit in religious experience and those implicit in moral experience? In my view there is none. The most obvious difficulty is that of reconciling the infinite power ascribed to God in religious experience with the self-initiation claimed in moral experience. But the difficulty, I believe, is apparent rather than real. It arises from a failure to be in earnest with the *mysterium* aspect of religious experience. If we are in earnest with it, we must recognize that translation of the infinite attributes of Deity into finite conceptual terms (e.g., causality) is in principle illegitimate. 'Power' and 'Goodness', as already argued, are ascribable to God only as *analogues* of finite power and goodness. Hence to speak of God as 'causing' a human action is not so much false as just meaningless. If we arrogantly insist upon trying to 'rationalize the suprarational', *of course* insoluble puzzles will emerge, including the morality-religion antinomy. But this thesis (which I have elaborated and defended elsewhere)[1] I cannot further develop in this paper.

[1] *Scepticism and Construction*, Ch. VIII.

PART II
PHILOSOPHY OF KNOWLEDGE

IX

CONTRADICTION:
'LAW' OR 'CONVENTION'?

To the present writer (and, he believes, to a good many other persons) one of the most puzzling aspects of the contemporary scene in philosophy is the continued attraction, for an important minority, of the doctrine that logical 'laws', including what used to be called 'laws of thought', are in fact merely conventional rules of linguistic usage, which we generally find it convenient to agree to adopt, but which, being conventions only, have in them no inherent necessity. The case against such a view seems, at first sight at any rate, so crystal clear and so compelling. The gist of it might perhaps be stated as follows. Granting that logic has to do with 'discourse', that discourse must be *intelligible* discourse. Hence any speech conventions which a specific logic prescribes must be such that if we speak in terms of them we speak intelligibly. But *do* we speak intelligibly—do we convey any determinate meaning even to ourselves—if we adopt a convention such as 'p does not exclude not-p'? If, for example, you say 'Ayer is a philosopher', and this proposition is, in accordance with your convention, compatible with 'Ayer is not a philosopher', is it not obvious beyond argument that what you are saying has no significance whatever? But if so, it would seem that, in logic, we are *obliged* to accept the rule 'p excludes not-p'; and if we are obliged to accept it, it is not a *convention*. It is a necessary rule for intelligible discourse—'necessary', because we are just not able to think save in terms of it. But this is really equivalent to saying that it is a 'law of thought'.

I want to raise this topic once more in connection with a passage in the BBC debate on Logical Positivism between Professor Ayer and Father Copleston (now for the first time available in print[1]). Whether the debate was scripted or unscripted I do not know; but in any event its publication presumably implies, in the absence of specific disclaimers, that the participants are reasonably satisfied that what appears represents their considered views.

[1] In *A Modern Introduction to Philosophy*, edited by Paul Edwards and Arthur Pap, pp. 586–618.

F*

In the course of the debate Ayer agrees that one can't admit the possibility of a piece of paper's being white and not-white at the same time 'given existing conventions about the use of the word "not"'. He goes on 'But of course you could perfectly well introduce a convention by which it would be meaningful. Suppose you chose, when the paper was grey, to say it was white and not-white. Then you would have altered your logic. But given that you're using a logic in which you exclude "p and not-p", then of course you exclude the paper's being white and not-white.'[1]

It seems to me that this argument is plausible only to the extent that it is ambiguous. It is intended, I take it, to show by an example (the grey paper) how it *is* possible to assert a self-contradiction intelligibly, if you alter your logic. Now it is true that the proposition 'this piece of (grey) paper is both white and not-white' can be given a meaning in which we should all agree that it is intelligible to assert it. But in this meaning, unfortunately, the proposition is not self-contradictory, and the example is therefore irrelevant to the question whether we can intelligibly assert what is self-contradictory. If, on the other hand, the proposition be interpreted, more naturally, in a way in which it *is* self-contradictory, nothing that Ayer here says, so far as I can see, has any tendency to show that it is intelligible to assert it.

A possible meaning of the proposition which would make its assertion intelligible is this. We are all familiar with the mixing of paints on a palette, and we know that by mixing 'white' with 'not-white' (e.g., black) we get 'grey'. We can, therefore, 'choose to say'—and still talk good, if slightly peculiar sense—that a piece of grey paper is both white and not-white (at the same time), meaning thereby that the grey appearance of the paper comes about by the physical mixing of white and not-white constituents. Since, however, the proposition as so understood can be intelligibly asserted in a perfectly straightforward way—with no 'alteration of our logic', for no self-contradiction is involved—the fact that we can 'admit the possibility of a piece of paper's being white and not-white at the same time' in *this* sense has no bearing on Copleston's problem.

Doubtless one could invent other unusual meanings for the proposition about the grey paper, in terms of which we could also 'choose to assert' it and still talk sense. But unless the proposition,

[1] *Op. cit.*, pp. 598–9.

in such meanings, involves a self-contradiction, its intelligibility will be irrelevant to any attempt to exhibit a kind of 'thinking' which abandons existing conventions in favour of a new convention by which p does not exclude not-p.

The 'plain' meaning of the proposition about the grey paper is, of course, that the paper has, at the same time and all over, the sensory appearance 'white' and the sensory appearance 'not-white'. What we want to know is how it is possible to assert the proposition intelligibly in *this* meaning; and my difficulty is to see how Ayer's argument helps us in any way.

For it is no good telling us that we can intelligibly assert it if only we adopt the new convention that p does not exclude not-p, unless we are also told how we *can* adopt this new convention—can adopt it, that is to say, as a 'logical' convention, a rule for conducting intelligible intercourse, not just a rule for manipulating marks on paper. The marks as mere marks, presumably everyone will agree, have no interest for logic. For logic their significance is as *symbols*; and, on this account, what is said about them, or what we are told to do with them, must be capable of intelligible translation in terms of what the symbols symbolize. A 'rule of use' which cannot be so translated ought not, it seems to me, to be called a 'logical' rule, for the marks are then *not* being treated as symbols. It may be a rule for playing a more or less interesting game, but the game is not logic. To apply this to the case before us, a convention like 'p is to be treated as not excluding not-p' is apt to *seem* intelligible because, as a rule governing the permissible moves in a game in which 'p' and 'not-p' are mere 'counters', it *is* intelligible. But to ascertain whether it is an intelligible rule for *logic*, we have to ask ourselves whether it makes sense when 'p' and 'not-p' are regarded no longer as mere counters but as symbols. The situation then becomes very different. When we translate the symbols in terms of what they are supposed to symbolize we find, it seems to me, that the 'game' is not playable according to the proposed rule. The rule is ostensibly a rule for intelligible discourse, but what we seem to find is that discourse just ceases to be intelligible if we try to treat any given proposition's being true as compatible with that same proposition's being false.

There is one way, of course, in which we *could* intelligibly assert 'p and not-p'; namely, by giving a *new meaning* to the word 'not'. We might agree to understand by 'not', say, 'either identical with or different from'. Then certainly it is intelligible to assert 'p and not-p'. If *that* is the sort of thing that is meant by altering 'existing conventions about the use of the word "not" ', then of course, by such alteration, we *can* intelligibly assert that a piece of paper is at the same time both white all over and not-white all over. But what we shall be doing in this manoeuvre is not to alter our logic, but merely to alter the English language. We are *not* adopting a new convention whereby a proposition does not exclude its contradictory, for, on the new meaning of 'not', 'not-p' is no longer the contradictory of 'p'. The question whether we can intelligibly assert a contradiction—'p and not-p' in the ordinary sense of 'not'—is therefore not touched. If, on the other hand, the 'conventionalist' logician is prepared to agree that in the *ordinary* meaning of 'not' we cannot meaningfully assert 'p and not-p', why, that is surely all that advocates of the traditional view have meant when they argued that there is a *law* of contradiction, and that it is a law of *thought*.

X

SELF-EVIDENCE

Others besides the present writer must have been struck at times by the curiously ambivalent attitude of so many philosophers towards the notion of 'self-evidence'. Almost all philosophers, when they raise in a formal way the question of rival criteria of truth, dismiss the claims of self-evidence with decision—not seldom, indeed, with derision. 'Self-evidence', they tell us, signifies no more than a subjective feeling of assurance, and is worthless as a test of objective truth. Yet one gets the strong impression that very few philosophers are prepared to forgo altogether the use of this criterion in their own personal practice. In informal debate and discussion, where a certain linguistic licence is excusable, references to propositions as 'self-evident' can be heard frequently. But they turn up surprisingly often even in the more circumspect language of the printed page. Moreover, it is perfectly clear that, when they call a proposition 'self-evident', these philosophers are not intending to inform us merely about the quality of their own psychical attitude to the proposition. They take themselves to be naming a characteristic of the proposition itself in the light of which that proposition ought to be acknowledged to be objectively true.

This is not a very satisfactory state of affairs. It suggests—what further reflection amply confirms—that the term 'self-evident' is liable, even in philosophical usage, to important shifts of meaning, and that it stands in much need of elucidatory analysis. It suggests also that there may be a meaning of the term (inexplicitly operating in the minds of philosophers on the occasions when they are disposed to accept a proposition as true on the ground of its 'self-evidence') in which self-evidence as a criterion of truth has a good deal to be said for it, and in which it is at least not obviously vulnerable to the staple objections listed in the textbooks.

The first half of this paper, roughly speaking, will be concerned with the *meaning* of 'self-evidence'; the second half with (*a*) its *validity*, and (*b*) its *value*, as a criterion of truth. In Part I my main object will be to discover what precise meaning one ought to give to 'self-evidence' if one is to be in the best position to put up a defence for it as a valid criterion. In Part II (*a*) I shall argue that, in this meaning, the claims of self-evidence are, in fact, extremely hard to rebut. My final contention, in Part II (*b*), will be that, while there are difficulties about the practical applicability of the criterion as so understood, and hence about the criterion's value, there is no reason to suppose these difficulties insurmountable.

I ought at once to draw attention, however, to a somewhat severe restriction which I have had to impose upon myself in this paper. I shall be concerned with self-evidence in the theoretical sphere *only*—not at all with self-evidence in the *practical* sphere (not, e.g., with the self-evidence claimed by ethical intuitionists for their ultimate moral principles). A discussion comprehending both spheres might, as I see it, proceed along lines common to both for a part of the way. But before very long divergences of a fairly fundamental character would force themselves upon us, and would compel the extension of the paper to unmanageable length.

I

I begin with one or two general points upon which clarification seems essential if the problems before us are to acquire sufficient sharpness of definition to make a satisfactory treatment possible.

That the term 'self-evidence' is capable of bearing a diversity of meanings is manifest. The first of the term's two components, the word 'self', does not normally lead to much trouble in this context, and we need not linger over it. Waiving the further analysis which would for some purposes be desirable, we may be content here with the simple statement that to be *self*-evident a proposition must be evident from its own nature, without regard to anything beyond itself. (For this reason, we may note in passing, no one supposes that self-evidence is the *sole* criterion of truth. It is offered as a criterion only in respect of such propositions [if there are any] as are true in their own right—i.e., are 'intrinsically' true.) Where difficulties arise is in the second of the term's two components, the word 'evident'. For 'evident' is a relational word, which remains indeterminate until supplemented, explicitly or implicitly, by some answer to the question 'evident *to whom*?' Now to this question, plainly, a number of different answers are abstractly possible. Yet even those who allow themselves to speak fairly freely of 'self-evident propositions' are by no means always careful to specify which answer to the question they are assuming.

The use of the term 'self-evident' without any clear indication of what answer is intended to the question 'self-evident to whom?' is one obvious source of philosophical confusion. But there is inherent in the term another, less obvious, source of confusion which calls for a rather more extended consideration at this juncture. In ordinary usage, the word 'evident' carries with it a very strong presumption of the *truth* of the proposition said to be 'evident'. We do not say 'It was evident to Smith that p was the case' unless we believe that p *was* the case. If we believed that it was *not* the case, the mere fact that Smith assured us that he was absolutely certain about it would not be felt to justify us in saying that it was 'evident' to him. Now if this be so, if we can properly call a proposition 'evident' to anyone only on condition that it is (to the best of our belief) a *true* proposition, it would seem to follow that, strictly speaking, there can be no problem about whether a proposition's being 'self-evident'—no matter to whom—is a guarantee of its (intrinsic) truth. *Of course* it is. The (intrinsic) truth of the proposition being part of what we mean when we say that a proposition is 'self-evident', it is an analytic statement that a proposition's being self-evident is a guarantee of its (intrinsic) truth.

Appreciation of the linguistic convention we have just been noticing requires, in the interests of clarity, that the customary formulation of the question before us undergo some revision. It now appears that the question cannot be whether *being* self-evident, but only whether *seeming* to be, or *being taken* to be, or *being believed* to be, self-evident is a valid criterion of truth, and if so, *under what conditions*. And in point of fact, in actual discussions of the question, the recognition that there is no problem about whether 'being' self-evident is a valid criterion is usually implied; as, for example, when criticism takes the form of arguing that what *seems* self-evident may not really *be* self-evident. The critic is manifestly assuming—rightly—that to say that a proposition *is* self-evident is to imply that, in the speaker's view, it is true.

The distinction between 'seeming' evident (or self-evident) and 'being' evident (or self-evident) is, of course, a familiar one in English idiom. We do often say 'it seemed evident that' where we should think it incorrect to say 'it was evident that'. Nevertheless, 'seeming evident' is not altogether a simple notion, and we must pause to try to make its meaning precise. Its complexity is due to the bi-polar character of the word 'evident', the conjunction in it of a logical with a psychological reference. Its logical reference (which we have already remarked) is to the implication of objective truth in the proposition which is called 'evident'. Its psychological reference is to the feeling of certainty entertained towards the proposition by the person who finds it 'evident'. What requires to be made plain is how exactly the word 'evident', so understood, is modified when there is prefixed to it the word 'seeming'.

The answer is, I think, that the modification affects only the *logical* reference, and not at all the psychological reference. Thus when we say 'it seemed evident to him that', we do not mean that it only *seemed* to him that he felt certain. If he tells us he felt certain, then, in the absence of special grounds for distrust, we accept his report; but we do not find in it any objection to our continuing to say 'it *seemed* evident to him that'. On the other hand we do mean, when we speak in this wise, that it remains open to question whether the proposition towards which this subjective certainty is felt is objectively true. I suggest, accordingly, that when we say 'it seemed evident to him that p was the case', rather than 'it was evident to him that p was the case', what we wish to convey is that while we recognize that he felt certain that p was the case, we also recognize that it is open to doubt whether p was the case.

A slight complication in the use of the expression occurs where the person to whom the proposition is said to 'seem' evident is the *user* of the expression, and the statement is made in the present tense. If we say 'it seems evident to me that p is the case' (intending a distinction from 'it is evident to me that p is the case'), we are implying, as before, that it is at least an open question whether p is the case. But, by the same token, we are obviously *not* implying that we feel certain that p is the case. On the contrary, we choose our mode of locution just because we do *not* feel certain. The psychological reference of 'evident' is of course still operative; but it cannot indicate on our part more than a strong inclination to believe the proposition true—a state, perhaps, of 'near-certainty'. 'It seems evident to me that p is the case' can, I think, be fairly enough rendered as 'I feel almost certain that p is the case, and I see at present no positive ground for doubting it, but I am unable to rule out altogether the possibility that I am 'missing something', and that *p* is in fact *not* the case'.

This linguistic complication, however, will not in fact trouble us in our enquiry into self-evidence as a test of truth. For the advocates of this test have never pretended that it is any guarantee of a proposition's intrinsic truth that someone (no matter how defined) should have towards it an attitude in which he feels it appropriate to say merely 'It *seems* self-evident to me that *p* is the case'. The *only* cases of interest for our problem are those in which the person to whom a proposition *seems* self-evident would say that to him it *is* self-evident—cases where he feels not just 'almost', but 'absolutely', certain of its intrinsic truth.

The main upshot of these preliminary considerations is twofold. The problem of self-evidence as a criterion of truth makes sense only if it be formulated (1) in terms primarily of what *seems* self-evident, not of what *is* self-evident; and (2) in terms of some determinate answer to the question 'seems self-evident to *whom*?'

We are now in a position to get under way. For in the light of the foregoing considerations it has become tolerably clear what the Self-evidentialist must do if he is to establish a case for his criterion; and one may add, what any philosopher must do if he is to justify the occasional appeals to 'self-evidence' he makes in his own practice. It is common ground to all parties that a proposition can seem self-evident to some subjects and yet not be intrinsically true, and perhaps not true at all. What the Self-evidentialist must try to do is to provide a determinate answer to the question 'seems self-evident to whom?' of such a kind that it will be defensible to say that a proposition which seems self-evident to a subject so characterized must be intrinsically true, and that a proposition which seems not to be self-evident to a subject so characterized cannot be intrinsically true. Or again his task might be said to be to specify the precise conditions under which a proposition's 'seeming self-evident' will be a guarantee of its being intrinsically true, and its seeming not to be self-evident will be a guarantee of its not being intrinsically true. There is no difference of substance, I think, between these two formulations. For the 'conditions' which require to be 'specified' will in fact all be subjective conditions, relating to the credentials of the subject-mind by which the proposition is taken to be, or not to be, self-evident, and sufficing (in so far as the specification is successful) to constitute that subject mind a 'competent judge' in matters of intrinsic truth.

Clearly the Self-evidentialist has a formidable task before him. On the other hand, some progress towards accomplishing it he can quite certainly and quite easily make. For there are a number of specifiable conditions the presence of any one of which in a subject can be clearly seen to disqualify that subject for the rôle of 'competent judge'. Thus every serious defender of the self-evidence test has gone out of his way to make it plain that he is not concerned with what seems to be, or seems not to be, self-evident to imbeciles, the intellectually immature, and the like. There is room, however, for a more systematic enumeration of these disqualifying conditions than the Self-evidentialist has, to the best of my knowledge, as yet supplied. The further we can go with the uncovering of these disqualifying conditions, the nearer we should be getting to the definition of 'competent judge' which the Self-evidentialist ideally desiderates. The nearer we should be getting, at the same time, to a meaning of the term 'self-evident' in which 'self-evidence' as a criterion of truth is invulnerable to at least the common objections advanced against it.

We begin with the most obvious disqualification—failure to understand the proposition whose intrinsic truth is in question. Ignorance, stupidity, inattention, mental immaturity can all, severally or together, prevent a man from grasping the precise meaning of the terms and relationships in their propositional unity. One need hardly elaborate the truism that the first essential of a 'competent judge' is that he should correctly understand the proposition he sets out to appraise.

'Seems self-evident to whom?', then, may receive as its first considered answer, 'to a subject who correctly understands the meaning of the proposition upon which he professes to be adjudicating'. This takes the Self-evidentialist a little way forward. But not very far. For it is a commonplace that a man may very well understand the meaning of a proposition and yet have his judgment about it warped by the intrusion of emotive factors which are irrelevant to the question of the proposition's truth or falsity. Everyone would agree that where a man approaches a proposition with a strong emotive bias in its favour, its seeming self-evident to him is no kind of guarantee of its intrinsic truth; and that should he approach it with a strong contrary bias, its seeming not self-evident to him is no kind of guarantee that it is not intrinsically true. Clearly, if the self-evidence criterion is to have any real force, the answer to the question 'seems self-evident to whom?' must be developed in a way that will provide against irrelevant emotional intrusions. The answer might perhaps now take the form 'seems self-evident to a subject who correctly understands the given proposition, and whose judgment upon it is unaffected by bias imparted to it from the side of the emotions'.

It should be observed, however, that the condition named in the first clause of this answer is, strictly speaking, rendered otiose by the second clause. For the initial words of the second clause—'whose judgment upon it' (i.e., upon the given proposition)—of themselves imply that the given proposition is correctly understood. If a man *mis*understands the proposition upon which he is ostensibly adjudicating, then it is not *that* proposition which is before his mind at all when he passes judgment, but another proposition which he mistakes for the given proposition. In other words, his judgment is not a 'judgment upon *it*' (the 'given proposition'). It is enough, therefore, that the answer to the question 'seems self-evident to whom?' should (at this stage) take the form 'to a subject whose judgment upon the given proposition is unaffected by bias imparted to it from the side of the emotions'. At the same time, it is as well to bear in mind that in this form the answer *does* carry with it the implication that the given proposition is correctly understood, and that the first disqualifying condition (misunderstanding) is eliminated as well as the second (emotive bias).

The definition of 'competent judge' which this stage implies is certainly an improvement. But it is still seriously defective. For it is apparent on a little reflection that the emotions (or what are ordinarily so called) are not the only sources of a bias that can vitiate a man's judgment. There is an equally powerful source of bias of which we have as yet taken no cognizance, namely, 'intellectual habituation'. I mean by this the disposition of the mind to run in certain determinate grooves of thought fixed more or less rigidly by mere custom. Force of habit, we are all aware, is by no means confined to the behaviour of the body. It is constantly operative upon our mental behaviour likewise. Where a man has been intellectually nurtured within a certain climate of ideas, where his own experience over a wide range has offered much which seems to

confirm these ideas and nothing which has moved him to call them
in question, where in consequence he has persistently over a long
term of years carried on his thinking through the medium of these
ideas, these ideas tend to become, as it were, woven into the very
texture of his mind, so that only by the most strenuous effort is he
able to free himself from their control. The feeling which habit thus
engenders of a compulsion to think in certain determinate ways it is
extremely easy for a man to misinterpret as a compulsiveness inherent in the propositions themselves; and it is extremely easy for
him, therefore, to take these propositions to be 'self-evident'.

It seems plain that we have here a source of bias which can be,
and often is, no less prejudicial than the emotions to the right discernment of truth. Little weight, obviously, can be placed upon
pronouncements that a given proposition is (or is not) self-evident
if they are delivered by persons strongly suspected of being intellectually habituated by sheer custom to accept (or reject) that
proposition. Moreover, although intellectual habituation has, as a
rule, received a great deal less attention than have the emotions as a
source of biased judgment, it would appear to have a rather special
importance for our present undertaking. For it may reasonably be
held to account in large part for a phenomenon which Self-
evidentialists have always found particularly hard to reconcile with
their acceptance of 'self-evidence' as a valid criterion. I refer to the
notorious disagreements among philosophers themselves about
which propositions, if any, are in fact self-evident. Such disagreements have naturally been something of a scandal for the cham-
pions of 'self-evidence', and an obvious trump card in the hands of
their adversaries. For it is seldom that they can be ascribed with
any plausibility to differences in the meaning attached by the
philosophers concerned to the propositions whose intrinsic truth
they dispute. Nor does it seem much more plausible, save in rare
cases, to suggest that emotive prejudices must have been at work
on one side or the other. It is, after all, an occupational characteristic of philosophers to be constantly vigilant against such intrusions; and in any event a great many of the propositions in
question (e.g., in logic, in epistemology, and in metaphysics) are
not of a kind to carry strong emotive overtones. Descartes thought
it self-evident that the transmission of light was instantaneous, and
self-evident, again, that every event has a cause—propositions
which no one today finds self-evident. But it would not be at all

convincing to argue that Descartes's judgment was either clouded by misunderstanding of the meaning of these propositions or subjected to improper interference from the side of the emotions. On the other hand, it *is* plausible, I think, to suggest that philosophers, like other folk, succumb at times (though perhaps less often than other folk) to the far subtler and less easily detectable influence of intellectual habituation. Looking back on the history of philosophy, it is by no means difficult to believe that different schools of philosophy, inheriting, and long habituated to entertaining without question, different philosophical assumptions, often misinterpreted the sense of subjective compulsion felt towards the acceptance of their own assumptions as though it denoted objective necessitation, and were in consequence induced to proclaim as self-evident many different and mutually inconsistent sets of propositions.

Having taken cognizance of this further factor which disqualifies a subject from assuming the rôle of 'competent judge', viz., intellectual habituation, we are now in a position to fortify considerably the Self-evidentialist's answer to the question 'seems self-evident to whom?' The revised version of the answer might now run 'seems self-evident to a subject whose judgment upon the given proposition is unaffected by bias imparted to it either by irrelevant emotions or by habits of thinking induced by mere custom'.

Do there remain any further disqualifying conditions of which a satisfactory definition must take account, any further influences from the side of the subject which might impart an improper bias to the judgment of self-evidence? It is doubtful whether there are others that can be very precisely specified. But it is not doubtful, I fear, that the disqualifying conditions so far enumerated fail to be completely exhaustive. What, e.g., of the dynamics of the human subconscious? The mere mention of this shadowy, still largely uncharted, realm is a sufficient reminder of how rash it would be to assume that the categories of emotive disposition and intellectual habituation—comprehensive as these undoubtedly are—embrace all possible judgment-perverting agencies. If the Self-evidentialists' 'competent judge' is to be 'competent' beyond reasonable cavil, he must certainly be defined in a way which will take care of the possibility of such additional, even if as yet undetermined sources of bias. The amplification of the answer to our question 'seems self-evident to whom?' which is now demanded is of a kind that is, by reason of its high generality, somewhat unwelcome. In order to be really 'safe', the new answer will require, I think, to take some such form as this: 'seems self-evident to a subject whose judgment upon the given proposition is unaffected by bias imparted to it (not only from irrelevant emotion and from habits of thinking engendered by mere custom, but) *from any source whatsoever*'.

This further elaboration is, I say, a somewhat unwelcome one. For if it makes, or helps to make, the criterion of self-evidence water-tight in point of theoretical validity, it also very much weakens it—conceivably beyond redemption—in point of practical applicability. It is hard enough in all conscience (the critic may reasonably urge) to be sure that one's judgment on a proposition is swayed neither by irrelevant emotion nor by mere intellectual habit; it is quite *impossible* to be sure that it is unaffected by further influences of a sort which we are not even in a position to specify.

Though the difficulties with respect to the criterion's applicability are without doubt formidable, they can, I believe, be met. I should like, however, to defer that question meantime, and to ask, rather, 'Have we at length reached a stage of definition of the term "self-evident" at which it can be claimed with some confidence that self-evidence (so defined) is a theoretically valid criterion of intrinsic truth?'

I believe this to be the case. It will be easier to establish it, however, if we first translate into positive terms the definition of 'competent judge' which has so far been only negatively formulated. 'A subject whose judgment upon the given proposition is not affected by bias imparted to it from any source whatsoever.' Now what is this but 'a subject whose judgment upon the given proposition *is the pure, unadulterated expression of the intellect*'? For a judgment to which 'bias' has been imparted is nothing other than a judgment in which the intellect is prevented by some alien influence from finding its proper expression; just as an '*un*biased' judgment is, in its very essence, a judgment into whose determination nothing whatsoever enters save the intellect itself. I suggest, therefore, that the 'competent judge' at whose negative characteristics we have somewhat laboriously arrived can be positively defined as 'a subject whose judgment upon the given proposition is the pure expression of the intellect operating, as it were, *proprio motu*'. And since, again, such a 'subject' is in no wise different from a subject functioning *qua* pure intellect, the 'competent judge' reduces, in the last resort, to 'the pure intellect', 'the intellect as such'.

If this be so, the claim of the Self-evidentialist, as we have now come to understand it, may be positively stated in the following simple form: 'Where a proposition seems self-evident to the (pure) intellect, it is intrinsically true.'

II (*a*)

When the criterion is so formulated, I submit that all reasonable ground disappears from the charge which constitutes the heart of the orthodox objections to it—the charge that 'self-evidence' signifies no more than a merely subjective assurance. In a sense, of course, the appeal is still to a 'subjective' assurance. An alternative formulation to that given above would be 'Where a strictly intellectual assurance, i.e., an assurance which derives solely from the functioning of the intellect, is felt towards a given proposition considered in and by itself, that proposition is intrinsically true'. But—and this is the point—an assurance of *this* kind, *intellectual* assurance, cannot be regarded as 'subjective' in any *pejorative* sense of that term. It is not subjective, that is to say, in a sense which is prejudicial to its objectivity. It is subjective only in the harmless sense in which *any* function pertaining to a 'subject' of experience can be called 'subjective'. Where (in the context of judgments) we call anything 'subjective' with pejorative intent, there is always a reference to some factor operating in the judging subject which is irrelevant to the determination of objective truth, and the operation of which, accordingly, may lead the mind into error. But obviously one cannot regard the *intellect* as such a factor, since the determination of objective truth is precisely *the intellect's job*. Indeed, it would be hard to define the 'bad' subjective (in the realm of factual judgments at any rate) save in terms of *contrast* with the intellect. A mental function entering into the determination of a judgment is 'subjective' in the pejorative sense, one might reasonably contend, if, and only if, it is a function *extraneous to the intellect*.

I think, then, that at least the 'routine' criticisms of the self-evidence criterion on the score of its supposed subjectivity lose their force when that criterion is understood in terms of self-evidence to the *intellect*. There remains, however, one rather special line of argument along which a challenge might still be developed to our view that strictly *intellectual* certainty is not subjective in any pejorative sense; and though the challenge is not, in my opinion, really hard to rebut, it does raise some interesting and somewhat perplexing points, and deserves serious consideration.

A critic might conceivably argue along the following lines: 'When you assert that a particular proposition is self-evident to the intellect, you do so, and can only do so, on the basis of its seeming self-evident to *your* intellect. But by what right do you assume that your intellect and that of other people always function in accordance with identical principles, and that disagreement is therefore possible only where at least one of the disputing parties is influenced in his judgment by non-intellectual factors? That "self-evident to *your* intellect" and "self-evident to *any* intellect" are one and the same thing is an *assumption*; and it may be a false one. Should it happen to be a false assumption, the criterion manifestly breaks down. If it is possible for intellects to vary in the principles of their functioning, it is possible for one person to have a strictly intellectual certainty about a proposition's intrinsic truth while another person has an equally strict intellectual certainty that the actual contradictory of this proposition is intrinsically true. The two "certainties" cannot both be objectively valid; but there is no way, in terms of your criterion, of discriminating between them. Your criterion, therefore, fails—unless, of course, you can justify your assumption that "the intellect" to which it makes appeal is not merely *your* intellect, but *any* intellect.'

Now one might reply to this, in the first place, that the assumption that the intellects of different persons are not differently constituted but function according to identical principles is one that underlies all rational intercourse between persons. In the second place, and more importantly, one might point out that, even if argument of great apparent cogency were to induce one reluctantly to abandon this assumption, acceptance of this argument would not entail, and would indeed be irreconcilable with, the view that the principles upon which one's own intellect functions in discerning truth and falsity are untrustworthy. For the argument which one accepts as establishing that intellects can function on different principles is (like any other argument) so accepted only in so far as one takes one's own intellect to *be* trustworthy in appraising it. One must still, therefore, even in admitting a diversity of intellects, insist upon the special authority of one's own. And as for any *direct* argument against the trustworthiness of one's own intellect, this, of course, must involve a *direct* self-contradiction. A man can attach weight to reasons for distrusting his intellect only in so far as he *trusts* it.

It is plain, however, that to leave the matter here would be extremely unsatisfactory. If there really are compelling arguments for the recognition of a diversity in principle of intellectual functioning, one obviously cannot hold that intellectual certainty as such is everywhere infallible. It is small consolation to know that one cannot logically distrust one's own intellect, and that other people cannot logically distrust their intellects, if in fact intellectual certainty can be entertained by different persons towards propositions that are mutually incompatible. Manifestly the criterion 'self-evident to the intellect' has, on this hypothesis, ceased to have meaning. For there is now *nothing* that can be called 'the' intellect.

And I think it must be granted that there are some disturbing, and perfectly familiar, facts which, prima facie, are none too easy to reconcile with the postulate of universal identity in intellectual functioning; nor, consequently, with the doctrine that strictly intellectual functioning is everywhere infallible. I lay no great store by certain anthropological reports which are sometimes supposed to show that the intellects of primitive peoples may function 'a-logically'; for it does not appear to me that the 'facts' here are anything like definite enough or detailed enough to warrant any such confident interpretation. But even in our ordinary, everyday, lives have we not all found ourselves, on occasion, complaining of so-and-so's 'illogical mind'? Is it not a commonplace that some intellects are 'defective', even to the point of imbecility? And do we not frequently observe persons that are so afflicted entertaining towards a given proposition a certainty that is genuinely 'intellectual', in the sense that it is founded solely upon their reflection upon it, but which is directly opposed to the intellectual certainty felt towards the same proposition by minds that function (as we should ordinarily say) 'more efficiently'?

It seems to me, however, that it is only on a somewhat superficial view that such facts as are here referred to are taken to imply that different persons can have conflicting intellectual certainties about the same proposition. Suppose we take the case of a man confronted by the problem of determining what is entailed by a given complex of related propositions a, b, c, d, e, f, g, where the given complex in fact entails X. It must be conceded, I think, that the man may, on the basis of strictly intellectual reflection on the problem, come to judge with a feeling of complete certainty that Y is entailed—even although Y directly contradicts X. But—and this is the core of the matter—that Y is entailed by *what*? He himself supposes, of course, and he will so declare, that it is the given complex of propositions which he has found to entail Y. But is it really the case that, in the intellectual act which is his judgment, it is *precisely this given complex* which he is attending to, and which he is so completely certain entails Y? May it not be that his 'illogicality of mind' (as we are apt to describe it) consists at bottom of a failure to comprehend, clearly and distinctly and all at once, the total complex as it is given, and that the complex which he *does* comprehend, and which he is certain (on genuinely intellectual grounds) entails Y, is a slightly *different* complex—with perhaps one proposition in the given complex overlooked, and another, perhaps, unwittingly identified with a proposition which only more or less closely resembles it? If that should be so, it is not the case that he enjoys intellectual certainty about the *false* proposition that a, b, c, d, e, f, g, entails Y. His intellectual certainty is about the proposition that a, b, γ, d, e, g, entails Y. And *this* proposition may perfectly well be true.

There is, I think, nothing fanciful in this interpretation of the situation. That something of the sort described occurs frequently seems quite clear. And I am much inclined to believe that this interpretation can be generalized, without undue strain, to meet all cases in which there is a certainty, genuinely derived from purely intellectual apprehension, which *looks* as though it were directed to a false proposition. In all such cases, I suggest, it is really a different proposition about which the intellectual certainty is felt. There has been an (unrecognized) failure to comprehend, clearly and distinctly and at all once, the actual given complex that sets the problem, and an unconscious substitution for that complex of one resembling it.

There would seem to be three typical ways in which intellectual weakness in coping with a problem reveals itself. First, in the way just described, where the given propositional complex is unconsciously replaced by another, and an entailment perceived in the latter complex is confusedly assumed to be an entailment pertaining to the former complex. Secondly, there may be a failure, of which the subject is himself aware, to comprehend the given complex adequately; in which case no claim is made to intellectual certainty about what it entails. Thirdly, the given complex may come to be adequately comprehended, but only after a lapse of time appreciably longer than would be required by an 'average' mind confronting the problem under like conditions; in which case the perception of what the given complex entails will be unduly delayed, but not incorrect. The second and third of these are probably at least as common as the first. Only the first, however, is relevant to the difficulty we are trying to deal with, since in neither of the other two is there any question of intellectual certainty being felt about a false proposition. And with the first we have dealt.

But is there, perhaps, a difficulty for our theory concealed in what we referred to as the subject's 'unconscious substitution' of a different propositional complex for the propositional complex that was given? For clearly the subject is committing an error in taking these two different things to be one and the same. Have we not, at best, succeeded in rescuing the 'weak' intellect's infallibility at one point only at the cost of admitting its fallibility at another point? But I do not think there is any real difficulty here. Our thesis has been that whenever there is genuine intellectual certainty, i.e., a certainty derived solely from the functioning of the intellect, about a proposition p, then p is true—the judgment is infallible. Now in making the mistake of identifying the two different complexes, it is not the case that the subject has, or would claim to have, intellectual certainty that the complexes are identical. Without doubt a judgment which is false, and which is nevertheless accompanied by subjective certainty *of a sort*, *is* present in the acceptance of a, b, γ, d, e, g, as identical with the complex which was given. But the judgment that is here present seems clearly to be of the nature of 'taking for granted that'; and the sort of subjective certainty involved in 'taking for granted that' is about as different as well can be from an *intellectual* certainty—a certainty 'derived solely from the functioning of the intellect'. The only judgment in the hypothetical situation we have been examining for which a claim to *intellectual* certainty is made is the judgment that a, b, γ, d, e, g, entails Y. And there is no reason to suppose that *this* judgment is false.

I have in the foregoing deliberately chosen to illustrate from the intellectual apprehension of entailments from a given *complex* of propositions; for it is in this kind of context that what is commonly called 'illogicality of mind' (or, for that matter, plain stupidity) most conspicuously manifests itself, and in which the essential nature of the intellectual defect stands out most clearly. But the principle is the same, I think, in respect of those simple, categorical judgments about which the question of 'self-evidence' is more usually raised in philosophy. If a man declares a proposition p to be self-evident, and therefore intrinsically true, when in fact p is not intrinsically true, the most *likely* explanation is, no doubt, that the certainty he feels is *not* founded solely upon intellectual processes, but is determined in part by such extraneous factors as we enumerated earlier in this paper. But if, as I think it must be admitted *may* be the case, his certainty is a strictly intellectual certainty, if it really is to his intellect that the proposition seems self-evident, then my suggestion is that the proposition about which he has this intellectual certainty is not p—which he has failed to grasp properly—but a different though resembling proposition π, which he has unwittingly identified with p, and which *is* in fact intrinsically true.

I conclude, therefore, that our criterion of intrinsic truth is not really imperilled by the admission that the intellect to which appeal is made is at bottom one's own. For there is no adequate ground for disbelieving (what we all in our rational intercourse with other persons assume) that the intellect functions everywhere according to identical principles.

Is this perhaps also—as I suggested at the beginning of this paper might be the case—the meaning of 'self-evidence' which is inexplicitly operating in the minds of philosophers on those occasions in their own practice when they apparently accept the self-evidence criterion? I am much inclined to believe that, at least generally, it is. This is not a matter that can be proved, and I do not propose to waste many words upon it. One is obliged to rely primarily upon interrogation of one's own experience. Yet I should be a little surprised if self-interrogation by others did not confirm my impression that the reason why one sometimes feels so completely confident that a proposition is true on the ground merely of its self-evidence is that on these occasions one is convinced that one's certainty about the proposition derives *solely* from intellectual discernment, and is in no wise influenced by emotive prejudices, intellectual habits, or any other extra-intellectual factor;

this coupled, it should be added, with implicit acceptance of the premise—which I have earlier tried to defend—that it does not make sense to doubt that of which one is *intellectually* certain.

II (*b*)

I pass now from the question of the *validity* of the criterion to the question of its *value*; meaning by this its practical applicability. Clearly a criterion may be perfectly valid, and yet be of little or no value, because it is difficult, or even impossible, to apply it in practice. The criterion 'self-evident to the intellect' is open to rather obvious challenge on this score. For it would be idle to deny that a man may very easily be deceived when he supposes that the certainty he feels about the intrinsic truth of a given proposition has a strictly intellectual basis, and that it really is to his *intellect* that the proposition seems self-evident. Non-intellectual factors may well have insinuated themselves without his being aware of it. We must ask, therefore, whether there is any way of ensuring beyond reasonable doubt that one is *not* deceived when one thinks that one's certainty is strictly intellectual. Unless there is, the critic will be fully entitled to complain that, even if 'self-evidence (to the intellect)' is a valid criterion, its importance is negligible, since one is never in a position to apply it with a justifiable confidence.

For my own part I am persuaded that, though the danger of self-deception is real enough, it is by no means impossible to protect oneself effectively against it. In order to defend this opinion I must begin by inviting attention to a characteristic which seems to me to be of the very essence of whatever can properly be said to be 'evident to the *intellect*'.

It will doubtless be agreed that that which seems evident to the intellect (or to reason, or to thought) is in all cases a *proposition*. Now we call a proposition 'evident to the *intellect*', so far as I can see, if, and only if, it is taken to be an *intellectually necessary* proposition. We do not call a proposition 'evident to the *intellect*' where the connection of its subject with its predicate is for the intellect merely *de facto*; as, for example, in the proposition that a blackbird is singing in yonder bush, or in the proposition that Glasgow is 44 miles distant from Edinburgh. No one supposes in such cases that he is affirming the proposition on the basis of *intellectual* insight. We call a proposition 'evident to the intellect', I think, only where

—as in the proposition that, on Euclidean premises, the three angles of a triangle are equal to two right angles—the subject-predicate connection is such that we feel ourselves under *intellectual* compulsion to affirm it; where, in other words, the proposition has for us 'intellectual necessity'.

In most cases the propositions to which this intellectual necessity can be ascribed are propositions which express entailments between other propositions or sets of propositions. They are such propositions as '*if* A-B, *then* X-Y'. In these cases the entailed proposition, X-Y, while intellectually necessitated, is not of course itself an intellectually necessary proposition, since that which necessitates it is something merely hypothetical. At least the abstract possibility must be allowed, however, of intellectually necessary propositions which are categorical and do *not* merely express entailments between other propositions or sets of propositions. Consider, for example, any chain of entailments. Obviously one (or more) of the entailing propositions must be accepted for some reason other than its being entailed by previous propositions; and the reason *could* be that it is taken to be intellectually necessary in itself (as Euclidean axioms in the chain of geometrical entailments were once universally taken to be). And it *could* also be that the entailing proposition is *correctly* so taken. If so, we should have a categorical proposition which possesses intrinsic intellectual necessity.

For purposes which will appear shortly, it is desirable to distinguish also propositions which have not *intrinsic* but *derivative* intellectual necessity. In '*if* A-B, *then* X-Y', we saw, X-Y is not itself an intellectually necessary proposition. But what if A-B is, and is seen to be, a proposition with intrinsic intellectual necessity? It will then be a case not of '*if* A-B, *then* X-Y', but of '*because* A-B, *therefore* X-Y'. In such a case, X-Y, as the entailment of an intrinsically necessary proposition, will be itself an intellectually necessary proposition. Since, however, it is an intellectually necessary proposition not *in* or *of* itself, but only in virtue of its being entailed by A-B, we must say that it (and other propositions of the kind) have 'derivative' as distinct from 'intrinsic' intellectual necessity.

Now if there be such a thing as a 'self-evident' proposition, i.e., a proposition evident to the intellect of its own nature, it is obvious what kind of intellectual necessity it must possess. Since its necessity is discernible irrespective of any reference to other propositions, its necessity must be of the intrinsic sort. We may say, therefore, that to be a self-evident proposition is to possess intrinsic intellectual necessity.

Let us then consider in this light the problem of how we can ever be sure that a proposition really is self-evident to the intellect. A proposition is self-evident to the intellect, we have suggested, if, and only if, it possesses intrinsic necessity for the intellect. Now a proposition possesses intrinsic necessity for the intellect, it seems clear, if, and only if, confronted by it, we 'can think no other'; and that means if, and only if, the contradictory of the proposition is incapable of being conceived at all. What we have to ask ourselves, therefore, when we are testing the claim of a given proposition, to be self-evident to the intellect, is this: 'Is the proposition such that when we try to think the contradictory of it we find that we cannot conceive it at all?' If on due trial we find that we cannot, we may assert with justifiable confidence that the proposition has indeed intrinsic necessity for, and is thus self-evident to, the intellect.

It may perhaps be asked, however, does this not just raise in another form the difficulty of being quite sure that a proposition is self-evident to the intellect? For is it not often difficult to be sure whether one is or is not able to think the contradictory of a given proposition?

Now I cannot for myself see that this is really difficult—*always provided that* 'conceiving' or 'thinking' is taken in an ordinary, straightforward meaning, as I am taking it here. There *is* a difficulty, I fully admit, where 'conceive' is given the more technical meaning which is usual when 'inconceivability of the contradictory' is proposed (as it often was during the reign of the Idealist philosophy) as a test for necessary propositions *in general*, and not (as for us) only for *intrinsically* necessary propositions. In that wider context it has been found imperative, if the test is to have any pretensions to validity, to mean by 'conceive' not just 'think', but 'think *out*'—think into all its entailments. And if 'conceive' be taken in the latter meaning, the test 'inconceivability of the contradictory' *is* often difficult to apply with confidence. This point, however, stands in need of some elaboration.

As a test of intellectually necessary propositions in general, 'inconceivability of the contradictory' has virtually no plausibility so long as by 'inconceivable' we mean 'incapable of being thought at all'. For intellectually necessary propositions include those which we earlier distinguished as having 'derivative' intellectual necessity, and it seems clear that we are quite often able to conceive (in the ordinary sense) the contradictory of propositions that have only a derivative intellectual necessity. For example, assuming for the sake of the argument that Euclid's axioms are intrinsically necessary propositions, the proposition that the three angles of a triangle are equal to two right angles is a derivatively necessary proposition. Yet we are quite well able to 'conceive' its contradictory—to 'frame it in our minds'. The advocates of the test, however, have not been so naïve as to overlook this elementary point. They have always insisted that (as already indicated) 'inconceivable' must be taken to mean not just 'incapable of being thought' but 'incapable of being thought *out*'—thought into all its entailments. And they could urge, not without force, that in the above illustration we cannot think the contradictory of the given proposition into all its entailments, since we eventually come to an entailment which we cannot think *at all*. But the trouble *then* is that, in acquiring plausibility, the test loses all ease of practical application. For it is often extremely hard to be sure whether one can or cannot think out into all its entailments the contradictory of a given proposition. We may be confident enough that we can think it out into all the entailments that on a careful scrutiny occur to us; but doubts may justifiably linger as to whether we may not have failed to notice some entailment which, had we noticed it, would have made it impossible for us to 'think it out', and would accordingly have required us to deny the 'necessity' which (as things stand) we are disposed to affirm.

But now notice. Difficulties of this sort (and, so far as I can see, difficulties of any other sort) are *totally absent* where our concern is with putatively *self-evident* propositions, which we are testing for *intrinsic* intellectual necessity. For a proposition which has intrinsic intellectual necessity is one which is intellectually necessary in its own right, in complete independence of its relations to other propositions. The test of a given proposition's intrinsic intellectual necessity, therefore, cannot involve the consideration of its relations to other propositions. Accordingly no question arises of whether we can 'think out into all its entailments' the contradictory of the putatively self-evident proposition. The sole question is whether we can think the contradictory of the proposition *at all*.

And this question, I must insist, is not really difficult to answer; or not difficult, at any rate, with respect to any of the propositions whose claim to self-evidence has ever been matter for dispute among philosophers. One *could*, of course, construct a complicated proposition the contradictory of which it would be difficult to be sure whether we could think, for the reason that its intricate composition would make it difficult to be sure that we had fully and precisely grasped its meaning, and difficult to be sure, therefore, just what it is that we are to try to do when we are called upon to try to think its contradictory. But, as we should expect, the candidates for self-evidence in the history of philosophy have not been of this complicated character. In their case the critical test-question above formulated can be asked, and answered, with ease. And if only they *had* been tested in this way, very few of them indeed would have escaped the axe—to the considerable profit of subsequent philosophy. Had Descartes, for example, ever seriously asked himself concerning the proposition that the transmission of light is instantaneous, 'Does this proposition possess intrinsic intellectual necessity, so that its contradictory—that light takes time to travel—is something which I cannot even conceive, can attach no intelligible meaning to?' he would surely have found himself obliged to admit that it was *not* so, and obliged in consequence to allow that the proposition was *not* self-evident. The so-called 'axiom of universal causation', and a large number of other propositions which philosophers from time to time have deluded themselves into supposing self-evident, would, if subjected to the same test, have suffered the same fate.

And now consider, by way of contrast, a proposition which probably most people, and certainly I myself, still regard as genuinely self-evident, viz., 'S cannot, at the same time and in the same relation, both be and not be P'. Is, or is not, this proposition such that we cannot think its contradictory at all? Surely the answer of anyone not inhibited by the pressures of preconceived theory must be that it *is* such? If we try to think S as being P and at the same time and in the same relation as not being P, we find, at best, that our mind oscillates with great rapidity between thinking S as being P and thinking S as not being P; never that we can think them both together. In other words, we find that the proposition

G

formulating the principle of contradiction possesses 'intrinsic intellectual necessity', and we are entitled accordingly to pronounce it 'self-evident to the intellect'.[1]

It would be out of place in the present paper to say more in defence of this view of the epistemological status of the principle of contradiction.[2] It may be permissible, however, before leaving the topic—and in concluding the paper—to point out that *if* the view here taken of the principle's status is sound, there may well be highly important implications for the evergreen problem of the possibility of synthetic *a priori* knowledge. Those philosophers who are willing to allow that there are such things as intrinsically necessary propositions are seldom prepared to admit into this category any but 'analytic' propositions; meaning thereby propositions whose denial is self-contradictory, like 'all equilateral triangles are triangles'. But is the principle of self-contradiction itself an analytic proposition? I very much doubt it. It does not appear to me that the denial of the principle of contradiction is self-contradictory. The principle is, I believe, a synthetic proposition; and if, as I have urged, intrinsically necessary, then a synthetic *a priori* proposition. Let me briefly try to justify this contention.

The principle of contradiction, as we have here formulated it, is 'S cannot, at the same time and in the same relation, both be P and not be P'.

The proposition which is the formal contradictory of the principle of contradiction is 'S can, at the same time and in the same relation, both be P and not be P'. For brevity's sake we shall denote this 'denying' proposition by the letter D.

The question at issue is whether D is a self-contradictory proposition.

---

[1] If, of course, we choose to express the principle of contradiction in the defective, but despite Joseph's warning (*Introduction to Logic*, p. 46) still not uncommon, form of 'S cannot at the same time be both P and not-P', it is perfectly easy to conceive its contradictory. Manifestly we can think a cherry (S) as being at the same time both red (P) and sweet (not-P). Misunderstanding on this point seems to be responsible for Mr Krishna Daya's difficulties over the applicability of the law of contradiction to empirical reality (*Discussion Note* in *Mind*, April 1957, pp. 250-257).

[2] Its most influential rival today is, I suppose, the 'conventionalist' view. I must confess that this view seems to me quite desperately unplausible, and to owe its appeal almost wholly to its obvious congruence with the general philosophical stand-point that happens to be now most in vogue. I have ventured to say something on this topic in *Analysis*, Vol. 18, No. 4, pp. 73-6, under the title 'Contradiction: "Law" or "Convention" ?'

The mark of a self-contradictory proposition is that it denies what at the same time it affirms. Now what D affirms is the possibility that mutually contradictory propositions may both be true. But it does not conjointly deny this possibility. D must not be mistaken for the proposition 'S both can and cannot, at the same time and in the same relation, both be P and not be P'. This proposition, of course, does at once affirm and deny the possibility that mutually contradictory propositions may both be true, and *is* self-contradictory. Nor should D be mistaken for the proposition (with which it is perhaps more liable to be confused). 'S both can and cannot, at the same time and in the same relation, be P.' This proposition too involves self-contradiction (at one affirming and denying the possibility of S being P). Both of these latter propositions have some resemblance to D in respect of verbal form, as also in the fact that they are both necessarily false. But clearly neither of them is equivalent to D. The difference which is especially relevant in our present context is that D does not, unlike the other two, conjointly affirm and deny anything—and is therefore not self-contradictory.

I submit, then, that the proposition which denies the principle of contradiction, though it is (I think) nonsense, is not self-contradictory. It follows that the principle of contradiction is a synthetic proposition. It further follows, if I have been correct in claiming for the principle the status of intrinsic necessity, that we have here *one* instance at any rate of a valid synthetic *a priori* proposition.

Whether there are any other instances, and if so what they are, it is not the business of this paper to enquire. The question is one that can be settled only by a thorough and uncommitted enquiry into the respective credentials of the different candidates. But if even one indisputable instance has been acknowledged, the need for such an enquiry can hardly be gainsaid.

XI

COMMON-SENSE PROPOSITIONS
AND PHILOSOPHICAL PARADOXES

I

Like many, perhaps most, students of philosophy in this country, I have long been troubled by a number of points in Moore's famous paper, 'A Defence of Common Sense', in the Second Series of *Contemporary British Philosophy*.[1] Just why is Moore so certain that he 'knows' the common-sense propositions listed? Just what is it he thinks he is knowing when he knows them? Just how does he conceive the bearing of what is thus known upon the solution of philosophical problems? These are some of the questions to which it has seemed to me hard to find satisfactory answers in the paper. Nor did much real help appear to be forthcoming from the commentators. These philosophers, despite the close acquaintance which most of them enjoyed with the technique of Moore's philosophical thinking, were hardly less ready than one's self to confess perplexity. Moreover, these philosophers, however puzzled they might declare themselves to be about Moore's meaning, almost all seemed to feel in their bones that he was saying something of extraordinary importance—a circumstance which made one's failure to understand the more disquieting.

From the state of intellectual frustration thus induced, the recent volume on Moore[2] by nineteen eminent students of his philosophy naturally held out good promise of relief. Somewhere in this massive work one might surely hope to discover at least some of the missing clues. And, certainly, I do not think that anyone can read this stimulating set of essays with attention and not gain a much clearer insight into many aspects of Moore's thought. I am bound to confess, however, that on the particular points upon which I especially desired enlightenment, such enlightenment as has ensued has in the main been evoked indirectly, through the medium of rather violent disagreement with contentions of the

---

[1] London: George Allen & Unwin, 1924.
[2] *The Philosophy of G. E. Moore.* Except where otherwise stated, all page references in my paper will be to this work.

essayists. And as this has been most conspicuously the case with regard to the very contribution which Dr Nagel, in his review in *Mind*,[1] judges to be 'the best and most rewarding in the final group of papers, if not in the whole volume' exhibiting 'a penetrating grasp of Moore's method of philosophizing' and giving 'a most persuasive and illuminating account of the rationale behind his defence of "common sense" '—the essay by Mr Norman Malcolm entitled 'Moore and Ordinary Language'—I think it may be of some interest to others besides myself to attempt a rather detailed study of this ingenious, but, as I think, misguided composition. I shall hope to show that, although Malcolm may conceivably be giving a valid *account* of Moore's thought,[2] he is certainly not, as he and apparently Dr Nagel believe, giving a valid *justification* of that thought. The criticisms I have to offer will pave the way for some final reflections of a rather more positive character upon the relationship between common-sense propositions, language, and analysis.

II

In this Section I propose to describe the way in which Malcolm envisages the problem of his paper and the general line of argument which he adopts for its solution. Criticism will be deferred to the two following Sections.

Malcolm begins with a series of twelve philosophical statements, whose common character is that they are all paradoxical to common sense. They are such propositions as 'There are no material things' (1); 'Time is unreal' (4); 'There are no other minds—my sensations are the only sensations that exist' (7); 'We do not know for *certain* the truth of any statement about material things' (10).[3]

To each of these propositions in turn Malcolm then opposes a very short common-sense argument which in his opinion is the sort of argument *Moore* would give, 'or at least which he would approve'.[4] Thus (to take the two propositions about which there

---

[1] *Mind*, Jan. 1944. Quotations are from p. 70.
[2] The fact that, in his 'Reply to my Critics' at the end of the volume, Moore does not expressly dissent from Malcolm's suggested 'rationale', cannot be taken as conclusive evidence of acceptance: but it does suggest that Moore has not felt that Malcolm misinterprets his mind very seriously.
[3] Pp. 435–6.   [4] P. 346.

will be most to say in the sequel) the reply to Prop. 1 is 'You are certainly wrong, for here's one hand and here's another; and so there are at least two material things'.[1] The reply to Prop. 10 is 'Both of us know for *certain* that there are several chairs in this room, and how absurd it would be to suggest that we do not know it, but only believe it, and that perhaps it is not the case'.[2]

Malcolm's problem is, are these common-sense arguments valid refutations of the philosophical paradoxes they attack, and if so, why? Malcolm believes that they are, and that he can show why.

'I hold that what Moore says in reply to the philosophical statements in our list is in each case perfectly true; and furthermore, I wish to maintain that what he says is in each case a good *refutation*, a refutation that shows the falsity of the statement in question. To explain this is the main purpose of my paper.'[3]

The next paragraph indicates what is to be the cardinal principle in Malcolm's explanation, and the two stages which will be involved in the full development of the argument.

'The essence of Moore's technique of refuting philosophical statements consists in pointing out that these statements *go against ordinary language*. We need to consider, first, in what way these statements do go against ordinary language; and, secondly, how does it refute a philosophical statement to show that it goes against ordinary language.'[4]

At this point we may be said to have reached the beginning of the argument proper. Malcolm is undertaking to show us that the philosopher in uttering his paradoxes is using words and phrases in a way which conflicts with ordinary usage, and that in denying certain common-sense propositions what he is really doing is

---

[1] P. 346.

[2] P. 347. It may be mentioned that Malcolm's opinion that his common-sense arguments would be approved by Moore is substantially borne out by Moore himself. In his 'Reply to my Critics', p. 669, he accepts all twelve arguments as *good* arguments; qualifying his approval only by the remark that in one case (Prop. 8) he would hesitate to say that the argument, though good, *proves* the falsity of the proposition against which it is directed.

[3] P. 349.   [4] P. 349.

'asserting the impropriety of an ordinary form of speech'. If this can be shown, the second stage of the argument will give little difficulty. It is an easy matter to show that *ordinary* language is *correct* language. It will then follow that the paradoxes of the philosopher are without justification.

In what way, then, do these philosophical statements 'go against ordinary language'? Malcolm develops his argument in greatest detail in connection with Prop. 10—'We do not know for *certain* the truth of any statement about material things.' In giving this argument, I shall quote Malcolm's own words as fully as regard to limitations of space will permit.

This paradox, Malcolm notes, has been a particularly popular one among philosophers. He chooses to concentrate, however, upon the version of it given by Mr Ayer in his *Foundations of Empirical Knowledge*; presumably because 'Mr Ayer is one who realizes that when he makes this statement he is not making an empirical judgment, but is condemning a certain form of expression as improper'.[1]

In that work, from which Malcolm quotes at length, Ayer gives as the ground of the paradox the fact that material-thing statements can never be fully verified, 'since the series of relevant tests, being infinite, can never be exhausted'.[2] Ayer goes on to contend that since the state of 'being sure' about a material-thing statement is one the attainment of which would require us to have completed an infinite series of verifications, and since the conception of such a state is self-contradictory, to say that 'we can never be sure'—a statement which suggests that the state of 'being sure' is in this context conceivable—may be objected to on the ground that it is misleading. 'What we should say,' Ayer decides, 'if we wish to avoid misunderstanding, is not that we can never be certain that any of the propositions in which we express our perceptual judgments are true, but rather that the notion of certainty does not apply to propositions of this kind.'[3]

At this point Malcolm steps in. What Ayer has said, he thinks, is tantamount to an admission that the disagreement between the philosopher and the plain man is only about the use of language.

'He [Mr Ayer] thinks that the phrase "known for certain" is properly applied only to *a priori* statements, and not to empirical

[1] P. 353. [2] Quoted by Malcolm, p. 454. [3] *Ibid.* p. 353. Italics Malcolm's.

statements. The philosophical statement "We do not know for certain the truth of any material-thing statement" is a misleading way of expressing the proposition "The phrase 'known for certain' is not properly applied to material-thing statements". Now Moore's reply "Both of us know for certain that there are several chairs in this room, and how absurd it would be to suggest that we do not know it, but only believe it, or that it is highly probable but not really certain!" is a misleading way of saying "It is a proper way of speaking to say that we know for certain that there are several chairs in this room, and it would be an improper way of speaking to say that we only believe it, or that it is highly probable". Both the philosophical statement and Moore's reply to it are disguised linguistic statements.'[1]

And it is Moore, Malcolm argues, who is right ' in this as in all the other cases'.[2]

'By reminding us of how we ordinarily use the expressions "know for certain", and "highly probable", Moore's reply constitutes a refutation of the philosophical statement that we can never have certain knowledge of material-thing statements. It reminds us that there *is* an ordinary use of the phrase "know for certain" in which it is applied to empirical statements; and so shows us that Ayer is wrong when he says that, "the notion of certainty does not apply to propositions of this kind".'[3]

In this last paragraph Malcolm is anticipating the second stage of his argument—that *ordinary* language is *correct* language—and as the second stage will be irrelevant if the first stage breaks down, we had better pause here to examine the first stage—that philosophical paradoxes 'go against ordinary language'.

III

No one can look after Mr Ayer's interests one-half so well as Mr Ayer, and I do not propose to try to anticipate what his reply might be to Malcolm's criticism. Ayer's argument (which I accept) can quite well be treated in detachment from his general philosophical position—as indeed Malcolm has treated it. When so

[1] P. 354.   [2] P. 354.   [3] P. 355.

regarded, it seems to me not at all difficult to show that it is merely perverse to suggest that the implication of this argument is that the dispute between the philosopher and the plain man, between paradox and common-sense statement, is a matter of 'linguistics'.

For, consider. Certainly it follows from Ayer's argument that 'the phrase "known for certain" is properly applied only to a *priori* statements, and not to empirical statements'. So too we could say, if we liked, that from some argument designed, let us say, to demonstrate the internal activity of physical bodies, it follows that 'the phrase "internal immobility" does not apply to physical bodies'. But surely this would be an altogether inept and unnatural way to express the consequence of the argument in the one case as in the other? For it seems perfectly clear that what each argument is concerned with is the proper understanding of the *facts* of the situation, and not with any problem of linguistics: and that there is a 'disagreement about language' with the plain man *only because* there is a disagreement about the correct reading of the facts. The plain man thinks that in certain situations there is no possible room for doubting the truth of such and such a material-thing statement: he therefore, very properly, applies the phrase 'known for certain' to that statement. The philosopher thinks that when we bear in mind certain considerations which the plain man has not taken into account, more particularly the never wholly eradicable possibility of hallucinations and dreams, we can see that there *must* always be room—however slight—for doubt: and he therefore, equally properly, says that we can *not* apply the phrase 'known for certain' to material-thing statements. In short, the 'disagreement about language' is wholly consequential upon a 'disagreement about the facts'. So that instead of it being the case, as Malcolm contends, that the philosophical statement, 'We do not know for certain the truth of any material-thing statement' is a misleading way of expressing the proposition 'the phrase "known for certain" is not properly applied to material-thing statements', precisely the *reverse* is true. The latter proposition is a misleading, a *highly* misleading, way of expressing the former proposition.

Let us get quite clear about this business of 'disagreement about the use of language'.

A small child, just learning the use of simple words, points to a cow close by, clearly outlined in the sunlight, and says, 'Look at the horse!' We say to him 'That's not a horse, it's a cow'. Here it is
G*

natural and proper to say that the disagreement is 'linguistic'. There is no difference, or none of substance, in the facts apprehended. The child sees much the same features as the adult, the features characteristic of the cow. He simply 'applies the wrong label', having mistakenly assigned to the name 'horse' characteristics which he should have assigned to the name 'cow'.

Suppose, on the other hand, two adults walking in the fields by night, and confronted by a dark shape, dimly silhouetted against the grass. One says, 'There's a horse!' The other replies, 'No, it's a cow', and he may add 'I can see its horns'. Here we would regard it as quite ridiculous to speak of the disagreement as 'linguistic'. The two men attach precisely the same meaning to the terms 'cow' and 'horse'. Their disagreement is about the facts: and naturally a different form of words is required to express differently apprehended facts.

The principle seems perfectly plain. A difference between statements is properly attributable to a disagreement about the use of language only in so far as that difference is *not* determined by a different reading of the facts of the situation and *is* determined by the assignment of different meanings to constituent words or phrases.

Let us apply this principle to the difference between the philosopher's paradox and the common-sense proposition. Is there, in the first place, no difference in the 'reading of the facts'? Of course there is. I have already indicated what it is. The philosopher's reading of the facts includes the apprehension of what he regards as a legitimate ground for doubt ignored by the plain man. So far as I can see, there is only one expedient by which it could be maintained, as Malcolm wants to maintain, that there is no disagreement about the facts. That is, by confining the 'facts' to the sensory presentations which occasion the statements. But Malcolm does not explicitly resort to that expedient, and it is not difficult to understand his reluctance. For if *that* is what we are going to mean by 'the facts', then 'the facts' are properly expressed *neither* by the statement 'We know for certain that . . .' *nor* by the statement 'We cannot know for certain that . . .' but only by some quite different statement such as 'We have a sensory presentation of . . .'

In the second place, *is* there a difference between the philosopher and the plain man about the meaning assigned to constituent words and phrases? It seems to me equally clear that there is *not*.

The plain man understands just as well as the philosopher that knowing for *certain* means knowing in a way that excludes the possibility of doubt. It is only because on his reading of the facts there is no possibility of doubt—or else for another reason, to be discussed in a moment, equally consistent with acceptance of the philosopher's meaning of 'knowing for certain'—that he is content to use the phrase he uses.

If anyone should feel the need of a proof that the plain man really understands that 'knowing for certain' means 'knowing in a way that excludes the possibility of doubt', I don't think he will need to search far to obtain it. Let him show the plain man hitherto unsuspected grounds for doubt in the case of any proposition at all which the plain man has been in the habit of thinking and saying, he 'knew for certain'. If the plain man appreciates these grounds, he will at once confess that he does not, after all, know for *certain*; though he may very well add, should the ground suggested be ground for only a very faint degree of doubt, that he is still '*practically* certain'. Indeed, there must surely be very few, if any, teachers of philosophy who have not performed this kind of 'experiment' upon beginners in the subject; and performed it, moreover, in relation to precisely the kind of common-sense propositions here in dispute. I should be profoundly surprised to learn that the results of their 'experiments' differ significantly from mine. Almost universally, in my experience, the student recognizes that he is mistaken in saying that he 'knows for *certain*'; though he may, as I have said, go on to insist that the ground for doubt is so clearly negligible that he remains 'practically' certain. But 'practically certain' is *not* 'certain': and nothing but confusion can result in philosophy from their identification.

This notion of 'practical certainty', however, calls for a closer consideration. Examination of it will point to the need of a qualification to the general statement that the plain man always means by 'knowing for certain', 'knowing in a way that excludes all possibility of doubt'.

I think it would probably be agreed that what we normally mean by a proposition being 'practically certain'—at least where we use the phrase with any degree of care—is that the proposition is one about which the ground for doubt is so slight that it may safely be ignored in our actual behaviour, i.e., in 'practice'. Now, if a proposition is such that any doubt about its truth may be legitimately ignored 'for all practical purposes', then, *should we be speaking in a context in which it is clear that the sole interest of the proposition to us is its practical interest*, it would be by no means unnatural to *drop* the word 'practically'—since it would be taken as understood—and to speak simply of the proposition as 'certain'. The ellipse seems a perfectly justifiable one, and the practice of it is exceedingly common. Thus the philosopher himself is quite ready to say, in the ordinary traffic of life, 'I am certain there are several chairs in this room'. He *is* certain—for all practical purposes. And since it is quite evidently in the context of practical purposes that the proposition is uttered, he does not deem it necessary to make explicit this qualification to his certainty.

Malcolm's treatment of our problem seems to me to suffer rather seriously from his omission to take any account of this notion of 'practical' certainty. Had he done so, and had he observed how natural it is in certain circumstances to elide the word 'practical', it would, I think, have made a difference to some of the inferences he thinks it legitimate to draw from common speech. Thus he tells us that 'Moore's reply [to Prop. 10] reminds us of the fact that if a child who was learning the language were to say, in a situation where we were sitting in a room with chairs about, that it was "highly probable" that there were chairs there, we should smile, and *correct his language*'.[1] So we should. We should no doubt say to him that it was 'certain'. Not, however, because we believe it to be *absolutely* certain, but because we believe it to be *practically* certain, and because we consider that practical certainty is all that matters to the child—or indeed to the adult—in that practical context.

It follows from this discussion that a trifling modification must be admitted to the principle that the phrase 'knowing for certain' has the same meaning in common-sense propositions as in philosophical paradoxes. In the former case we *may* be meaning by 'certainty' only 'practical certainty'. But it must be insisted that the modification *is* only a trifling one, which in no way prejudices our criticism of Malcolm's argument. For in the common-sense propositions which Moore and Malcolm are interested to defend, 'certainty' is taken in the sense of 'absolute', not 'practical', certainty. Were it otherwise, indeed, *cadit quaestio*. For no philosopher that I know of has ever seriously disputed that these

[1] P. 354–6.

common-sense propositions have 'practical certainty'. The pro-
pounders of the 'paradox' that we do not know for certain the
truth of any statements about material things assuredly have no
thought of denying that in numberless cases the ground for doubt
may safely be ignored 'for all practical purposes'.

IV

We have, I hope, seen adequate reasons for rejecting, at least in
the case of the example to which Malcolm has chosen to give most
attention, the view that philosophical paradoxes 'go against
ordinary language'. If that stage of his argument fails, it becomes,
strictly speaking, a work of supererogation to consider the second
stage—the demonstration of how a philosophical statement is
refuted by showing that it goes against ordinary language.

Nevertheless, I think it will be profitable to give a good deal of
attention to this stage of Malcolm's argument also. And this for two
reasons. First, because it may with some justice be felt that we
have so far concentrated too much upon a single example; and we
shall have an opportunity in 'stage two' of widening the field. And
secondly, because in formulating the key proposition of 'stage
two', the proposition that 'ordinary language is correct language',
Malcolm seems to me to slip into the acceptance of a criterion of
'ordinary language' which makes that proposition not true but
false. And I rather fancy that it is largely *because* he is thinking in
terms of this criterion of ordinary language that he finds it so easy
to persuade himself that philosophical paradoxes go against
ordinary language.

This suspect criterion first makes its appearance in a passage
designed to show how absurd it is for a man knowingly to use
language in a way contrary to established custom. Malcolm
supposes the case of two men (we shall call them A and B) looking
at an animal. A says it is a fox: B says it is a wolf. Yet B, according
to the hypothesis, agrees with A not only 'as to what the characteristics of the animal are, but furthermore *agrees that that sort of
animal is ordinarily called a fox*'.[1] If B were to continue to insist that
it is a wolf, Malcolm goes on, 'we can see how absurd would be his
position. He would be saying that, although the other man was
using an expression to describe a certain situation which was the

[1] P. 357.

expression ordinarily used to describe that sort of situation, never-theless the other man was using incorrect language. What makes his statement absurd is that ordinary language *is* correct lan-guage.'[1]

I agree about the absurdity of B's statement. But I am not at all happy about the criterion of 'ordinary language' which seems to be implied in Malcolm's formulation of this absurdity. It looks as though Malcolm is saying that in any given situation the mark of 'ordinary language' is that the expression used to describe it should be 'the expression ordinarily used to describe that sort of situation'. Now, if this implies that language is being used in a sense *out of* the ordinary wherever a *different* expression is used from that ordinarily used to describe the situation, it seems to be plainly false. Suppose a situation X, ordinarily believed to have the characteristics *abcd*, and therefore ordinarily described by the expression which symbolizes the characteristics *abcd*. Does it follow that anyone who describes X by the expression which symbolizes the characteristics *abfg* is using language out of its ordinary sense? Not at all. For it may well be that this person disagrees with ordinary opinion in his analysis of X, and is con-vinced that it has the characteristics *abfg*. If so, his use of the expression symbolizing *abfg* is the ordinary and correct use of language.

B's position, of course, remains absurd. For B, *ex hypothesi*, agrees with A that the situation is characterized by *abcd*, and yet rejects as incorrect the ordinary expression, symbolizing *abcd*, used to describe that sort of situation. What I am anxious to make clear, in view of what immediately follows in Malcolm's paper, is that the use of language may be ordinary and correct even if it describes by an expression symbolizing *abfg* a situation *ordinarily* described by an expression symbolizing *abcd*.

What 'immediately follows' in Malcolm's paper is an attempt to show that the philosopher who says that we can never really perceive material things is committing the very same absurdity as B, 'though in a subtle and disguised way'. It will be best to give the crucial passage in full:—

'But the philosopher who says that the ordinary person is mistaken when he says that he sees the cat in the tree, does not mean that he

[1] P. 357.

sees a squirrel rather than a cat; does not mean that it is a mirage; does not mean that it is an hallucination. He will agree that the facts of the situation are what we should ordinarily describe as "seeing a cat in a tree". Nevertheless, he says that the man does not *really* see a cat; he sees only some sense-data of a cat. Now, if it gives the philosopher pleasure always to substitute the expression "I see some sense-data of my wife", for the expression "I see my wife", etc., then he is at liberty thus to express himself, *providing* he warns people beforehand so that they will understand him. But when he says that the man does not *really* see a cat, he commits a great absurdity; for he implies that a person can use an expression to describe a certain state of affairs, which is the expression ordinarily used to describe just such a state of affairs, and yet be using incorrect language.'[1]

Is our sceptical philosopher really as foolish as all that? I am quite sure he is not.

Does the philosopher agree 'that the facts of the situation are what we should ordinarily describe as "seeing a cat in a tree" '? In a sense, yes. He agrees that here is a situation X ordinarily described by the expression symbolizing *abcd* ('I see a cat in the tree'). But this does not in the very least imply, as it would have to imply for Malcolm's argument to be effective, that he agrees that X has in fact the characteristics *abcd*. On the contrary, the sceptical philosopher's analysis of the situation leads him to believe that X is characterized by *abfg*, not *abcd*. He therefore, very rightly, uses the expression symbolizing *abfg* to describe it. And of course he does *not* go on to say, or to imply, that the ordinary man is using incorrect language. For he knows that the disagreement is not about language at all, but about the facts. The philosopher would agree that the plain man is using perfectly correct language to describe the facts as he apprehends them.

It is worth while pointing out also that the philosopher would not demur in the indiscriminate and unqualified way that the passage quoted suggests to the statement of the plain man who says 'I see a cat'. On ordinary occasions the philosopher will freely make such statements himself. He objects to them only *in the context of philosophical discourse*, where it is vital that our words should *accurately* describe the facts. If our sceptical philosopher

[1] Pp. 357–8.

chose to make a detailed reply to Malcolm's criticism, incorporating this point, I think it might run somewhat as follows:—

'No doubt we do ordinarily describe this situation by saying, "I see a cat". In ordinary life no harm is done thereby. For practical purposes this expression serves very well to secure the desired behaviour-adjustments—much better, indeed, than the technical statement of the philosopher, which would certainly be cumbrous and probably be unintelligible.[1] So I take no objection to the ordinary statement in the context of ordinary discourse. But if we are talking *philosophy*, if our interest is in the accurate and precise description of the real facts, and not in mere practical effectiveness, then I must demur. For I cannot agree that the statement "I see a cat" does accurately and precisely describe the facts as these appear on an analysis of them more thorough than is appropriate to everyday life. The ordinary statement suggests, *e.g.* that through visual sensing alone we cognize the cat. And this seems not to be the case. There are good grounds for holding that several factors besides visual sensing (though precisely what they are is admittedly controversial) enter essentially into cognition of the cat. There are good grounds for holding that visual sensing gives us at most certain "sense-data" of colour, shape, and size, and that the sense-data seen at any one time are not only not identical with the cat (since there is much in what we mean by a "cat" which these sense-data do not cover), but may not even be identical with the surface of the cat. In short, the real "facts of the situation" are very different from anything that can be said to be accurately described by the statement "I see a cat": and we must not therefore allow the practical convenience of this kind of statement to beguile us into supposing that it is other than inept in philosophy.'

Is there any valid reply to this defence of his 'paradox' by the philosopher? I can only say that I cannot find one in Malcolm's pages.

[1] Berkeley has said about all that needs to be said on this matter. 'In the ordinary affairs of life, any phrases may be retained, so long as they excite in us proper sentiments, or dispositions to act in such a manner as is necessary for our well-being, how false soever they may be, if taken in a strict and speculative sense.' (*Principles of Human Knowledge*, 1st Ed., Para. 52.)

V

In the light of what has been urged in the last two Sections, I venture to conclude that Malcolm has failed in the main purpose of his paper. If Moore's defence of common-sense propositions against the paradoxes of philosophy is to be justified at all, it cannot be done on the ground that philosophical paradoxes 'go against ordinary language'. The division is far deeper than one of 'linguistics'.

In this final section I want to pass from Malcolm's paper in order to give attention to a very important type of common-sense proposition which plays a prominent part in Moore's writings. The statement 'I see a cat' may be said, in virtue of its form, positively to clamour for philosophical correction if it is made within the context of philosophical discourse. This is not, or not so obviously, the case if the perceptual judgment is formulated in the statement 'This is a cat'. Has the philosopher anything to condemn here? I gather that a good many persons think that the sceptical (which we may here take as including the immaterialist) philosopher *has* something to condemn; and that this proposition contradicts, by implication if not directly, such propositions as 'There are no material things', and 'It is doubtful whether there are any material things'. I believe this view to be mistaken. In what follows I shall attempt a brief analysis of the proposition in question designed to bring this out, and also to bring out certain other important facts about this type of proposition.

Let me indicate in advance the general ground upon which I hold that the sceptical philosopher has no reason to quarrel with the proposition 'This is a cat'. It is that in this (and in any similar) proposition, as asserted in common speech, nothing whatever is asserted or implied as to the being or not-being of material things in any sense of 'material things' in which their existence has been a subject of philosophical controversy. Berkeley would not have considered it in the least way inconsistent with his immaterialism to assert 'This is a cat': and he would have objected to the assertion of the proposition by others only if he had some special reason to suspect from the context that the speaker intended his words to imply that the cat was a 'material thing' in a sense not resolvable into a cluster of 'ideas'. In ordinary contexts, it seems to me, there is no such implication. Nor, of course, is there a contrary implication. The specific point of the proposition is, as I see it, quite neutral towards the philosophical issue. I do not doubt, indeed, that if the plain man were asked, after he had uttered his statement, whether he means by the cat a cluster of ideas (in some sort of relationship) or a non-mental entity, he would reply unhesitatingly that he meant the latter. But that does not imply that the 'materiality' of the cat was any part of what he asserted in his original proposition. All the plain man would mean, I think, would be, that *had* the question been raised at the time he made his assertion, that is how he would have answered it. But he would agree that neither question nor answer was at that time in his mind at all.

I have said that the specific point of this type of proposition is neutral towards the philosophical issue. This I believe to be true, and to be the real justification of the contention of Moore and his school that propositions of this sort are proof against any of the paradoxes of the philosopher. But to see that, and in what exact sense, it is true, we must now examine more closely what precisely it is that is being asserted, whether by the plain man or by the philosopher in the ordinary context of life, in the proposition 'This is a cat'.

First, as to the 'this'. At first glance it might seem as though the 'this' were what is presented in sense. But a moment's reflection suffices to show that such is not the case. The sensory presentation contains a certain complex of sensible features, but the speaker assuredly does not believe that the 'cat', which he identifies with the 'this', is exhaustively characterized by the limited features in this complex. The meaning which the term 'cat' has for him includes many more constituents than can be presented in any single sensory apprehension. Evidently, then, the 'this', though it 'has' these sensibly presented features, is taken to be an entity of wider scope, which 'has' also many other features.

The importance for the proposition of the sensibly presented complex is, of course, that the speaker recognizes therein certain features which are characteristic, in a more or less central way, of what is ordinarily meant by a 'cat'. He recognizes, perhaps, a characteristic shape, size, and mode of movement, and a colour that falls within the rather wide range characteristics of cats. And he apprehends in the complex no features which he recognizes as incompatible with the characteristics of cats. Then, having reason to believe, either from experience or from hearsay, or from both, that an entity which sensibly presents this particular group of features is almost, or almost always, an entity which in the appropriate empirical situations exhibits all the other features characteristic of what we mean by a 'cat', he proceeds to identify the 'this' with the 'cat' in the proposition 'This is a cat'.

If, then, we attempt to articulate the precise meaning which the proposition 'This is a cat' has for the speaker who asserts it, we might do so in some such form as this:—'The entity which I sensibly apprehend as having certain of the features characteristic of what is meant by the term "cat" is an entity so constituted that it will exhibit in the appropriate situations all the other features characteristic of what is meant by the term "cat".' This statement, so far as I can see, includes everything that the speaker intends, and nothing that he does not intend, when he asserts 'This is a cat'.

Two omissions from the statement call for special notice. Nothing appears there as to *how* the entity is supposed to 'have' these features. This is as it should be. The speaker, in asserting the proposition, holds no view as to 'how'. The entity may 'have' these features as real constituents of a 'thing', or as members of a 'family' of sense-data, or as 'representations' of real constituents of a thing—in what way is a matter of complete indifference from the point of view of the proposition being asserted. The proposition's truth or falsity is not affected by the truth or falsity of any view about 'sense-data' and 'things'. The speaker regards his proposition as verified or falsified according as the entity which somehow 'has' these sensible features does or does not exhibit in the appropriate empirical situations the other features characteristic of a 'cat'. Nothing else matters. That is the 'point' of the proposition. There is no reference, implied or otherwise, to *how* precisely the entity has the sensibly apprehended features.

Much the same has to be said about the second omission. Nothing appears about the relationship supposed to hold between the 'other features' and either the entity judged to have them or the sensibly presented features which the entity also has. Again it seems to me that nothing *should* appear, that the speaker has no views on the matter. That the entity should exhibit these 'other features' on the occasion of the appropriate empirical tests—that is all the speaker is concerned to assert. These empirical tests are recognized by the speaker as sufficient to verify or falsify his proposition. But it is clear that they cannot verify or falsify any view as to how these other 'features' are related to the 'entity' on the one hand or to the sensibly presented features on the other. What the truth may be about these matters is irrelevant to the truth or otherwise of the proposition.

Now, if this analysis be accepted as sound in substance, there are a number of comments which seem worth making as to its bearing upon contemporary philosophical controversies.

1. We have established our view that the sceptical philosopher has no quarrel with propositions of the type 'This is a cat'. The proposition 'There are, or at least may be, no material things', and the proposition 'This is a cat', are not contradictory of one another. It follows that no appeal can be made to propositions of the latter kind (in so far as they are true) in order to disprove propositions of the former kind. Of course, if the plain man were to say not just 'This is a cat', but 'This is a cat: and a cat is a material thing',[1] then his proposition *would* be in contradiction with that of the sceptic. But on this situation two remarks fall to be made.

(*a*) The contradiction *may* be only verbal. The plain man may very well be meaning, when he calls the cat a material thing, merely that under certain appropriate conditions relating to the entity he and others will have certain definite sensible experiences, primarily of a tactual character: that, in fact, it is a 'tangible' as distinct from an 'intangible' entity. If that *is* all the plain man means, the sceptic has no reason for dissent. Their respective propositions are only in verbal, not in real, contradiction. And certainly the plain man seems to think, with Dr Johnson, that a thing's materiality is at least *established* by the possibility of tactual sensations with regard to it.

(*b*) I agree, however, that the plain man may mean more than this. He may mean that the cat is a material thing in a sense of 'material thing' in which its existence *is* in dispute among philosophers. In that case his proposition is in real contradiction with that of the sceptic. But in that case I really fail to see why we should regard his proposition as a *common-sense* proposition, and entitled on that account to claim special authority. For if a common-sense proposition is entitled to special authority at all, it is

---

[1] Malcolm's 'common-sense reply' to his Prop. 1 is of this general character, but it is only given by him by way of illustration, and not developed. Moore appears to approve it.

surely only in virtue of the great mass of past experience through which it is supposed to have established and sustained itself. But the proposition which the plain man is now asserting is not established or sustained by anything of the sort. There seems no reason to suppose that the 'mass of past experience' is either more, or less, consistent with his proposition than with that of the sceptic. If we are going to prefer it to that of the sceptic, it ought therefore to be only because it is more capable of being supported by philosophical argument—not because of some peculiar authority enjoyed by common-sense propositions.

2. I want to say something now about the relationship between the kind of analysis attempted above and the kind of analysis which Moore gives of the same type of proposition in his 'Defence of Common Sense'.

There is, I think, no great mystery as to how our own kind of analysis is connected with the proposition it analyses. Its aim is, keeping consistently within the mental orbit of the speaker, to unfold and give detailed expression to, what the speaker himself means when he asserts the proposition. It is of the essence of this kind of analysis that the speaker should be able to recognize that this *is* what he meant by his assertion. There was no reason, of course, why he should himself trouble to say it in this elaborate way. The simple words 'This is a cat' are the accepted way of expressing the meaning in question, and give rise to no mis-understanding. But in so far as the analysis is a sound one, it will contain nothing which the speaker cannot recognize, and every-thing which the speaker can recognize, as relevant constituents of his proposition.

In some respects this is very similar to Moore's kind of analysis. And in point of fact the analysis of 'This is a cat' given above seems to fulfil pretty completely the conditions of analysis in his own sense which Moore lays down in his most recent statement on the subject.[1]

On the other hand, it does differ in at least one important respect from analysis as Moore actually practises it in the context referred to. This becomes manifest when we remind ourselves of the special difficulty in the analysis of common-sense propositions which led Moore to declare that although we know these propositions for certain, 'no philosopher, hitherto, has succeeded in suggesting an

---

[1] P. 663, and later on p. 666.

analysis of them, as regards certain important points, which comes anywhere near to being certainly true'.[1] When we try to analyse a proposition such as 'This is a hand' Moore finds, we are able to say some things about it with tolerable certainty. But one particularly obstinate problem holds us up. What is it in such propositions that we are knowing with regard to the 'sense-datum', and more particularly with regard to its relation to that of which it is a sense-datum? Moore examines what he believes to be the only possible alternative types of solution of this problem: but to each of them he finds objections which seem to him sufficiently grave to warrant him in saying that 'no philosopher has hitherto suggested an answer which comes anywhere near to being certainly true'.[2]

But it is clear that this kind of difficulty can arise only for a kind of analysis which refuses to confine itself to what the speaker himself means in his assertion of the proposition. No such difficulty arose for us; because (so it seemed to us) the speaker is not, in asserting the proposition, in the least way concerned with the nature of the relationship between the sense-datum and that of which it is the sense-datum. The speaker is of course aware of presented sensible features and of an entity which somehow 'has' them. But as to the special nature of the 'how', he has no view. For no view on this subject is relevant to what he is concerned to assert. The truth or falsity of what he is concerned to assert does not depend in the smallest degree upon the truth or falsity of any view about the relationship of the sense-datum to that of which it is the sense-datum.

It seems to me, therefore, that Moore's analysis is not, in this instance at any rate, an analysis of what the speaker means in asserting the proposition. This conclusion would still hold even if I am mistaken in my view that the speaker is asserting nothing about the relation of the sense-datum to that of which it is a sense-datum. For suppose he *is* asserting something about this. If he is, then, if he really is a plain man, there is only one kind of relationship he *could* be asserting; for there is only one kind of relationship the possibility of which has ever entered his head, viz., the inherence of the sense-datum as a real constituent in that of which it is a sense-datum. Hence if Moore's analysis were really analysing common-sense propositions of plain men from the point of view of what plain men assert in them, he would have to rule

[1] *Cont. Brit. Phil.*, p. 216.   [2] *Ibid.*, p. 219.

out *ab initio* all other alternative answers about this relationship. That he in fact is far from doing this confirms our view that he is not, or not consistently, concerned to bring out what the speaker himself means in asserting his propositions.

I must confess that it seems to me difficult to hold that an analysis which makes problems of this sort central can be called, in any intelligible sense, an analysis of 'common-sense' propositions. This kind of problem, I should have said, belongs essentially to the metaphysics of perception. The question to which an answer is being sought in the discussion of this problem is, at bottom, 'What is the true nature of the sensory presentation which occurs in perception of objects and how is it related to the object that is perceived?' That is a question of first-rate interest and importance: but I cannot think that the answer to it is capable of throwing any light upon the problem of what is being asserted in 'common-sense' propositions.

3. I should like, finally, to stress, though it must be briefly, a main element of value in our kind of analysis, which remains consistently at the point of view of the speaker himself.

This kind of analysis, in elucidating for us precisely what we are asserting, and thus what precisely we are claiming to know, seems to me to be an indispensable condition of our forming a worthwhile judgment as to whether we really *do* know what we claim to know. It is a commonplace that people frequently think they know with certainty all sorts of propositions which are in fact false, and which they therefore cannot 'know': and that this failing is not confined to the plain man, but extends even to philosophers gifted beyond the ordinary with powers of self-criticism—Descartes, for example—the history of philosophy amply attests. Fairly early in the Modern era, however, philosophers (largely through the influence of Descartes himself, despite the occasional aberrations of that philosopher's practice) learned to view with acute, and wholesome, suspicion propositions backed by nothing more substantial than strong personal conviction. That lesson seems to me to be in danger of being unlearned. Perhaps the pendulum had swung too far in the direction of scepticism. Certainly it is swinging back now with a vengeance.[1] I think it is a good deal more than time to call a halt. When, for example,

---

[1] Consider, e.g., the favour now so widely accorded to 'intuition'—not so long ago, for excellent reasons, the bogy-word of philosophy.

Moore says to us, in answer to his own question whether it isn't possible that he merely *believes* common-sense propositions, or knows them to be *highly probable*, 'I think I have nothing better to say than that it seems to me that I *do* know them with certainty',[1] I could wish that philosophers would have the courage to retort, with all respect, 'If indeed you have nothing better to say, we are not interested. For this is a matter upon which there obviously *is* something better to say.' For surely there is something a *great deal* better to say: first and foremost, what precisely is being asserted in the proposition claimed as known. Once we are clear about *that*, we shall generally (perhaps always) be in a position to see the kind of evidence that is relevant to the verification of the proposition. Then, and only then, we shall be able to form a critical judgment as to whether the evidence in our possession really does entitle us to claim that we know the proposition for 'certain'.[2] But to insist that we know for certain the truth of a proposition before we have even tried to make clear to ourselves what is being asserted in the proposition—that is an attitude for which no defence seems to me possible.

Let me illustrate by reverting, in a last word, to our old proposition 'This is a cat'. Are we entitled to say that we know for certain a proposition of this sort? It is evident that analysis can assist us enormously towards giving the correct answer. It enables us to appreciate that at least some of the objections which philosophers have directed against the possibility of knowing such a proposition are groundless. We can see the irrelevance of objecting that there are, or at least may be, no material things; or again of objecting that nobody yet knows how a sense-datum is related to that of which it is a sense-datum. On the other hand, in revealing to us the kind of evidence that *is* relevant to the truth or falsity of the proposition, analysis seems to me to make it clear that even under the most favourable conditions absolute certainty is impossible. I at least cannot see any way of evading the force of

[1] *Cont. Brit. Phil.* p. 206.

[2] The view expressed in this paragraph is not meant to imply the view that there is no rational certainty without 'proof', or that where we cannot prove a thing acceptance of it becomes a mere matter of faith—a view which Moore justly condemns in the concluding paragraph of his British Academy Lecture. I at least should agree that proof presupposes something known without proof. My point in this paragraph is that we cannot know whether or not the proposition in question is the kind of proposition for which grounds are needed until we analyse it and find out what precisely it is that is being asserted in it.

Ayer's contention that the series of relevant tests is infinite, and can thus never be exhausted. Doubtless we can in certain cases attain to a degree of probability that is quite fantastically high. But the distinction between even fantastically high probability and *certainty* remains. And though such distinctions are of little interest to 'common-sense', I do not think they can be slurred over in philosophy without disaster.

XII

THE MIND'S INVOLVEMENT IN 'OBJECTS': AN ESSAY IN IDEALIST EPISTEMOLOGY

The present paper calls for a few preliminary observations. I shall make as few of them as possible.

1. I appear in this volume[1] as a representative of the 'idealist' tradition; but there have been many brands of idealism, and the cleavages between them are often deep. The standpoint from which I shall be writing is that of the post-Kantian idealism that dominated the philosophy of the English-speaking world in the late decades of the nineteenth century and the first two decades of this. Rightly or wrongly, I am convinced that post-Kantian idealism has still much that is of value to offer to philosophers today and that the main reason why this is not recognized is that what it has to offer is so little known.

2. For (post-Kantian) idealism the theory of *mind*—to which the present volume is devoted—and the theory of *reality* are, in the last resort, one. It would be futile, therefore, within the limits prescribed for this paper, to try to deal with the idealist theory of mind in its full scope. To readers with any knowledge of idealist philosophy the treatment could not appear intolerably superficial; to the uninitiated it would mean little or nothing. Even on the restricted topic I have elected to write about—the idealist view of the mind's involvement in 'objects'—I have found myself obliged to accept the further restriction of eschewing metaphysical argument and adopting an almost exclusively epistemological approach. Nevertheless, the topic chosen is one so central to idealist thought that it ought to be possible, despite these limitations, to bring out a great deal of what is most important in, and most distinctive of, the idealist theory of mind.

3. Within post-Kantian idealism itself variations are very far from negligible. Hegel is no doubt the prototype: but it is a serious

[1] *Theories of the Mind.* (See Preface to present volume.)

error to suppose that later idealists have been simply Hegel's disciples. There is a strongly individual flavour about the respective versions of idealism offered by outstanding modern representatives of the movement like Green, Bradley, Royce, Bosanquet, and Pringle-Pattison. Perhaps only Bosanquet among them could with any strictness be called an 'Hegelian'. The differences are less strongly marked, I think, in epistemology than in metaphysics, which is one reason why I have here preferred the epistemological approach. But I shall not deny that there may be occasions in the following pages where what I refer to as 'the idealist theory' might with greater accuracy be described as 'the version of idealist theory that to me seems the soundest'.

Adoption of the epistemological approach entails that I shall be constantly talking in this paper about 'cognition': indeed, the paper will in large measure be an exposition and defence of the idealist theory of cognition. Unfortunately, 'cognition' (with its derivatives) is one of the less satisfactory words in the philosopher's vocabulary. It carries misleading suggestions that one would fain avoid. Perhaps a brief terminological note on 'cognition' at the outset will be the best way of ensuring that in what follows no great harm will come from its use.

The need of a word to do what 'cognition' is intended to do is hardly open to question. Almost everyone is agreed that there is a mode of mental activity whose specific aim is truth, and whose instances exhibit very varying degrees of success and failure in the realization of that aim. We want a word to denote this mode, applicable to the whole range of its instances irrespective of considerations of their actual success or failure, their truth or falsity. 'Knowing' obviously will not do, since a knowing that is false is a contradiction in terms. The word that has on the whole won most general favour is 'cognizing'. Yet it must be confessed that if what we are searching for is a word that is neutral as between truth and falsity in its significance, 'cognizing', though less conspicuously unsuited to the office than 'knowing', still leaves much to be desired.

The trouble is, of course, that 'cognition' retains in ordinary usage a good deal of its original etymological significance of actual knowing; so that to speak of 'false cognitions' excites a discomfort closely akin to that which we feel toward an expression like 'false knowledge'. Here before me is an elm tree which I mistakenly think to be an oak. Can my thinking that the tree is an oak properly be described as a *cognizing* that it is an oak? It is hard not to feel that so to describe it comes very near to being an abuse of the English language. You cannot 'cognize', one is inclined to say, what is not the case. You can 'cognize' that the tree is an elm, since it *is* so, but not that it is an oak.

Could the language of 'cognition' in such cases be defended on the ground that, though we are in error in thinking this to be an oak, and though 'cognizing' does imply apprehending correctly, we *are* nevertheless correctly apprehending *something*—namely, the false proposition that this is an oak tree? But clearly there is no help to be had in this direction. Instances are easily enough conceivable, no doubt, in which what we are doing is simply apprehending correctly a false proposition. But, of course, that is not all a proper description of what we are doing when we think that this tree is an oak. The essence of what we are doing is not correctly apprehending a false proposition, but mistakenly thinking that the false proposition is true; and the whole trouble is to see how, without violating ordinary usage of the word, we can call this mistaken thinking a *cognition*.

And yet, are the possible alternatives to 'cognition' that might occur to one in any better case? One might perhaps be tempted at first to fall back on 'thinking', which is at least free from the particular disability we have noticed in 'cognizing'. Most people would agree that we can think erroneously as well as think truly. But the term 'thinking' has specialized associations that fit it very ill for the generic use proposed. It is sufficient to remind ourselves that we commonly distinguish between, and even contrast, thinking and *perception*. Yet perception is certainly among the most important of the mental acts which we should want our general term to cover. Clearly we cannot conveniently use to cover it a term from which it is commonly, and as a rule rather sharply, distinguished.

Could we do any better with 'believing', which shares with 'thinking' the advantage that either truth or falsity can be predicted of it? I think we should fare even worse. Whatever ought to be understood by 'belief' (and on this philosophers by no means speak with one voice) it is at least common ground that it is not an *act* or *process*. We talk of 'belief' in terms of states occasionally, and of dispositions more often, but no one talks of 'acts' of belief, or of believing 'processes'. Yet it is precisely a mode of mental *activity* for which we are seeking an appropriate name. Central among the phenomena to which the name is to be applied are judgments and inferences, which are neither states nor dispositions, but acts or processes. (A judgment or an inference may be, perhaps must be, *accompanied* by a belief, but neither a judgment nor an inference can be regarded as an *instance* of belief.)

On the whole it seems best just to 'make do' with 'cognition' as probably the least objectionable of the several unsatisfactory candidates. But it will require to be borne in mind throughout what follows that the word is being used as a technical term and not in all respects in conformity with its ordinary usage. Its etymological connection with actual knowing is to be forgotten. It is to be taken as applying indifferently to *all* instances of the mode of mental activity whose specific aim is knowledge or truth, without regard to whether or not that aim is fulfilled.

In deciding how best to expound the idealist theory of cognition, one has to face at the outset a difficulty at which I have already hinted. Acquaintance with even the general character of post-Kantian idealism cannot safely be taken for granted among philosophers today. That this is the situation, in English-speaking countries at any rate, is hardly disputable. Naturally it makes no easier the task of giving an account of a fundamental aspect of idealist philosophy which will be at once brief and intelligible.

On the whole, the problem of presentation this entails will perhaps be best solved if we approach the idealist theory of cognition indirectly, allowing it to emerge as far as possible by way of critical reaction to the kind of views about cognition which are most familiar and most widely approved at the present time. This is not quite so paradoxical a procedure as may appear at first sight. Contemporary theories about cognition have to do in the main with *sensory* cognition; and though these theories do of course incorporate in their superstructure many novel conceptions, their basic premises seem to me very seldom to be substantially different from those of the empiricist thinkers with whom the old-time idealists did battle, and in so doing defined in large measure their own positive epistemology, several generations ago.

Indeed, if an old-time idealist were to return from the shades, he would, I fancy, be somewhat taken aback to find, on so crucial a question as the role of 'sense' in sensory cognition, a position commonly adopted today which at least looked as though it lay open to criticisms the same in principle as those by which he fondly supposed he had demolished the 'sensation' of the old-time empiricist. He would seek eagerly for evidence in modern empiricist writings that his criticisms had been pondered and answered, not just sidetracked; but I am bound to say that, in my opinion, his search would be largely in vain. It seems to me, therefore, that a restatement of these criticisms, directed specifically to the contemporary situation, may not be altogether without profit, quite apart from its topical usefulness in serving to introduce the idealist's positive theory of cognition which it is our business to expound.

Our procedure, then, will be to consider the analysis of sensory cognition which is typical of present-day theory, explain just where and on what grounds a critic bred in the idealist tradition would find this analysis unacceptable, develop therefrom the main features of the idealist's own theory of cognition, and, finally, exhibit the implications of the idealist theory in respect of 'the mind's involvement in objects'.

We shall take our start from, and indeed long continue with, sensory cognition in its simplest form; for it is on the correct analysis of this that almost everything turns. I am referring to such cognitions as are popularly described as 'the seeing of a colour', 'the hearing of a sound', and so on. They could also be indicated by saying that they are such cognitions as most philosophers today would regard as instances of the 'sensing of sensa'. A formal definition is, however, obviously desirable; and it is not too easy to give. The trouble is that a definition of 'simple' sensory cognition is very liable to beg questions which ought to be decided only in the light of the subsequent analysis. A definition that avoids question-begging must do so, I fear, at the cost of being cumbrous; and I certainly cannot claim elegance for the attempt which follows. By simple sensory cognition (hereafter, for brevity's sake, I shall drop the prefix 'simple' save where misunderstanding might thereby arise), I propose to mean 'the unmediated cognition of those *qualia* which are commonly classed as "sensible" on the ground that experience gives good reason for believing the cognition of them to be in all normal cases specifically conditioned by stimulation of our organs of sense'.

We can list as follows the most important issues that are not prejudged by the way the definition is framed:

1. Whether there is—as the title 'sensory cognition' tends to suggest that there is—a distinctive cognitive mode of pure 'sensing'.

2. What sort of 'being' belongs to the *qualia* cognized in sensory cognition (hence our adoption of the noncommittal term *qualia*).

3. Whether the *qualia* are objects cognized by *direct inspection* (for though all direct inspection is unmediated cognition, it can by no means be assumed that all unmediated cognition is a matter of direct inspection).

4. Whether there can be sensory cognition in which *nothing besides* what is sensible is cognized; and if there cannot, what is the relation of the 'something besides' to the 'sensible' in the cognition.

Now to each of these questions, which are of course closely interlocked with one another, most philosophers during the last thirty or forty years have been ready with a pretty definite and confident answer. They maintain that:

1. Pure sensing is a distinctive mode of cognition;

2. The *qualia* cognized by sensing are actually existing entities of some sort;

3. The *qualia* are cognized by sensing as objects of direct inspection; and

4. Sensory cognition of the *qualia* does not essentially involve the cognition of anything besides.

The sensible *qualia*, since it is through sensing and sensing alone that they are supposed to be cognized, these philosophers usually call 'sensa', or alternatively 'sense-data' (the latter term being especially appropriate to emphasize the virtual passivity of the mind in their apprehension—their aspect of 'givenness').

It will be convenient to label the theory which returns the above answers to the above questions the 'sense-datum' theory of sensory cognition.

I shall now try to explain why the idealist thinks that none of the sense-datum theory's answers can be accepted. An accurate analysis of what is involved in sensory cognition, it will be argued, is completely destructive of the whole notion of 'sensing sense-data'.

It matters very little what example we select for special analysis, and we may as well accept the one which is so often invoked by the devotees of sense-data to illustrate their theory, namely, the sensory cognition of 'a patch of red'. We are supposed to be able, by sensing pure and simple, to cognize a patch of red. *Can* we?

Difficulties arise at once concerning the relation of the 'red' to the 'patch'. Let us suppose for the moment that we sense the red, and (still more difficult to suppose) that we also sense some spatial configuration that can answer to the term 'patch'. Clearly these two apprehensions—of the red and of the patch—even if they occur simultaneously do not give us the apprehension of a *red patch*. To apprehend a red patch, if the apprehension is to be a *cognition*, we must apprehend the red patch *as* a red patch; and for this to occur, we must apprehend the red as characterizing the patch or the patch as characterized by the red. In other words, cognition of a red patch implies an apprehension of the subject-attribute relationship. But such apprehension is certainly not included in the sensing of the red plus the sensing of the patch; and it seems absurd to suppose that the lack can be made good by some further operations of sensing. No one, so far as I know, has ever suggested that the subject-attribute relationship is the sort of thing that can be a 'sensum'—a direct object of 'sensing'.

In point of fact sense-datum theorists quite often betray understandable symptoms of discomfort about their own choice of 'patches' of colour to exemplify 'sensa'. Beginning with talk about 'a patch of red' being the sort of thing of which we are directly aware in sensing, they tend later to drop the 'patch' and speak of the sensum as though it were just the 'red', or (sometimes) '*this* red'. And it may be that they would justify their earlier language on the ground that it was intended as no more than a preliminary description which would sufficiently serve its purpose if it drew the reader's attention to the sort of thing that is meant by the term 'sensum'. It was not intended as a precise statement of that which is directly sensed. This, the sensum proper, is just the 'red'.

But at least equal trouble then threatens the sense-datum

theorist from another direction. If all that is present to sense (or to the mind *qua* sensing) is just the 'red', then the experience, whatever else it may be, is not a *cognition*. Cognition, we must remind ourselves, is the mode of mental activity whose specific concern is to *know*. As such, it presupposes (just as knowledge does) independently existing objects to be known; and every cognition is an attempt, successful or unsuccessful, to 'know' this objective world, i.e., to characterize it correctly. If what is apprehended be not taken as characterizing the objective world or some constituent thereof, then the apprehension is, from the standpoint of actual or possible knowledge, and therefore from the standpoint of *cognition*, as good as *nothing*. Of this it seems to me that anyone can convince himself by simple experiment. Let him contemplate (or try to) just 'red', *without* the acceptance of it as in any way or under any conditions characterizing the world which in cognition he is seeking to know. If he contemplates it to the end of time he will still not find it conveying to his mind any information of any sort about anything. To call such an experience a *cognition* would be absurd. Only if, and in so far as, the 'red' as experienced is taken as characterizing something in the world which in cognition we are seeking to know, can our experience of it even begin to have a relevance for the business of *cognition*.

Later we shall have occasion to elaborate considerably the point we have just been trying to make. But in principle it seems to me to be sufficiently made already, and I shall take it as at least provisionally established that even the most elementary sensory cogniton is 'cognitive' at all only if its sensible *quale* is cognized as characterizing something in an independently existing objective world. How far removed this is from the view of the *quale* as a sensum directly apprehended by sensing, I need not stress.

Let us turn now to a different, and perhaps simpler, objection to sensory cognition as the sensing of a sensum.

What of the 'red' itself in sensory cognition—quite apart from any relation it may bear to something which it characterizes? It will be agreed, I suppose, that the red, if it is to be anything for *cognition*, must be apprehended *as* red; or at all events as *some* determinate colour—for we have to allow for cases where we do genuinely cognize the determinate colour to which the name 'red' is conventionally affixed but do not yet know the correct name

H

for it, nor even, perhaps, that it *has* an agreed name. But to apprehend it as red, or as some determinate colour, involves discriminating it from (and accordingly relating it to) other actual and possible colours in our experience. Now this is precisely the kind of operation which is commonly regarded as distinctive of *thought*, not of *sense*. 'Sensing', we are given to understand, consists in the direct apprehension of its so-called 'sensum', the 'red'. If the mind has to go *beyond* the red in order that there should be cognition *of* the red, then it has to go beyond sensing also. The operation involved, as already remarked, is of the kind normally attributed to thought; and there seems no reason why we should not frankly acknowledge that it is thought that is at work here.

The same criticism applies, with double force, if the sensum is supposed to be not just 'red', but '*this* red'. Just as for 'red' to be cognized it must be apprehended '*as*' 'red' (or at least as some determinate colour), so too for 'this' to be cognized it must be apprehended *as* 'this'. But to be apprehended as 'this' implies that it is apprehended as 'not-that'. The 'this' has meaning for us as 'this' only in so far as it is distinguished from (and thereby related to) a 'that'. Accordingly a discriminatory operation of the intelligence is necessarily involved. Not of course, that the meaning of 'this' for a cognition ever consists solely in its negative relationships. As a demonstrative adjective prefixed to a *quale* in sensory cognition it signifies at least 'the particular *quale* to which I am now attending' (in contradistinction from other *qualia* to which I might be, but am not, now attending). This is, I think, the minimum positive significance it carries in sensory cognition. The point of immediate importance, however, is that, whatever meaning the 'this' carries, that meaning presupposes an operation of *thought*.

Can we go on to say that an operation of thought is further involved in sensory cognition in that the sensory *quale* is always cognized as *an exemplification of a universal*?—meaning here by 'universal' a character capable of identical exemplification in an indefinite number of instances. Something of the sort is said at times by critics of empiricism, but it seems to me to be going too far. There is a good case for saying that in sensory *recognition* the sensory *quale* is so cognized. But not all sensory *cognitions*, surely, are sensory *recognitions*; although admittedly the great bulk of those that occur in adult life are. Cases to the contrary, however, are not even confined to childhood. There is nothing excessively rare in the experience of coming across a colour *x* that to the best of our knowledge we have never seen before nor even learned of indirectly. We are not on this account debarred from cognizing it as a determinate (though to us, of course, nameless) colour. It is true that in adult life, since we have by then gained possession of the general notion of 'universals', even a sensory *cog*nition may well be, perhaps usually is, a cognition of the *quale* as a universal. But it does not seem plausible to say this of our earliest sensory cognitions. In these it need not enter our heads, so far as I can see, to think of the *quale*-character we cognize as a character belonging to, or capable of belonging to, anything besides that which we here and now cognize as having it. Later on (probably stimulated thereto by subsequent cognitions of what seems to us to be the same character in other things) we may well come to regard a particular *quale*-character (and, generalizing, *any* particular *quale*-character) as something capable of identical exemplification in an indefinite number of instances. Then we do have the notion of it as a universal; and we are likely in future experience to have many cognitions of what we then take to be (identical) exemplifications of this universal. At this later stage, too, looking back, we could say with a certain justification that even our initial apprehension of the *quale* was 'the apprehension of a universal'. What we should *not* be entitled to say, however, is that it was the apprehension of the *quale as* (or as *exemplifying*) a universal. The initial apprehension is simply of something as having a determinate character.

The point is not one of major importance for the purpose of this essay, and I must not labour it. I have deemed it desirable to touch briefly upon it, however, if only because it behoves anyone who sets out to rebut the extravagant claims often made for sense in sensory cognition to guard himself against the counter-charge of making equally extravagant claims on behalf of thought.

From the idealist criticisms of the sense-datum analysis of sensory cognition that have been so far advanced we can perhaps begin to discern the lineaments of the idealist's own positive theory dimly emerging. They should come into much clearer vision, I think, at our next stage, even though what we are to consider there is, formally, not much more than a corollary of what has gone before.

Sensory cognition, we saw, is always the cognition of something as characterized by a sensible *quale*; the cognition, e.g., of *x* as red. Now is there any difference between cognizing *x* as red, cognizing *x* to be red, and mentally affirming (or accepting) the proposition '*x* is red'? So far as I can see, none whatever. They are three ways of saying the same thing. The third way has superficially a rather different look from the first (even when bridged by the second), but that the difference is only apparent, not real, seems clear enough when we attend closely to that in our experience to which the expressions refer. Nor is there anything in the least surprising about this. It seems even obvious that, if an experience is to be a cognition, it must be of such a kind as to find its appropriate verbal expression in the proposition. Presumably no one would be prepared to call an experience a 'cognition' if it were not *informative* (or *mis*informative) in some way about something. It must be an experience which the experiencing subject takes as contributing—it may be only negatively, it may be only indirectly, but contributing in *some* way—to the goal of knowledge which is the specific concern of the cognitive mode of the mind. But an experience which is *informative* about *x* is an experience for which the one proper verbal expression is a *proposition* in which *x* figures as subject and some quality or relationship is predicated of it.

The doctrine that is here being introduced might fairly be described as the lynch-pin of the idealist epistemology; the doctrine, namely, that all cognition, from the most rudimentary to the most advanced, involves *judgment*. It is a doctrine which, at the present time—the small contingent of idealists apart—some philosophers think to be false, others think to be true but trivial, and the great majority do not pretend to have thought about at all. I hope to show that the case for accepting it is a compelling one, and that, so far from its being trivial, it has implications of first-rate and far-reaching importance.

Let me begin by touching briefly on two matters on which some preliminary clarification seems desirable: first, on the idealist's predilection (which I share) for the term 'judgment' where most people would say 'proposition'; and, secondly, on the distinction between 'affirming' and 'accepting' a proposition.

It is well known, and the idealist does not attempt to deny it, that the term 'judgment' has a certain ambiguity. It stands indifferently *either* for the mental act of judging *or* for the content judged; either for the affirming or accepting that S is P, or for the proposition that S is P. With some plausibility the critics complain that since we have available to us the perfectly good and (in this respect at least) unequivocal term 'proposition' for the content judged, it is perverse of idealists, and an obvious source of confusion, to use for the content judged a term which can equally well direct the mind to the act of judging.

It is a partial, but I should agree not a sufficient, answer to this objection to point out that no real harm is done by using a term which has an inherent ambiguity so long as it is made clear by the user, either by *ad hoc* declaration or by context, in which of the two meanings he is using it. In point of fact it is, I think, very rare indeed for the term 'judgment' to occur in any of the standard idealist writings without the context making it clear to any reasonably careful reader which meaning is intended. Still, if 'judgment' has even a tendency, which 'proposition' has not, to mislead in this way, we ought certainly to prefer 'proposition' unless some special advantage can be shown in the former term which outweighs its disadvantage. *Is* there any such special advantage?

I think that there is; although only in those cases where the 'universe of discourse' is epistemological or metaphysical rather than (in the traditional sense) logical. The advantage is this. The content judged, the 'proposition', is an abstraction. It has no being in itself, but only in relation to a mind which affirms or denies or at least entertains it: and in an epistemological or metaphysical discussion it is vitally important not to forget this. The advantage of using the term 'judgment', which, as it were, 'looks both ways'—both to what is judged and to the judging—is that it becomes virtually impossible to forget it. To the logician this is a matter of indifference. He has no need to bear in mind that he is talking about abstractions, since none of the questions he raises about them, *qua* logician, will be affected whether he remembers or forgets it. There is nothing to be lost, and there is something to be gained, by *his* preference for 'proposition'. But if the epistemologist or metaphysician forgets that propositions are abstractions, the danger is very real. He may easily slip, and not seldom has slipped, into thinking of them as actually existing entities with some kind of 'reality' of their own .Then the fat is in the fire. All sorts of vexatious problems arise which are in fact pseudo-problems. What kind of reality or existence do propositions have, and what, above all, are we to make of *false* propositions? Pseudo-problems generated by the hypostatization of abstractions have had a long history in philosophy, but we can at least safe-guard ourselves against this danger in the case of 'propositions' if, save in strictly logical contexts, we abandon the term in favour of 'judgment'.[1]

Let us pass to the second matter for preliminary consideration. I have spoken above of judgment as (mentally) affirming *or* accepting a proposition. Idealist usage has generally been to speak of 'affirming' (sometimes 'asserting') and leave it at that. I believe this usage to be essentially correct, inasmuch as, in my opinion, 'accepting' a proposition is just an inexplicit 'affirming' of it. But it does seem to me that when judgment is described in terms of 'affirming', and it is not made clear that this is intended to cover not only affirming of which we are explicitly conscious, but also affirming the consciousness of which is very far from explicit, then the doctrine 'all cognition involves judgment' is apt to provoke avoidable objections that arise from mere mis-understanding. For it is in fact the exception rather than the rule in cognition that there should be an explicit consciousness of affirming. We are explicitly conscious of affirming only in regard to that small sector of the cognized world upon which, for one reason or another, our cognitive interest happens to be focused. In our normal, incurious 'taking in' of our familiar physical environment we mentally subscribe to a whole host of proposi-tions about its features, but almost all of them (and it could be *all*) are 'taken for granted' or 'accepted' rather than explicitly affirmed.

I do not think it is really open to doubt that by far the greater part of our cognitive experience consists in the accepting, or taking for granted, of propositions. But is it also the case that this 'accepting' is just implicit 'affirming'? It certainly appears so to me. I can find no difference at all between the common cognitive

---

[1] It is, of course, very well known that the so-called 'philosophical logic' in which idealist philosophers have been primarily interested is much closer akin to epistemology, and even to metaphysics, than to what has traditionally been called 'logic', which accounts for their preference for the term 'judgment' even in works that bear the title 'Logic'.

experience of 'accepting' a proposition and the much less common one of 'affirming' it except that in the former the affirming is something of which we are less clearly conscious. Sometimes circumstances occur which lead us to affirm explicitly a proposition which we had previously been just 'accepting'. When this happens, no difference of kind that I can discover is detectable between the cognitive attitudes to the proposition in the two experiences— only the difference in degree just alluded to. Whatever we can say that is of any *epistemological* significance about the one, we can equally well say about the other.

In what follows I shall usually conform to traditional idealist usage and speak of judgment 'affirming' propositions; but there will be certain contexts in which it will be desirable to mark the inexplicit nature of the affirming by the use of the word 'accepting'.

Having cleared the ground so far, we may now proceed with the defence and development of the idealist's 'judgment theory' of cognition: the theory (as it is in its present skeletal form) that in cognition of any sort whatsoever we are affirming that some subject S is characterized by some predicate P. I shall continue to conduct the argument, for the most part, in close connection with the sense-datum theory; for it is in the region of what we may call the 'low-level' cognitions of sensory experience that objection to the judgment theory is most naturally taken—almost no one would wish to deny that our high-level, reflective cognitions involve judgment. Moreover, the sense-datum theory, in one form or another, is still deeply entrenched in philosophy, and it constitutes, in my opinion, an outstanding obstacle to philosophical progress. The two rival analyses of sensory cognition clearly stand in the most fundamental opposition to one another. According to the sense-datum analysis, the sensible *qualia* cognized are objects directly apprehended by sense, and actual existents in their own right. According to the idealist analysis, their sole being is as characters predicated of some subject in a judgment. (Not, of course, that the idealist would wish to deny that we can *abstract* this element from its context in the judgment and consider it *per se*. But the crucial point for him is that, as so considered, it *is* an abstraction, and that to lose sight of this fact is productive of a stream of ruinous errors.) The difference between the two analyses is indeed so far-reaching that there is scarcely a problem of any philosophic interest about the external world that is not

profoundly affected by it. Some problems, of first-rate importance on the sense-datum analysis, simply disappear if the judgment analysis is accepted—the problems, for example, of the
ontological status of sense-data and the relation they bear to
'material objects', and in particular the problem whether material
objects so-called are properly to be interpreted as logical con-
structions out of sense-data. It ought to be unthinkable, therefore,
for a serious philosopher to accept either analysis without a
thoroughgoing attempt to appraise fairly the claims of the other.

Let us ask, then, how the judgment theory of cognition would
meet the kind of objections most likely to be urged as fatal to it
by the votaries of sense-data.

A convenient starting point will be a criticism which has been
found convincing by some able philosophers, but to which I must
confess I have never been able to attach much weight.

The critic concedes that whenever there is a sensory cognition
there may very well be also, and even always, judgment. The
'red' of a sensory cognition is, quite possibly, always judged to
have some shape and some size and to stand in some kind of
spatial relations to other items in our experience at the time. But
the fact (if it be a fact) that there is always judgment in sensory
cognition, he argues, has no tendency to disprove that there is
not always *also* in sensory cognition a 'given' which is merely
sensed—a 'sensum'. On the contrary, the judgments just mentioned *about* the red presuppose a red which is cognized *otherwise*
than through these judgments. And what can this 'red' be but
our old friend the sensum? Accordingly the judgment theory of
cognition, insofar as it aims to replace, and not merely to supplement, the sense-datum theory, must be rejected.

It seems to me that this criticism misses the essential point of
the idealist doctrine. Certainly any judgment which is *about* the
red presupposes the red as already otherwise cognized. But then
this judgment—let us call it judgment *B*—is *not* the judgment
which the idealist is referring to when he claims that judgment is
involved in sensory cognition. The judgment which the idealist
finds essential to sensory cognition is not one *about* a (cognized)
red, but one which first *constitutes* this red as a *cognized* red at all.
Obviously the *latter* judgment—let us call it judgment *A*—does
not presuppose a red already cognized. No doubt the idealist may
be wrong in his argument that judgment A is involved in all

sensory cognition. That is fair matter for debate. But since it is judgment *A* that the idealist is talking about, it seems a mere *ignoratio elenchi* on the critic's part to point out to him that judgment *B* presupposes an already cognized red. The idealist has no interest in denying this. What *he* is claiming is that the 'already cognized red' is constituted by judgment *A*.

Nevertheless, this criticism can easily be developed into something a good deal more formidable. The idealist must agree that judgments of type *B*, *about* the cognized red, can and do take place. It is perfectly possible to attend solely to the red in, say, a perceived tomato, and judge it to have certain qualities and relations. Now what we certainly *seem* to ourselves to be doing when we do this is attending to something *given*, to an entity 'out there' directly present to our inspection and continuing to present itself to our inspection merely on condition of our continuing to attend to it. Does it really make sense to say, as the idealist account of the matter would seem to imply, that what we are attending to (and judging about) is not this at all, but some character which we are predicating of a subject in another and contemporaneous judgment?

I think it has to be admitted that the idealist account does not have a very plausible look. For the mind which is attending to the cognized red, the only relation which the red seems to have to it is that of being attended to; and it is far from obvious how its appearance of 'givenness' can be reconciled with its 'really' standing in the very different relationship to the mind of being a predicate in a judgment. The required reconciliation can, I believe, be satisfactorily effected. But it is not a simple matter, and will involve our probing a good deal deeper than we have yet done into the nature of our sensory cognitions.

The first thing that must be made clear is this. In arguing that the intellectual act of judgment is involved in sensory (as in all other) cognition, I have by no means wished to defend the paradox that there is nothing in sensory cognition save an operation of the intelligence. I have not even wished to deny that there may be in sensory cognition something that can, in a legitimate sense, be called a 'sensibly given'. I have denied only that there can be any meaning in a 'sensibly given' which is, as such, an object of *cognition*. That sensory experience cannot as such yield sensory cognition does not entail that sensory experience is not an

H*

essential factor in sensory cognition. Indeed it is rather hard to believe that anyone has ever seriously supposed that in sensory cognition the intellect operates without a basis in sensory experience of *some* sort. The difficulty is to attach a clear meaning to this sensory experience, and to interpret in intelligible fashion the function it fulfils in sensory cognition.

The line of argument which has long seemed to myself the most hopeful on this perplexing question is as follows. In all sensory cognition the cognizing mind is aware of a *compulsion* to make the particular judgment it makes, and the compulsion is experienced as one that is not *intellectual* or *logical* in character. Judging in a given sensory situation that this is red, we do not feel free to judge it to be any other colour; and yet what compels us to judge it in this way is not, we know, any sort of *intellectual* necessity that it should be red. An 'extralogical' compulsion imposed upon the intellect in all sensory cognition must, I think, be accepted as sheer matter of fact. But *why* we feel so compelled, or what it is that does the compelling, is another story. Analysis of sensory cognition from the point of view of the cognizing subject affords, so far as I can see, very little help. The feeling of compulsion is not accompanied by any positive indication of its source. On the other hand, in the light of what we know 'from the outside' about the situation which exists when sensory cognition takes place—in particular the excitation of events in the sense organs and sensory areas of the brain—reinforced by what we can reasonably conjecture from the *inside* on the basis of certain 'internal' sensations which accompany sensory cognition and which have for us at least the appearance of being located in our sense organs, it does seem a fair enough assumption that the source of the felt compulsion lies in some kind of 'sensing'. But this 'sensing', we know, is not any kind of *cognizing*. If there is such a sensory 'experience' at all, it must be of the nature of *immediate* experience, or 'feeling'. The hypothesis that emerges is that the source of the felt extralogical compulsion in sensory cognition is the existing situation *as immediately experienced in sense*.

This hypothesis, it should be said, does not entail that, given an immediate sensory experience, the appropriate judgment *must* ensue. It is very probable that whether or not this ensues depends upon whether or not certain other conditions are fulfilled, upon whether, e.g., the sensory experience occurs in a mind which is at the time intellectually oriented to what is going on in the outside world. All that the hypothesis entails is that when (or if) immediate sensory experience of a situation occurs, this creates a feeling of compulsion in the mind to judge in a specific way *if it judges at all*; to judge, e.g., that this is *red*, and not that it is black, or white, or green, or any other colour.

Now how is all this going to help us to resolve the special difficulty which we acknowledged as confronting the judgment theory—the difficulty that when we attend, for purposes of closer examination, to a sensory *quale* which we have cognized, we seem to ourselves to be so manifestly attending to something that is just 'given' to us from without?

The hypothesis just offered to account for the feeling of extra-logical compulsion in sensory cognition was confessedly conjectural; but fortunately this does not matter. What matters for the argument now to be deployed is the *fact* of the felt extralogical compulsion, not any particular explanation of the fact. The relevant point is that in sensory cognition the mind feels itself to be subject to compulsion from without, and thus in great measure *passive* in respect to the cognition. The mind cannot be *wholly* passive, for it does perform the intellectual act of judging. But the intellect's role in such judgments is so meagre, its activity so formal, that it would not be surprising if it tended to be over-looked altogether. Now this *is*, I think, what actually happens in the type of case we are concerned to understand, where there supervenes upon a sensory cognition a period of attention to the sensible *quale* cognized with a view to making judgments about it. Throughout the duration of the attention, we may assume, the situation which evoked by extralogical compulsion the original cognition of the *quale* remains constant, and continues to evoke an identical cognition—we continue to cognize 'the same red'. And throughout this period (here is the crux of the matter) our feeling of compulsion from without in respect of our cognizing of the red, coupled with our awareness of ourselves as intellectually active in the different business of attending to and examining the red cognized, causes us to overlook completely the immeasurably slighter intellectual activity involved in the identically persisting judgments which consitute and sustain the red we are attending to *as* an object for our cognition.

Hence it is that we so confidently regard the cognized red as something just 'given' from without, whose only relation to the mind is the purely external one of being attended to and judged about. But we are deceived in so regarding it: and I have tried to show that the origin of the deception is not really mysterious.

We have now seen how the judgment theory would seek to repel the very plausible objections based on the appearance of givenness in the *qualia* cognized in sensory cognition, and, at the same time, that and how it is able to accept in the sensible *qualia* a genuine element of givenness. It is tempting to explore further the implications of this element of givenness, particularly in relation to the question of the incorrigibility often alleged to belong to simple sensory cognition. We cannot afford, however, to follow up even the most seductive bypaths while so much still remains to be observed on the main road.

Our early examination of the sense-datum analysis of sensory cognition from the standpoint of idealist criticism, together with our recent defence of the rival idealist analysis against criticism from the side of sense-datum theory, have contained by implication a good deal of the answer to the question why, and in what sense, 'the mind's involvement in "objects" ' is a central tenet of the idealist philosophy. For idealism, as we have seen, the mind's objects in even the most rudimentary sensory cognition are in large measure constituted and sustained by thought. Their qualities and relations, as cognized, have their sole being as elements within judgment, and are in that sense 'ideal'. On the *higher* levels of sensory cognition—let alone on the level of *non-*sensory cognition—the mind's involvement in its objects is certainly not likely to be *less*. But we have still some distance to travel if the idealist position on this matter is to be elucidated even to the extent that can reasonably be expected in the space at our disposal. There is a very relevant topic which has so far been little more than hinted at. Reference was made earlier (with a promise of later development) to 'an independently existing objective world' which, it was contended, all cognition postulates. Now if idealism accepts this as a postulate of cognition, it is apparently recognizing, in addition to 'objects' which the cognizing mind largely constitutes, 'objects' which are entirely independent of the cognizing mind. To objects in this latter meaning the idealist doctrine of 'the mind's involvement in its objects' would seem not to apply; and it certainly cannot apply in the sense we have so far given to 'the mind's involvement'. Evidently there is something here that must be cleared up. Just how, for the idealist theory, is 'object' in the one sense related to 'object' in the other sense? The answer (to the extent that the limited epistemological approach can give it) necessitates some consideration of the formal analysis offered by idealism of the nature of 'judgment', on which we have as yet said nothing; and to this analysis and its implications our remaining pages will best be devoted.

The first point of importance to be noted is a very simple one, namely, that there is a claim to *truth* inherent in the very form of judgment. If we say 'S is P', and someone retorts 'that's not true', this denial of the *truth* of our judgment we take as a matter of course to be a denial of a claim we are making in our judgment. It is not felt necessary to say expressly 'it is true that S is P', simply because it is assumed that everyone accepts this as implied in the form 'S is P'.

More interesting is the question of what exactly we *mean* when we thus claim 'truth' for our judgment.

The notion of 'truth' obviously presupposes recognition of the distinction between truth and error. Now this distinction, the idealist would contend, itself presupposes the recognition of another distinction; the distinction between, on the one hand, an objective 'order of things' with a permanent determinate nature of its own—a 'reality' independent of the judging mind—and, on the other hand, a subjective field of 'ideas', in the sense of 'ideal *meanings*',[1] which ideas, according to the manner in which they are brought together in the judgment, may *either* conform to *or* be discrepant with the nature of the independent objective reality. On the basis of the distinction between these two realms, the claim to truth inherent in judging is interpreted by idealists as simply the claim that the complex of related ideas (the 'ideal

[1] The reader may be reminded that there are two very different aspects in which 'ideas' can be regarded. Every idea has (*a*) a *psychical existence*, as a state or event in someone's mental history; and (*b*) a *meaning*, as the character or complex of characters which constitutes the 'objective content' of the idea. It is, of course, in aspect (*b*) that ideas are used in judging. Their aspect as mental states is quite irrelevant for the mind *qua* judging. In Bradley's characteristically pithy comment 'When I say "this horse is a mammal" it is surely absurd to suppose that I am harnessing my mental state to the beast between the shafts'. (*Appearance and Reality*, seventh impression, p. 164.) Idealist writers have usually sought to prevent misunderstanding by speaking of 'ideal content' when what is meant is 'idea' in aspect (*b*).

content') which we affirm in our judgment does conform to, or correctly characterize, the nature of the independent objective reality. To this interpretation I can, for my part, see no reasonable alternative.

This leads on, however, to a development of the idealist analysis which seems to have puzzled a good many people—the doctrine that in judgment the ultimate logical subject is always 'Reality'. Yet the reason for maintaining this seems plain enough when considered in our present context, i.e., in the context of what is implied by the claim to truth inherent in the judgment. If, in seeking and claiming truth, the judging mind is seeking and claiming to characterize correctly the objective reality, then the ultimate subject of judgment, that about which we are making the affirmation, is in a perfectly intelligible sense always 'Reality'. In further confirmation of this doctrine idealists have been wont to appeal to the significant fact that *any* judgment '*S* is *P*' can be reformulated, without change of meaning, as '*Reality is such that S is P*'. No change of meaning is detectable because what the reformulation does is merely to make explicit something that is left implicit in the customary formulation, namely, that the affirmation is 'about Reality'.

It must be presumed, I think, that the main reason why there is so much suspicion of this doctrine is the appearance it has of doing violence to the ordinary conception of the 'subject' of judgment with which the logician traditionally works. According to the doctrine, the *whole* ideal content of the judgment, *including* what is ordinarily distinguished as the 'subject', may legitimately be regarded as a predicate affirmed of Reality. Now it can very reasonably be insisted that no analysis of judgment is acceptable that does not find room for the *ordinary* distinction of subject from predicate. Even if it be justifiable to say that the judgment 'this tree is a poplar' predicates what is meant by 'the poplarity of this tree' (i.e., predicates the ideal content for which this expression stands) of 'Reality' as subject, it must surely also be recognized that there is a valid sense in which, in the same judgment, 'this tree' is subject and 'poplarity' is predicated of it?

In point of fact, however, the idealist agrees that this is so, and he makes specific provision for it in his analysis. According to his analysis, it is necessary to distinguish between the *ultimate* and the *immediate* subject of judgment. In all save a few exceptional cases, we are seeking in judgment to characterize not just 'Reality in general', but Reality in some specific aspect of it upon which our cognitive interest happens to be focused. The idealist view is that while the ultimate subject is Reality, there is, almost always, an immediate subject which is the specific aspect of Reality to which the mind's attention is at the time directed, and which is, as it were, the 'starting point' of the judgment. This immediate subject coincides with what is *ordinarily* called the 'subject', e.g., 'this tree' in the judgment 'this tree is a poplar'.

The 'immediate subject', it should be carefully noted further, is for the idealist analysis, in an important sense, *both* 'ideal' *and* 'real'. It is 'ideal' in the sense that it is always part of the ideal content affirmed of Reality as subject. It is 'real' in the sense that it is always *that* part of the ideal content which, on the basis of past cognitive experience, the judging mind *already accepts as correctly characterizing Reality*. Precisely on this latter account— because, though 'ideal', it is accepted by the judging mind as being, as it were, a valid representation of the 'real' so far—it serves in the judgment as the *basis* for the *further* characterization of Reality; i.e., serves as 'the immediate subject'. A return to our example 'this tree is a poplar' may help to make the position clearer. What this judgment essentially does is to affirm that Reality, in the *specific aspect of it accepted as already correctly characterized so far by what we mean by 'this tree', is correctly characterized further by what we mean by 'poplarity'*. The ground for the 'further characterization', it may be added (though there is no space to develop the point), is the detection in the immediate subject, 'this tree', of those marks—or at least a sufficiency of them—which serve to define 'poplarity'. And this procedure of establishing, through 'ideal identity', fresh links between our 'immediate subjects' and other elements in our experienced world, is for idealism typical of the development of human knowledge generally.

Overcondensed though this account of the idealist analysis of the judgment has inevitably been, it should, I think, enable us to see how in principle idealism reconciles the *mind-independence* of 'objects', which seems a postulate of all cognition, with the *ideality* of 'objects', which is a central tenet of its own philosophy.

The core of the matter is this. The term 'object' stands for two distinct, though closely related, notions. We may mean by the mind's 'object' that particular part of the presupposed independent reality which in our judging activity at any particular moment we are seeking to know. The object in this *first* sense has, *ex hypothesi*, a nature of its own which our cognizing mind does nothing to constitute. The mind has just *no* involvement in its object when 'object' is so understood. But we may also mean by the mind's 'object' that same part of the presupposed independent reality *in the character which it bears for our present cognition*. This character which it bears for our present cognition is a complex of ideal meanings which we accept, on the basis of many past judgments and inferences, as characterizing correctly the independent reality so far. In this *second* sense of 'object' there would seem to be no question of claiming for the object independence of the cognizing mind. Take such an object as a tree in the character it has for a present cognition (in which character it will probably serve as 'immediate subject' for judgments in later cognitions). Even if we were to concede (as of course we do not) that there are certain basic *qualia* here, such as determinate shapes and colours, which are directly 'given' to sensory inspection, these would be very far indeed from yielding us what we mean when we take the object to be a *tree*. By a 'tree' we mean an entity with a definitive and relatively permanent set of properties, most of which are *not*, on *any* theory of cognition, open to inspection at the moment of cognition. The 'invisible' properties are accepted as belonging to what is before us on the basis of past judgments and inferences relating to similar congeries of shapes and colours. Such 'interpretation' of the *qualia* has, as a rule, quite early in our lives, been established by custom as a virtually automatic mental response; but it still presupposes a long history of conceptual analysis and synthesis. We cannot indeed say without qualification that the mind 'constructs' or 'constitutes' its object in this character. That would be to ignore the 'given' element in sensory cognition whose importance we have freely acknowledged and even stressed. But it hardly seems to me possible to deny that, in *this* sense of 'object', the mind's involvement in its objects is at once profound and pervasive.

The distinction between the two senses of 'object' might also be formulated, in relation to the wider perspective of knowledge as a whole, as the distinction between *our* world and *the* world. Our world, the object world in the character it has for our cognition at any given time, is in large measure constituted and sustained by us through judging. But this is compatible with, and indeed is misleading if not supplemented by, the recognition that *our* world is not *the* world. *The* world is the independent reality which *our* world is a more or less successful attempt to characterize correctly. To the extent that the attempt succeeds, to that extent *our* world becomes indistinguishable from *the* world, except in the one all-important respect that it remains inescapably 'ideal'. In Bosanquet's words 'our world as existing for us in the medium of knowledge consists, for us, of a standing affirmation about reality'.[1]

But is it not the case, it may reasonably be asked, that *the* world, the objective reality we are seeking to know, even if it be acknowledged by the idealist philosophy to exist independently of the judging mind, is nevertheless for that same philosophy constituted by 'mind' in *some* sense—perhaps 'Mind' with a capital M? Undoubtedly this is so; for those idealists, at any rate, who (unlike myself, I fear) find the constructive side of Hegel's thought as convincing as its critical side.[2] For them, indeed, the ultimate reality *is* Mind. But to say anything worth saying about this aspect of idealism would require another paper at least as long as the present one, and a concentration upon just those metaphysical considerations which, the reader may recall, I gave notice at the outset I should be obliged to abjure.

Our space has run out, with the writer disturbingly aware of how much remains to be said by way both of clarification and of recommendation of the views he has been trying to present. But perhaps he might be permitted a very brief appendix on a matter that has, in his experience, been a source of much unnecessary confusion in debates about idealism.

One cannot help noticing that when a contemporary philosopher has occasion to refer to idealism, he seems much more often than not to be thinking in terms of *Berkeleyan* idealism.

[1] *Essentials of Logic*, p. 32.
[2] I must frankly confess that—as those who have done me the honour of reading my books will already know—I cannot for my own part regard as valid any of the metaphysical arguments for the identification of reality with Absolute Mind or Spirit. I cannot even accept Bradley's more general asseveration that reality is of the nature of 'experience'. I suppose I ought, on this account, to disclaim altogether the title of 'idealist'; though my strong conviction of the validity and basic importance of the epistemology of idealism makes me reluctant to do so.

In a way it is natural that this should be so. Certainly there would be no difficulty in explaining it in the light of the climate of philosophical opinion which has overwhelmingly prevailed, and has in consequence determined the general pattern of philosophic education, for something like three decades. Natural or not, however, it is extremely unfortunate. For Berkeleyan idealism and post-Kantian idealism are poles asunder. They are developed along quite different lines from quite different principles, and it is seldom that a criticism of the former brand of idealism has any relevance to the latter brand.

Berkeley, like most present-day philosophers, accepts (and hardly dreams of questioning) the general epistemological premise that cognition of the 'external' world starts from, and continues to be constantly supported by, direct apprehension of *something*. From the Representationalism current in his time Berkeley takes over the further premise that the 'something' is 'ideas', and in the main the criticisms offered of Berkeleyan idealism consist in arguing that this further premise is mistaken. The contemporary critic generally (though not invariably) takes the 'something' to be sense-data, which need by no means be interpreted as 'ideal'. But such criticisms do not touch post-Kantian idealism. As we have seen, it is of the very essence of the epistemology professed by the latter to deny the fundamental premise which Berkeley and his 'realist' critics share. According to the judgment analysis of cognition, we begin by directly apprehending neither ideas nor sense-data nor physical things nor anything else. We directly apprehend *nothing*. Every cognition, however elementary, is a *judgment*, in which the mind seeks to characterize correctly an objective nature of things, whose independence of the judging mind is necessarily presupposed in the judgment's inherent claim to *truth*. Hence, not only is post-Kantian idealism *opposed* to Berkeleyan idealism, its opposition is actually far more fundamental than the opposition of most of Berkeley's critics. Berkeley and these critics give different answers to the same question; the question, namely, how, if at all, we can justifiably pass from what is directly apprehended to the affirmation of an independently existing reality. For post-Kantian idealism the question itself does not arise. There is no point in asking how we 'pass' to an affirmation which, if all cognition involves judgment, is necessarily there from the beginning.

XIII

RYLE ON THE INTELLECT

As this paper is, I fear, in the nature of a sustained assault upon the central teaching of *The Concept of Mind*, I should like to preface it by saying that I share the opinion, from which I imagine very few dissent, that the author of that work is one of the most powerful, original and ingenious thinkers in contemporary philosophy. But, as history amply testifies, it is from powerful, original and ingenious thinkers that the queerest aberrations of philosophic theory often emanate. Indeed it may be said to *require* a thinker exceptionally endowed in these respects if the more paradoxical type of theory is to be expounded in a way which will make it seem tenable even to its author—let alone to the general philosophic public. That Professor Ryle has succeeded to admiration in expounding his theory persuasively, there can be no possible doubt. Few if any philosophical works of recent years have been greeted in this country with a comparable enthusiasm. But though I could myself applaud with sincerity many of the penetrating incidental discussions in which the book abounds, it seems to me a good deal more useful, in the present state of philosophic opinion, to draw attention to the truly mortal weakness (as I see it) of the general position which it is the concern of the book to establish. The 'one-world theory' (to use a convenient title) is in my opinion totally unable to survive a serious examination of the arguments upon which it is based. In the present paper I shall review one major field of its application, and I shall try to show that even so skilful an advocate as Professor Ryle can 'make a case' only by resorting to arguments that are invariably inadequate, frequently flimsy, and at times almost openly fallacious. It will be best to begin, however, with some brief observations about the character of the work as a whole.

The Concept of Mind is, as everyone knows, in its main purport an attack upon the traditional dualism of mind and matter. According to the traditional 'two-world' theory, the material and the mental are irreducibly different from one another; so different, indeed, as to be in some respects polar opposites, since extendedness and divisibility are commonly regarded as definitory characteristics of the one, and unextendedness and indivisibility as definitory characteristics of the other. Moreover, the two realms are known to us in sharply contrasting ways. In respect of the material, there is direct access of a 'public' nature, through the medium of the senses common to all of us. But in respect of mental happenings, direct access is a privilege reserved for the individual being in whom they happen. Apart from the possibility of telepathic information, the mental states and processes of others can be apprehended only inferentially on the basis of certain physical 'signs'. In this sense, then, and to use Ryle's terminology, mental happenings on the traditional theory are 'occult', and only material happenings are 'overt', or 'publicly observable.'

This dualism, Ryle wants to show, is radically false. The correct way to overcome it, however, is not (we are told) by reducing one side to the other side. 'The hallowed contrast between Mind and Matter', he claims in his opening chapter, 'will be dissipated, but dissipated not by either of the equally hallowed absorptions of Mind by Matter or of Matter by Mind, but in quite a different way' (p. 22).

What is this 'different way'? I think it turns out in the end to be not so *very* different. The mental and the material would appear to be for Ryle denizens of 'one world' of overt bodily behaviour, amenable to public observation by the ordinary senses: and the only ground I can discover for his denial that this involves the absorption of Mind by Matter is the surely insufficient one that the bodily behaviour to which we apply the term 'mental' has certain typical differences from other forms of bodily behaviour. Now of course if we choose to limit the term 'material' to *certain forms only* of bodily behaviour—e.g. to the 'mechanical' form—we can certainly say that Mind, even as Ryle understands it, is not 'absorbed by Matter'. But we shall be guilty of a departure, and one not easy to justify, from the ordinary use of words. For 'material' is a term which is ordinarily applied to whatever can be described as 'bodily', not merely to certain *specific* bodily forms. It would seem, therefore, that the claim that Mind is not being absorbed by Matter really rests upon a rather esoteric use of language.

That *The Concept of Mind* is, at bottom, a thinly disguised form of Materialism comes out perhaps most clearly in the final chapter, where Ryle devotes a short section to the relation of his view to Behaviourism. For the only distinction he is there able to point to is that the Behaviourist is in the habit of interpreting mental happenings in terms of a *Mechanistic* view of matter. The Behaviourist is right in denying the supposed 'inner life'. But (Ryle says) 'Man need not be degraded to a machine by being denied to be a ghost in a machine. He might, after all, be a sort of animal, namely, a higher mammal. There has yet to be ventured the hazardous leap to the hypothesis that perhaps he is a man' (p. 328). The implication is that the Behaviourist has gone wrong only in so far as he interprets such processes as, e.g., those commonly called 'intellectual', in terms of physical categories that are too narrowly conceived. There is nothing wrong in principle in his confining himself to *physical* categories. And this is surely Materialism, though not *Mechanistic* Materialism. Perhaps, adapting a term used elsewhere by Ryle himself, we ought to call it 'polymorphic' Materialism.

But perhaps it will be objected that Ryle's Materialism is, after all, of a very different sort from ordinary Materialism: so different that it is more misleading to say that he is a Materialist than to say that he is not. Ordinary Materialism, in recognizing only mechanical and chemical forms of bodily behaviour, or at most these *plus* an 'organic' form, finds no room for intelligent purpose. And it is precisely this omission which, by reason of its implication for human values, is felt by most people to constitute the real 'sting' of Materialistic philosophies. Now Ryle, it may be urged, *does* find room for intelligent purpose. There is for him, over and above even the organic form of bodily behaviour, the further form that is characteristic of distinctively *human* conduct: and of this 'further form', 'intelligent purpose' would seem to be of the very essence. But if Ryle thus repudiates that in Materialism which constitutes its real sting (viz., the denial of intelligent purpose), the mere fact that he is at one with the Materialist in denying an 'inner life' of 'consciousness' does not suffice to make appropriate the description of his philosophy as 'materialist'.

This rejoinder would be reasonable enough on one assumption —that it is possible for what is ordinarily meant by 'intelligent purpose' to survive when 'consciousness' is eliminated. But this assumption is surely false. 'Intelligent purpose' without 'consciousness of an end' seems to be about as near a self-contradiction as makes no difference. Later I shall be criticizing at length Ryle's attempt to give an account of 'intellectual acts' without reference to consciousness. But so far as 'intelligent purpose' is concerned, it is very hard not to feel that argument is sheer waste of time. Anyone who supposes that an act can be intelligently purposive in the total absence of consciousness of an end must just be using words in some queer way of his own. But if what is ordinarily meant by 'intelligent purpose' is not reducible to bodily behaviour, there is, after all, no room in Ryle's scheme for what is ordinarily meant by intelligent purpose. And if that be so, Ryle's Materialism would appear to differ from ordinary Materialism in none of the respects which would commonly be regarded as important.

To avert misunderstanding, let me add that if I have seemed somewhat to labour Ryle's 'Materialism', it has been by no means with the object of enlisting against him the unfriendly emotions which that term is apt to evoke. My motive is merely to clarify a situation which it is certain that a good many of Ryle's readers have found obscure.

There is one further preliminary point upon which I must dwell for a little. I assume in this paper that at least part of the object of *The Concept of Mind* is to make a contribution to our knowledge of the nature of mind; or at any rate of the nature of mental operations. When it is contended, for example, that (contrary to the orthodox view) mental operations are exhaustively describable in terms of overt behaviour, one can hardly suppose that a claim is not being made to enhance our knowledge of the nature of mental operations. We are being invited to substitute a true view of their nature for a false one. Yet there are prominent passages in Ryle's book, particularly in the early stages, which must give one pause. A disturbing contrast appears to be being drawn between knowledge of mental operations on the one hand, and knowledge of the 'logic' of mental-conduct concepts on the other; and Ryle seems to be saying that it is *only* with the latter that he is concerned. Thus he tells us in his *Introduction* that 'This book . . . does not give new information about minds', and that 'The philosophic arguments which constitute this book are intended not to increase what we know about minds, but to rectify the logical geography of the knowledge we already possess' (p. 7). A little later (p. 16), speaking of the 'myth' of the official doctrine which 'represents the facts of mental life as if they belonged to one logical type or category (or range of types or categories), when they actually belong to another', he goes on to say:

'In attempting to explode this myth, I shall probably be taken to be denying well-known facts about the mental life of human beings, and my plea that I aim at doing nothing more than rectify the logic of mental-conduct concepts will probably be disallowed as mere subterfuge.'

This seems to me very puzzling. *Can* the 'rectification of the logic of mental-conduct concepts' be divorced in this way from the knowledge of mental operations? 'Mental-conduct concepts' are, presumably, thoughts about mental operations. To 'rectify the logic' of them is therefore, presumably, to expose certain false ways of thinking about mental operations, and to expound the true way —to tell us how we *ought* to think about them. But knowledge of the true way of thinking about mental operations is surely inseparable from knowledge of the real nature of mental operations? If so, can the rectification of the logic of mental-conduct concepts fail to 'give us new information about minds', or to 'increase what we know about minds'?

Or again, from the other side, what is the procedure for 'rectifying the logic of mental-conduct concepts'? If (as I have suggested) the phrase quoted can only mean determining how we *ought* to think (i.e., how to think *truly*) about mental operations, there would seem to be no procedure of any sort of promise that does not involve the patient, critical and untendencious examination of the mental operations themselves. We all of us want, just as Ryle does, to assign mental operations to their proper logical categories. But it seems to me clear that we cannot do this until we know the nature of mental operations, and that we cannot know the nature of mental operations without directing attention upon them.

But here, I suspect, the myth that bedevils so much of the thinking of the linguistic philosophers is at its baneful work again. Is it possible that Ryle thinks we can 'rectify the logic of mental-conduct concepts' by discovering what is the 'correct' way of *talking* about mental operations; the 'correct' way of *talking* about them being itself discoverable by appeal to 'accepted linguistic usage'? If so (and it is hard to deny that we do have here one of the many strands of Ryle's thought), it seems sufficient to reply, first, that there is *no* 'accepted linguistic usage' in respect of most mental operations (accepted by *whom*, anyway?): and secondly, that even if there *were*, a 'correct way of talking' about something in the sense of a 'generally accepted' way of talking about it, must be distinguished from a correct way of talking about something in the sense of a way of talking about it *which describes it as it really is*; and that the *latter* is the *only* sense in which the 'correct way of talking' has any relevance to the aim of 'rectifying the logic of mental-conduct concepts'. But on this whole question of the philosopher's appeal to 'ordinary language' I would refer to Mr Heath's article in the *Philosophical Quarterly*,[1] which says incomparably well a number of things that have needed saying for a very long time.

I come now to the specific aim of this paper. To avoid the danger of vagueness which is always attendant upon generalized criticism, I have chosen to attack upon a limited front. But a break-through on this sector must, I think, have the effect of turning the whole enemy line. To drop metaphor, I shall be criticizing in some detail Ryle's application of his general thesis to a single, but central, topic, viz., the character of those happenings in our so-called 'mental' life which it is customary to group under the title of 'intellectual'. There is the more need to examine Ryle's treatment of this topic since it has so far, to the best of my knowledge, evoked singularly little critical reaction from those who have published comments upon his book: very much less, e.g., than his accounts of Will and Imagination. Yet it does not appear to me that his account of Intellect is in any degree less vulnerable.

Ch. IX of *The Concept of Mind*, it will be remembered, is devoted expressly, and exclusively, to 'The Intellect'; and to this chapter, in the main, I shall confine myself. There is, of course, material relevant to this question in the earlier parts of the book also, notably in the famous second chapter on 'Knowing how' and 'Knowing that'. But although this earlier chapter makes perfectly clear Ryle's view that 'knowing how' is neither preceded nor accompanied by a 'knowing that', and also his view that 'knowing how' is fully describable in terms of overt behaviour, his precise view of the nature of 'knowing that' is—reasonably enough—left somewhat in the air. And it is with 'knowing that' rather than with

[1] January 1952.

'knowing how' that 'intellectual activity' is, as a rule, primarily identified. It seems best that we should concentrate, therefore, upon Ch. IX, where most of the doubts the reader may have entertained earlier about just how Ryle understands 'knowing that' are resolved. But I shall occasionally find it necessary to draw upon, and I shall constantly have in mind, the discussions which precede it.

Let us then now address ourselves directly to the content of the chapter in question.

The purpose of the chapter is to show that there are no 'intellectual acts' in the sense given to that expression by orthodox epistemologists. Judging, inferring, and the like are not 'occult' happenings to which the person judging or inferring can alone have direct cognitive access, nor have they a special status in some sphere of their own totally different from that in which physical happenings occur. Properly interpreted, they will be seen to consist, as 'physical' happenings consist, of publicly observable behaviour through and through: though, as is to be expected, the behaviour of which they consist will turn out to be of a pattern different from that of the happenings we are accustomed to distinguish as 'merely physical'.

Now the intellect is usually taken to be concerned primarily with the discovery of *truth*. This suggests to Ryle that we shall be most likely to get a good view of 'intellectual acts' if we fix our attention upon the operation in which 'truth' is systematically sought; i.e., the operation of 'theorizing'.

Within 'theorizing', however, there is, he tells us, a very important distinction to be drawn. There is the process of *building* the theory; and there is the quite different process of *didactically expounding* the theory after it has been built. And here comes the first of the many surprising things that Ryle says in this chapter. Epistemologists, we are informed, constantly confuse these two processes. They

'very frequently describe the labours of building theories in terms appropriate only to the business of going over or teaching a theory that one already has; as if, for example, the chains of propositions which constitute Euclid's *Elements* mirrored a parallel succession of theorizing moves made by Euclid in his original labours of making his geometrical discoveries; as if, that is, what Euclid was equipped to do when he had his theory, he was already equipped to do when constructing it. But this is absurd' (p. 289).

It *is* absurd; but I confess I find myself quite unable to identify the peccant, though unnamed, epistemologists who have (apparently in considerable strength) committed the absurdity. I should have thought myself that, so far from this confusion being widespread, the distinction between 'the order of discovery' and 'the order of exposition' was something of a commonplace among reputable epistemologists.

However, to this alleged, but I think totally imaginary, confusion among the epistemologists Ryle attributes certain grave consequences. The importance of the distinction in our present context, he tells us, is that, once it is recognized, we see that we ought to raise the question, in *which* of the two sides of theorizing, the exploratory or the expository, are so-called intellectual acts like judging and inferring to be found? Traditional epistemologists have omitted to ask this for the obvious reason, so Ryle believes, that they have failed to make the above distinction. They therefore 'tend not to realize that such a question exists' (p. 291). What they commonly do, he continues:

'is to classify the elements of doctrines didactically expounded by theorists already at home in them, and to postulate that counterpart elements must have occurred as episodes in the work of building those theories. Finding premisses and conclusions among the elements of published theories, they postulate separate, antecedent, "cognitive acts" of judging; and finding arguments among the elements of published theories, they postulate separate antecedent processes of moving to the "cognizing" of conclusions from the "cognizing" of premisses. I hope to show that these separate intellectual processes postulated by epistemologists are para-mechanical dramatizations of the classified elements of achieved and expounded theories' (p. 291).

The relevance of Ryle's argument here to his main thesis I take to be as follows. Epistemologists have not *really* found direct evidence of 'occult' intellectual acts. They have *assumed* them in order to account for certain elements which they do find in the exposition of 'achieved theories'. If, therefore, it can be shown that the *exposition* of theories does not in fact imply the said intellectual acts, the whole case for their existence disappears. And Ryle believes, of course, as we shall see in detail later, that this *can* be shown.

But surely, in the first place, this story of how epistemologists have come to believe in 'cognitive acts' of judging and inferring is the sheerest fiction? It is perfectly true that epistemologists have not, as a rule, asked whether these acts are to be found in the building of theories or in their exposition. But the reason for that is simple; just that it has seemed obvious to them that such acts are to be found in *both* phases of theorizing, and not at all that they have failed to recognize any distinction between the two phases. It is certainly false that 'what they commonly do' is to postulate cognitive acts in the building process as 'counterparts' to elements discovered and classified in 'achieved and expounded theories'. Rightly or wrongly, they have at least *supposed* that there is no difficulty in finding any number of judgments and inferences quite directly in the building operation itself. Almost any text-book account[1] of how we set about solving a theoretical problem will testify to this. The usual account, very briefly, runs somewhat as follows. First we specify our problem as precisely as possible. Secondly, we look for likely hypotheses, guided by our knowledge of the relevant facts and of the laws and patterns pertaining to the given field. Thirdly, we consider in the case of each hypothesis what would follow if it were true. Fourthly, we test the hypothesis by observation of, and it may be experiment upon, the facts. Now such a procedure cannot possibly be described in any detail without constant reference to judging and inferring: inferring,

---

[1] Citation of instances, unless so voluminous as to be here impracticable, could prove little. But I may mention in passing that reference to the chapters on induction in a random half-dozen of popular text-books has discovered none that does not describe 'problem-solving' (generally under such heads as 'Explanation', 'Hypothesis', or 'Scientific Method') in the manner here summarized. All of the authors—Stebbing, Mace, Joseph, Latta and Macbeath, Welton and Monahan, Mellone—devote much space to the congnitive processes involved in the exploratory or building phase of scientific theory, and they manifestly believe that they are directly finding in that phase the judgments and inferences which they describe as constituent of it. I can see no trace of evidence to support the suggestion of 'postulation' (conscious or unconscious) of 'counterpart elements'.

e.g., in the consideration of what will follow from the alternative hypotheses; judging, e.g., in noting what facts are, and what facts are not, in accordance with the hypotheses.

There is, then, I submit, no mystery about where the traditional epistemologists have found their 'intellectual acts'. They have found them in *both* phases of theorizing, the exploratory and the expository. Moreover, so far from its being the case that they are exclusively concerned with the *latter*, I think that any survey of their actual writings[1] will show that it is to the *former* that they preferably turn for the clearest examples of intellectual acts. And naturally so. For it is evident that in exposition of a finished theory, especially when one has become very familiar with it, the mental activity involved is normally a good deal less intense, and its features, in consequence, are a good deal less easily distinguishable, than when we are still 'straining our minds' to discover a tenable theory.

This contention of Ryle's, that it is obviously to the expository, not the exploratory, phase of theorizing that we must look (if anywhere) for intellectual acts, is on the face of it so surprising that it is natural to ask whether he nowhere offers better justification of it than has so far appeared. In point of fact he does later in the chapter return to the topic and attempt some argument in its favour. The argument seems to be patently fallacious, but on this the reader must be given the opportunity to make up his own mind.

In this later part of the chapter, then, Ryle asks once more at *which* stage of theorizing are a man's acts of judging, inferring and the like supposed to be manifested, 'in his saying things when he knows what to say, or in his travailings, when he does not yet know what to say, since he is still trying to get this knowledge' (p. 297). Ryle's answer, of course, is that it is in the expository phase. He takes the case of the detective investigating the death of the squire and reaching the conclusion that he has been killed by the game-keeper.

---

[1] I find it as hard here as in the case dealt with in the previous footnote to name any instance to the contrary. Cook Wilson, Stebbing, and Mace are only among the more conspicuous of those who focus their account of 'inferring' upon the constructive, exploratory phase of mental operations. (Incidentally, each of these shows explicit awareness of the distinction between the exploratory and the expository phases.) Most notable of all, perhaps, is Blanshard, who in his *The Nature of Thought* (Part III especially) has studied the exploratory phase with a care and skill and completeness not equalled in any other work with which I am acquainted.

'If we are to use at all the odd expression "making a judgment", we must say that the detective makes the judgment that the game-keeper killed the squire, only when he is putting into indicative prose a piece of the theory that he now has, and that he keeps on making this judgment as often as he is called upon to tell this part of his theory, whether to himself, to the reporters or to Scotland Yard' (p. 298).

But the answer to this is surely obvious. Who would ever have thought of claiming that *this* judgment ('the gamekeeper killed the squire') was among the judgments belonging to the exploratory stage? No one ever supposed that we should find in the exploratory phase the *self-same* judgments and inferences that appear in the finished theory. The kind of judgment one has in mind as belonging to the exploratory phase of the detective's work is 'there is a small round hole in the squire's forehead': the kind of inference, 'this hole must, in view of its size and character, have been made by a bullet from a Service revolver'. To argue that the judgment 'the gamekeeper killed the squire' does not belong to the exploratory phase seems to me a clear case of *ignoratio elenchi*.

Actually Ryle seems to realize this himself. He seems to see that it is upon quite different judgments that the real issue turns. And in the very next paragraph he admits that in the 'preparatory ponderings' that precede there *may*, after all, be some thinking 'consisting of, or containing, the making of some judgments'. *But*—and here is the ingenious device he adopts to reconcile this admission with his thesis—these judgments which occur *en route* to the theory are just 'interim reports of sub-theories' which the investigation has already established. And so, despite appearances, they *really* belong to the expository stage after all!

This is clever; but it will surely convince nobody. One would have to use language in a very odd way to say that, e.g., the detective's observational judgment that there is a small round hole in the squire's skull is the 'exposition of a theory'—even of a 'sub-theory'. Not only is this a most unnatural meaning for the phrase, but it is not at all the sort of meaning that Ryle himself seemed to be attaching to it in the early part of the chapter.

However, the question of terminology is of little importance. Let Ryle call the judgments involved in the 'preparatory pondering' interim reports of sub-theories if he chooses. What *really* matters is that he has found himself forced to recognize at least the appearance of intellectual acts in a realm which he has seemingly hoped to be allowed to ignore, i.e., in the realm of what *most* people would regard as 'theory-building'. It follows that his initial programme must suffer some revision. It can no longer be adequate to the disproof of 'occult' intellectual acts to concentrate upon 'the didactic exposition of established theory' and show that there is no evidence of them *there*. Ryle is now obliged to attend also to those ostensible judgments and inferences that occur *en route*, and to show that they too involve no occult acts. This development is not unimportant. For although Ryle cannot by any means, in my opinion, show that even the didactic exposition of established theory is describable in terms of publicly observable behaviour alone, it is distinctly easier to make a case of sorts here than it is with regard to the more conspicuous manifestation of intellectual activity in the actual *constructing* of theories.

So far we have been considering little more than the framework within which Ryle's arguments against 'occult' intellectual acts are set. We turn now to the arguments themselves.

The argument which first emerges, however, is one upon which I shall not dwell at length; for although it is given some prominence by Ryle, I find it difficult to suppose that he can really attach much importance to it.

Ryle's view is, it will be remembered, that the terms 'judgment', 'inference', etc., are only by confusion taken to designate recordable acts of any kind—let alone occult intellectual acts. The 'reality', as it were, whose significance traditional epistemology misinterprets, is the *published theory*, classifiable into certain elements: and the 'misinterpretation' consists in postulating 'counterpart' elements in the mind (acts of judgment, inference, etc.) which 'must have occurred as episodes in the work of building those theories' (p. 291). In support of his contention that such episodes do not in fact occur, Ryle thinks it worth while to call to the witness-box Citizen John Doe. And John Doe, it appears, knows nothing of such happenings in his own life-history. He just 'cannot answer at all' if he is asked such questions as:

' . . . How many cognitive acts did he perform before breakfast,

and what did it feel like to do them? Were they tiring? Did he
enjoy his passage from his premises to his conclusion, and did he
make it cautiously or recklessly? Did the breakfast bell make him
stop halfway between his premises and his conclusion? Just when
did he last make a judgment . . . ', etc. etc. etc. (pp. 292–3).

Now I submit that John Doe's bewilderment before this formidable array of psychological posers offers not the slightest presumption against the occurrence of the psychical events referred to.
John Doe may be an admirable citizen, but there is no reason
whatever why he should be any good at introspection. *Nothing*
follows from his inability to answer questions which, in so far as
they are answerable at all, could be answered only by a person
highly skilled in introspective technique.

But, in the second place, the questions in almost every case are
either virtually or absolutely unanswerable even by an expert
introspectionist, *not* because the mental acts at issue do not occur,
but because of the way in which the questions are framed. 'How
many cognitive acts did he perform before breakfast?'—as if,
without the prior acceptance of some convention as to what is to
count as a cognitive 'unit', anyone could even begin to answer such
a question; or as if, waiving this difficulty, even an expert introspectionist could have had any conceivable interest in keeping a
numerical tally of all the thoughts that had occurred to him, and all
the routine and other observations he had made of his surround-
ings, between waking up and beginning his breakfast! As well ask
John Doe how many *breaths* he drew between waking and breakfast; and then, because he cannot tell us, conclude that he must really
have been dead! Certain others of the questions are unanswerable
absolutely, because they are asked about non-existent features of
mental acts. 'Did the breakfast bell make him stop halfway
between his premises and his conclusion?' A question like this
has no significance save on the assumption that, within inference,
there is a time-interval between apprehension of the premises
and apprehension of the conclusion. But this assumption is false
(as indeed Ryle himself later has occasion to stress). The question
asked, then, is unanswerable, not because there are no intellectual
acts of inference, but because inference is not characterized in the
way that the question implies.

I think we need analyse this passage no further. It is an entertaining sample of its author's wit, but its function is perhaps better regarded as one of light relief than of serious philosophic argument.

Let us hasten on, then, to Ryle's more important arguments. They can, I think, be reduced to three. The first two (which are closely connected) are concerned with the expository phase of theorizing, and try to show that this supplies no evidence of occult intellectual acts. The third is directed to what would normally be called the exploratory phase, or the phase of discovery, and tries to show that what admittedly *look* like 'acts of inferring' can and should be otherwise interpreted. We shall deal with each of these three arguments in turn.

It is Ryle's view, as we know, that in the finished and delivered theory there can be distinguished 'arguments which can be called inferences or reasonings'; but that it is an error to suppose that there is something called thoughts *in addition to* the written or oral form in which the theory is overtly presented. Traditional epistemologists, of course, have been guilty of this error. They have been tempted to suppose that:

'there must be mental acts of passing from premisses to conclusions, since the "because" and "so" sentences which feature in the statements of theories are significant and therefore express counterpart cogitative operations in the theorist's mind. Every significant expression has a meaning, so when an expression is actually used, the meaning of it must have been occurring somewhere, and it can have been occurring only in the form of a thought that took place in the speaker's or writer's private stream of consciousness' (pp. 294–5).

Ryle's first argument against this view is, in effect, that the implication of an expression's 'having significance' has been misunderstood by the epistemologists. Certainly, he agrees, significant expressions have *meaning*. This is a tautology from which nothing follows. But:

'this does not warrant us in asking, "When and where do these meanings occur?" A bear may be now being led about by a bear-leader . . . but to say that an expression has a meaning is not to say that the expression is on a lead held by a ghostly leader called a "meaning" or a "thought". . . . The very fact that an expression is made to be understood by anyone shows that the meaning of the expression is not to be described as being, or belonging to, an event that at most one person could know anything about' (p. 295).

The last sentence, I think, contains the essence of the argument. The fact that an expression is made to be understood by *anyone*, Ryle suggests, implies that the meaning which an expression expresses is not something belonging to 'the speaker's or writer's private stream of consciousness'.

The argument has some plausibility. I agree that the fact alluded to does entail that an expression's 'meaning' must, in some sense at least, be regarded as a 'public' rather than a 'private' phenomenon. What we must ask, however, is whether the sense in which an expression's meaning is 'public' is not compatible with an equally valid sense in which an expression's meaning is 'private'. It seems to me that it is not very difficult to see that the two *are* compatible. But in order to show this, a brief analysis of the ambiguous phrase 'the meaning of an expression' is indispensable. I shall conduct the analysis from the standpoint of common-sense and ordinary linguistic usage, which is (I think) the standpoint from which Ryle is himself arguing.

Consider such an expression as 'The Theory of Evolution has been established'. What is its 'meaning'? It is a commonplace (is it not?) that it may mean one thing to the speaker and another, significantly different, thing to the hearer. Thus the meaning which the words 'the Theory of Evolution' carry may include for the hearer, but not for the speaker, a mechanistic view about the origin of the variations which make evolution possible, and the hearer may on that account (and in fact often does) vigorously dispute the statement, supposing himself, quite erroneously, to be in disagreement with the speaker. And that, of course, is only one of many significant differences which might obtain between what the speaker meant by the expression and what the hearer takes it to mean. Obviously not only the words 'the Theory of Evolution' but also the word 'established' can be understood in a variety of partially conflicting ways.

There is, then, the speaker's meaning, and there is also the hearer's meaning. And to these we should add what might be

I

called (not perhaps very happily) the 'conventional' meaning. This may be described, sufficiently for present purposes, as the meaning which the expression would carry for a hearer who interpreted its constituent terms in as strict accordance as possible with the accepted usage of the words in the operative language, and in the case of specialist terms like 'Theory of Evolution', in accordance with the accepted usage of the appropriate specialists.

Now this analysis of 'the meaning of an expression', conducted at a common-sense level, may well be defective. It may be that it ought to be rejected in favour of a much more sophisticated and esoteric analysis. But *any* analysis no matter how sophisticated or esoteric, has got to give *some* account of the commonly recognized distinctions to which our simple analysis draws attention. I do not find any account of them given by Ryle. Yet until he tells us how he interprets what I have called 'the speaker's meaning', this item at least of the analysis stands out in unresolved contradiction with his thesis.

On the simple analysis we have here offered there is, of course, no difficulty at all in seeing how 'the fact that an expression is made to be understood by *anyone*' is compatible with the expression being the expression of a meaning in the speaker's private consciousness. The situation is that the speaker chooses the particular pattern of words which he hopes will excite the hearer (assuming him to be conversant with the language) to think substantially the same thought as *he* is thinking. To that extent the meaning is, or is intended to be, 'public'. But even where the speaker's intention is wholly successful, there is the speaker's thinking of his thought and the hearer's thinking of his thought, and the two 'thinkings' remain separate private episodes in the respective individuals' histories none the less because the objective content of the thinking is identical in the two cases.

It will be worth while to look also, in terms of our analysis, at Ryle's contention that 'to say that an expression has a meaning is not to say that the expression is on a lead held by a ghostly leader called a "meaning" or a "thought"'. This contention seems true or false according to which of the three senses of the term 'meaning' distinguished above we happen to have in mind. It is defensible if we have in mind the meaning for the hearer—what hearing the words excites the hearer to think; or if we have in mind the 'conventional' meaning—what certain hypothetical hearers would be excited to think. In these cases, evidently, the meaning of the expression pertains to events posterior to the utterance of the expression, and cannot, therefore, 'lead' the expression. But (at least at our present level of common-sense analysis) it seems equally evident that if we have in mind the meaning for the *speaker*—what the speaker thought, and sought to convey by the expression—the meaning does precede (though it may also accompany) the expression. And that it also (in a manner) *directs* the expression, so that it is a valid, if not specially helpful, metaphor that the expression is 'on a lead' held by a 'meaning', seems sufficiently established by the fact that what the speaker is aiming to express in the expression is precisely his 'meaning', or 'what he thinks'.

Ryle's first argument, then, would not appear to have much force against the orthodox view that the use of significant expression in the exposition of a theory indicates a meaning present in some form in the speaker's or writer's private stream of consciousness. The 'facts' to which he draws attention in our ordinary intelligent usage of the phrase 'what an expression means' are facts which comport perfectly well with the orthodox view. Evidently a new line of attack is required: in particular, one which will impugn the validity of that common-sense analysis of 'the meaning of an expression' which seemed adequate to rebut the first line of attack. And that is, in fact, what we now get.

This second argument (the most crucial, I think, in the whole chapter) seeks to establish that the so-called thought in the speaker's mind—what we have identified with 'the speaker's meaning'—turns out, when we attempt to give a description of it, to be indistinguishable in principle from the expression itself. It may, indeed, be a 'covert', rather than an 'overt', expression: for the overt expression may be preceded by a rehearsal of the words in the speaker's head—'silent speech', as Ryle often calls it. But that, for Ryle, makes no theoretical difference, since silent speech (so he appears to think) is in principle, if not in practice, publicly observable just as audible speech is.

I quote the key sentences of this second argument:

'When descriptions are proffered [of "the thought that corresponds with the word, phrase or sentence"], they seem to be descriptions of ghostly doubles of the words, phrases or sentences themselves. The "thought" is described as if it were just another more shadowy naming, asserting or arguing. The thought that is supposed to bear-lead the overt announcement "to-morrow cannot be Sunday, unless to-day is Saturday" turns out to be just the announcement to oneself that to-morrow cannot be Sunday without to-day being Saturday, i.e. just a soliloquized or muttered rehearsal of the overt statement itself' (p. 295-6).

Up to this point Ryle's position would seem to be that the speaker's 'thought' in significant expression cannot be distinguished from the utterance, audible or inaudible, of the words themselves. This is a simple and straightforward theory enough; but almost immediately Ryle goes on to add a qualification about which it is really rather difficult to know what to say. To express oneself significantly, it now appears, it is not enough merely to utter words in a certain order. One must utter them '*in a certain frame of mind*', viz., 'on purpose, with a method, carefully, seriously, and on the *qui vive*' (p. 296). Now this at least *looks* like readmitting by a back door the 'separate' intellectual activity just ejected from the front door. I think it will be best, therefore, to defer discussion of this seemingly suicidal development, and to ask first how far the theory can stand *without* the qualification as an intelligible account of the 'thought' commonly supposed to 'underlie' significant speech.

The theory as thus understood seems to be open to many criticisms.

1. It should be noted that by 'silent speech' or 'soliloquizing' Ryle means something more than the 'sub-vocal talking' which the Behaviourist identifies with thinking. Ryle remarks earlier (p. 35) on 'the technical trick of conducting our thinking in auditory word-images, instead of in spoken words'; and it is *imaging*—no doubt visual and kinaesthetic as well as auditory—which I think Ryle has primarily in mind rather than the concealed operation of linguistic mechanisms. In what follows I shall assume that this is the case. It is, I think, at least a more plausible doctrine that we mean *this* by thinking than that we mean sub-vocal talking. On the other hand, if the straight Behaviourist account be abandoned, and thinking identified with 'word-

imaginings', the inclusion of thinking within the category of the publicly observable is surely very hard to defend.

2. The mere fact that, if asked to describe the 'thought' to which a sentence corresponds, we tend to reply by repeating the words of the sentence, does not at all entail that we cannot distinguish the thought from the words. To reply in this way would admittedly be natural if we could not make that distinction; but it would also be natural if we *could*. For suppose that we *could* make the distinction—that our thought *is* for us something different from the words. This thought will have two aspects; the psychical occurrence which is the 'thinking', and the objective content which is 'what we think'. Now it is the *latter*, or 'what' aspect, not the *former*, or 'that' aspect, in terms of which the specific character of a thought is determined. Hence if we are asked to describe some *specific* thought (not 'thought in general'), such as the thought corresponding to the sentence, 'To-morrow cannot be Sunday unless to-day is Saturday', we shall naturally tend to reply with a description of the 'what' aspect of our thought. But to 'describe' the 'what' aspect is just to put into words 'what we thought'. And as this is precisely what we were already doing in our original sentence, it is inevitable that our description should more or less repeat the sentence itself.

I suggest, therefore, that the fact that our proffered description of a thought 'seems to be a ghostly double' of the words of the sentence tells us nothing one way or the other about the identity of the thought with the sentence.

3. Admittedly, all that our second criticism establishes is that a man's inclination to describe a specific thought in terms of the words of a sentence does not *entail* that he recognizes no distinction between the thought and the sentence. It is still *compatible with* his recognizing no distinction. But it seems clear that if the ordinary person, having given an answer in such terms to the request for a description of his 'thought', had the question actually put to him, 'Do you then agree that your "thought" was simply the words (perhaps the soliloquized words) of your sentence?', he would most emphatically dissent. No doubt he would find it far from easy to explain clearly just what it was, other than the words, that he *did* mean by the 'thought' that to-morrow cannot be Sunday unless to-day is Saturday. But he would not, I think, be wholly at a loss. I think a very little Socratic interrogation would

speedily elicit his agreement that the 'thought' was *the appre-hension of a certain relationship*: of a certain relationship, moreover, not between words or groups of words (such as might interest the grammarian), but between what the words or groups of words *mean*; a relationship, namely, between what we mean by 'the to-morrowness of Sunday' and what we mean by 'the to-dayness of Saturday'. Now the saying (or imaging) of words, in whatever pattern, includes nothing that can be even remotely identified with this 'apprehension of a relationship'; not even if the 'relation-ship' apprehended were a relationship between words, which (in this instance at any rate) it certainly is not.

4. Perhaps the clearest proof that the 'thought' or 'meaning' in a speaker's mind cannot be identified with the verbal expression is the fact that the self-same thought can be expressed in different languages. 'The king is dead.' '*Le roi est mort.*' How is this possible on the hypothesis that the thought and the verbal expression are indistinguishable?

The odd thing is that Ryle does *notice* this very familiar objec-tion to the kind of view he is holding, but apparently does not think it worthy of examination. He admits that a man 'might have uttered a sentence to the same effect in a different language, or in a different form of words in the same language' (p. 296). I quote the reply—the *sole* reply—which he gives:

'Knocking in a nail is not doing two things, one with a hammer and another without a hammer . . . for all that the carpenter could have knocked in his nail with another hammer instead of with this one' (*ibid.*).

This seems to call for a comment of equal brevity. I shall only observe that a single sentence of rather obscure metaphor is hardly an appropriate form of reply to a criticism so determinate in character, so frequently advanced by reputable philosophers, and, at least in appearance, so utterly deadly to the theory criticized.

5. The words of a sentence, whether uttered audibly, soliloquized inaudibly, or imaged in auditory imagining, succeed one another in time. But in a thought which is, as here, the seeing of an impli-cation, there can be *no* time interval between the apprehension of the premisses and the apprehension of the conclusion. The seeing that the 'to-morrowness of Sunday' entails the 'Saturdayness of

to-day' cannot be divided into a stage in which we apprehend the to-morrowness of Sunday and a temporally later stage at which we apprehend the Saturdayness of to-day. We should not under these conditions be 'seeing the implication' at all. We may, of course, in an *earlier* phase of our reflections, apprehend *simply* the tomorrowness of Sunday. But that is *before* we 'see the implication'—not a constituent *in* the 'seeing the implication'. At any point at which the apprehension of the premisses and the apprehension of the conclusion are temporally external to one another, there can be no seeing that the premisses *entail* the conclusion. How this fact is to be reconciled with the temporal sequence in which the words of the sentence occur, on the hypothesis that the thought and the words are identical, it is hard to see.

The above criticisms seem to me more than sufficient to refute the doctrine that a speaker's 'thought', in 'significant expression', is indistinguishable from his 'words'. There is no obligation upon the critic, *qua* critic, to go on to develop his own view of the nature of the 'inner act'—of the thought on its 'that' side as well as on its 'what' side. And I shall not attempt this here. It may be worth while, however, to point out in passing the special difficulty which the traditionalist must always have in giving a description of thought that will satisfy a 'last-ditch' opponent. The fundamental reason is that consciousness is indefinable. We can go some way towards describing cognition, as a specifically directed *mode* of consciousness, distinguished in certain ways from other modes of consciousness. But if anyone likes to say, 'This means nothing to me, for I don't know what "consciousness" is', I doubt whether one can do very much about it. One cannot force a man to become aware of the direct experience or 'enjoyment' through which consciousness is known to almost everyone but himself. Perhaps the most one can do is to show him that attempts to interpret the states and processes to which 'consciousness' and its derivatives are normally applied in terms of some *other* notion break down in intolerable paradox. But the fact is that in the case of ultimates and indefinables generally, the last and most important step in understanding cannot be initiated from without. The final appeal must be to the sceptic's own experience.

We must now take notice of the rather puzzling qualification, already mentioned, which Ryle makes to the straightforward theory which identifies thinking with the use of words. When we

are told that the 'thought' which we think we 'express' in significant speech is 'just a soliloquized or muttered rehearsal of the
overt statement itself', we know pretty well where we are. I think
we find it difficult to know where we are when Ryle goes on to
describe saying something significant, in awareness of its significance, as saying it 'on purpose, with a method, carefully, seriously
and on the *qui vive*' (p. 296). 'Saying something in this frame of
mind', he proceeds, 'whether aloud or in one's head, *is* thinking the
thought'. What are we to make of these adverbial qualifications—
'on purpose', 'carefully' and the like—all of which seem to get
their ordinary meaning from the very thing they are here supposed
to be helping to define, viz., thinking? Indeed, when one considers
the generic character of these adverbs and adverbial expressions
one feels that Ryle might just as well have added the adverb
'thoughtfully' to the list while he was about it. But to define
thinking a thought as 'saying something thoughtfully' might have
been too obviously unhelpful.

But Ryle is not to be caught out so easily as this. The ultimate
question at issue is evidently whether these adverbial qualifications
can be understood as denoting only publicly observable features of
behaviour, or whether they must be taken, as on the common view,
to denote 'occult' processes of 'thinking'. And Ryle has prepared
the way for acceptance of his present paradox by a systematic
attempt in an earlier chapter to establish the former of these
alternatives. I refer to Section 4 of Chapter V, which is concerned
primarily with the analysis of what Ryle calls 'heed concepts'.
Ryle is aware that such concepts—e.g. of 'noticing', 'taking care',
'attending' and the like—at least *seem* especially difficult to
reconcile with the theory that there is nothing going on in our so-
called 'minds' save publicly observable happenings; and he
addresses himself to the task of showing that a reconciliation is
nevertheless attainable.

The problem which the 'heed concepts' set for the 'one-world'
theory is that they appear to designate something more than is
capable of inclusion in what we sensibly observe in the activities
qualified by heed adverbs. As Ryle puts it, 'When a man is described as driving carefully, whistling with concentration or eating
absent-mindedly, the special character of his activity seems to
elude the observer, the camera, and the dictaphone' (p. 138).
Hence we seem at first sight:

'forced to say either that it is some hidden concomitant of the operation to which it is ascribed, or that it is some merely dispositional property of the agent' (p. 139).

But either alternative seems untenable. For:

'to accept the former suggestion would be to relapse into the two-worlds legend. It would also involve us in the special difficulty that since minding would then be a different activity from the overt activity said to be minded, it would be impossible to explain why that minding could not go on by itself as humming can go on without walking. On the other hand, to accept the dispositional account would apparently involve us in saying that though a person may properly be described as whistling now, he cannot be properly described as concentrating or taking care now; and we know quite well that such descriptions are legitimate' (*ibid.*).

Before going on to consider how Ryle seeks to escape from this dilemma, let me pause for a moment to point out the inadequacy of the two reasons he has given for rejecting the former of the two alternatives (that minding is a 'hidden concomitant of the overt process').

The first reason is that it involves 'relapse into the two-worlds legend'. But of course that the two-worlds theory *is* a legend is an *hypothesis*, the tenability of which must largely depend upon whether a satisfactory account can be given in terms of a one-world theory of just such refractory phenomena as set the problem of this Section. This reason, therefore, does not seem to carry much weight.

The second reason, that it would then be 'impossible to explain why that minding could not go on by itself', carries, in my judgment, even less. It is not at all clear why the acceptance of two processes as enjoying a different ontological status should entail the rejection of any intrinsic connection between them. Surely we can perfectly well, and frequently do, mean by 'minding', something of different ontological status from what is being minded, and *yet* recognize that, since minding necessarily has for its object something that is being minded, the minding 'could not go on by itself'. Indeed, this is to understate the case. Since on the traditional view, mind, *qua* consciousness, is of its very essence 'intentional', it does not make sense to ask why on *this* view mind-ing cannot go on by itself—without an 'object'. It is precisely on *this* view of mind that the inseparability of minding and what is minded is *not* open to question. Admittedly we do not know *how* the two are connected; least of all, perhaps, where what is being minded is a 'physical' process. That is just the Mind-Body problem. But we do not require to *understand* a connection in order to be satisfied that a connection exists. So far as I can see, only on one supposition would the 'two-worlds' theory support the suggestion that, where what is being minded is a physical process, 'the minding could go on by itself'; the supposition, namely, that we understand by 'two worlds' (with some of the early Rationalists) two absolutely self-subsistent entities. But who among all the philosophers of the last 200 years and more who have insisted upon the different ontological status of 'mind and matter' have had any interest in sponsoring a dualism of that kind?

Let us see, however, how the *one*-world theory fares with heedful operations. How does Ryle meet the admitted difficulty of bringing these within the orbit of a 'one-world' theory?

His solution consists essentially in a development of the 'dis-positional' interpretation. According to the 'straight' dispositional interpretation, to say that a person is 'reading carefully' is to mention one overt occurrence (reading), and to 'make some open hypothetical statement' about the person reading. This account, Ryle contends, has obviously *some* truth. For one of the tests that a person is reading carefully is that certain true hypothetical statements can be made about him; as, e.g., that if he is asked to give the gist of what he has read he will be able to satisfy us. But the trouble is that heed concepts seem to have something *episodic* as well as something dispositional in their reference. As Ryle frankly points out, 'it is proper to order or request someone to apply his mind, as it is not proper to order him to be able or likely to do things' (p. 140). How is this 'episodic' aspect of the situation to be incorporated in the analysis?

The following passage gives (I think) the clearest statement of Ryle's solution.

'To say that someone has done something, paying some heed to what he was doing, is not only to say that he was, e.g., ready for any of a variety of associated tasks and tests which might have cropped up but perhaps did not; it is also to say that he was ready for the task with which he actually coped. He was in the mood or frame of mind to do, if required, lots of things which may not have been actually required; and he was, *ipso facto*, in the mood or frame of mind to do at least this one thing which was actually required' (p. 141).[1]

That is to say (if I understand the passage aright), the requirement that the episodic reference of heed concepts be recognized as well as the dispositional is met by locating the dispositional factor *not only* in those *other*, associated acts of the agent to which the appropriate hypothetical statements will refer, *but also* in the actual doing of the act under immediate observation. To say that someone has done something 'heedfully' is 'not only to say that he was, e.g., ready for any of a variety of associated tasks . . .; it is also to say that he was *ready for the task with which he actually coped*'.

Now my quarrel with this solution of the problem is, in a sense, not with its analysis of heedful action at all. The analysis seems to me, on the contrary, most instructive. My whole trouble is that I cannot see how the analysis is to be understood in terms of the 'one-world' theory which it is Ryle's concern here to justify. The crux, of course, lies in the interpretation of that 'readiness', or 'ready frame of mind' which is declared (rightly, I think) to find expression in the heedful act itself. Ought this not to be something publicly observable if the one-world theory is to be saved? And how *can* it be? There are, admittedly, certain sensibly observable physical signs which we have all come to associate more or less closely with heed, care, concentration and the like. But Ryle has himself earlier agreed that these do not constitute what we *mean* by the 'heed-terms' in question. They are not even conclusive *evidence for* it. As he puts it, 'Perhaps knitted brows, taciturnity and fixity of gaze may be evidence of intentness; but these can be simulated, or they can be purely habitual' (p. 138). Yet if we rule out these physical signs, what is there sensibly observable left of which 'readiness of mind' can consist? So far as I can see, Ryle has given no answer: and certainly I cannot supply one.

From the ordinary standpoint, of course, there is no need whatsoever for all this mystery. Puzzles arise only if our preconceptions compel the attempt to interpret 'readiness of mind' in

[1] See also p. 147 ('To describe someone . . . called on to do').

terms which exclude 'inner' happenings directly knowable only by the subject of them. Lift this gratuitous ban on the so-called 'occult', and everything is plain sailing.

The simple, natural interpretation of heedful acts in terms of the *two*-world theory—or as I should much prefer to call it, less tendenciously, the *different-status* theory—ought perhaps to be briefly illustrated. Let us take as example a heedful act of one's own; since it is only in respect of one's own acts that there can be any claim to be directly aware of constituents of *each* of the two worlds. Suppose, then, I am set to transcribe from a long list of names prefixed by 'Mr', 'Mrs' or 'Miss' the names *only* of persons of the female sex. After a little my attention 'wanders', and I write the next three names 'automatically'. By sheer good fortune, however, they happen to be the names of females; the same, therefore, as they would have been if I had been paying heed. Now in my overt action there is nothing whatever to show that I was not acting heedfully, in 'a ready frame of mind'. But if some-one should come along and say to me at this juncture, 'I hope you're taking proper care', I should of course at once realize that I was *not* heeding what I was doing. How can I know this if there is no discernible difference in my overt activity? Quite easily, because what I mean by 'heeding' is not an 'overt' activity, but an inner, 'occult' activity which is known to me in introspection; and I am aware that it is, and for some moments has been, lacking. I am aware that my overt acts had temporarily ceased to be con-sciously directed towards the end to be accomplished—the trans-cription of the names of females only. By noting the presence or absence from my mind of such a process of conscious direction I have no difficulty in distinguishing my 'heedful' from my 'heedless' activity. Without this clue the distinction would, I think, be altogether baffling.

In the case of other persons, of course, I do not enjoy the direct access to the mind which would enable me to determine in the same way (or, very significantly, with anything like the same confidence) whether they are acting heedfully or not. I am obliged to be content with the evidence of their overt behaviour. But I am certainly *not* obliged on that account to *mean* by the term 'heedful', when I apply it to others, characteristics of their overt behaviour. (That would be to confuse 'evidence for' with 'meaning of'—a confusion of which it is difficult to satisfy oneself that Ryle is always guiltless.) Indeed, so far from my being *obliged* to mean this, the truth is that I am obliged *not* to mean this, on pain of being convicted of using the term 'heedful' with one meaning in its application to myself and with another meaning in its application to other people. And it must surely be agreed that we at least *intend* that our use of the term should be univocal when used of ourselves and when used of others?

I venture to conclude, therefore, that we are amply justified in dismissing as a failure Ryle's attempt to interpret heed concepts in terms of his 'one world' theory. It follows that Ryle's qualified account of thinking as using words 'heedfully'—apart from other grounds for criticism—must be rejected on the ground that while his adverbial suffix does make the theory rather more plausible as an account of thinking, it destroys the claim of the theory to be an account of it in terms of 'one world'.

I turn now to the third and last of the three main arguments which Ryle advances against 'intellectual acts' as ordinarily understood. This argument (it will be remembered) is directed against intellectual acts in the *exploratory* phase of theorizing. It is (ostensible) acts of *inferring* that give him especial concern. Ryle seems confident that he has already disposed of acts of *judging* in this phase to the satisfaction of the reader, but is evidently apprehensive that the reader will prove less docile about acts of inferring. For according to the traditional view, he recognizes, it seems 'part of the very notion of a rational being that his thoughts sometimes progress by passages from premises to conclusions' (p. 299). It is necessary to take some pains over the rebuttal of a dogma so strongly entrenched.

I think it may be helpful to begin by getting better acquainted with the 'one-world' account of inference in favour of which Ryle asks us to jettison the traditional notion of intellectual acts of inferring. Such acts, it will be remembered, Ryle regards as gratuitously postulated by his *bêtes noires* the espistemologists to explain certain features discoverable in expounded theories. 'Finding arguments among the elements of published theories', this muddle-headed breed of men invent the fiction of separate, antecedent, 'counterpart' processes of 'inferring'. The only 'reality' to which the term 'inferring' bears witness, it would seem, is for Ryle the saying or writing of the words of the argument. As in his account of thinking in general, however, Ryle complicates what would otherwise be a very simple theory by a qualification which makes it look more plausible. Here too, we discover, the operation is one of using words '*in a certain frame of mind*'.

'An argument is used, or a conclusion drawn, when a person says or writes, for private or public consumption, "this, so that", or "because this, therefore that", or "this involves that", provided that he says or writes it knowing that he is licensed to do so' (p. 301).

Now the last clause of this passage tends to create the impression that Ryle *is*, after all, talking about something recognizably akin to what ordinary folk mean by 'inferring'. For to most of us a man 'knows that he is licensed' so to speak or write if, and *only* if, he sees the logical implication of conclusion with premises. But of course this cannot be the way in which Ryle is understanding the clause. On Ryle's principles, a man's 'knowing that he is licensed' to make the transition in question must *itself* be something 'publicly observable'. We must therefore ask what features of overt behaviour Ryle is prepared to identify with 'knowing that one is licensed' to say or write 'because this, therefore that'. And to this question Ryle's answer is, to say the least of it, inexplicit. It is possible, however, that the following passage may contain the clue:

'If he [any "thinker"] is to merit the description of having deduced a consequence from premises, he must know that acceptance of those premises gives him the right to accept that conclusion; and the *tests* of whether he does know this would be *other applications of the principle of the argument*, though he would not, of course, be expected to name or to formulate that principle *in abstracto*' (p. 300).

Now we may freely grant that the *test* of whether a man knows that acceptance of certain premises gives him the right to accept a certain conclusion lies in the way in which he deals with problems involving the same ratiocinative principles. And this will mainly be manifest in the 'overt behaviour' of speech or writing. But the fact that the evidence for another person's 'knowing' is some form of overt behaviour, does not, of course, entail that his 'knowing' is itself a form of overt behaviour. One is hesitant, once again, to impute to Ryle a confusion of 'evidence for' with 'meaning of': but it is very hard to see how otherwise he supposes himself able to identify the mode of 'knowing' that is here at issue with publicly observable behaviour.

However, the unconvincing character of Ryle's own 'one-world' account of inference does not of itself invalidate, though it may fairly raise a presumption against, his criticisms of the orthodox account. The orthodox account is, roughly, that 'inferring' is a dateable, and frequently occurrent, intellectual act, the essence of which is the seeing of a logical implication between premisses and conclusion. What does Ryle find so mistaken about this notion?

The first point he makes is that inference does not involve *discovery* (p. 299). For we still call an inference an *inference* even though it is being made for the twentieth time, by which time, obviously, there can no longer be any question of 'discovery'.

This contention seems to me to be sound. One's difficulty with it is merely to appreciate its relevance as criticism of the orthodox view. Granted that inference is not necessarily discovery, what then? If it followed that inference is therefore not 'the seeing of a logical implication', that *would* be helpful for Ryle's critical purpose. But this does not follow, unless on the assumption that the seeing of a logical implication is held by those who believe in such acts always to involve 'discovery'. And this assumption is surely false. Certainly I should not myself hold, and I fancy few 'traditional' epistemologists would hold, that seeing a logical implication involves discovery, save on the occasion when one 'sees' it for the first time.

And in any event, what about this 'first time'? How does Ryle deal with the case when 'the light first bursts' upon a thinker? Is there not the seeing of a logical implication, which is likewise 'discovery', on *this* occasion? Must he not admit an 'act of inferring here at least?

At this point Ryle becomes more than usually elusive. He first tells us that there *need* not 'have been any occasion on which the light first burst upon him' (p. 299). It may only have 'dawned' upon him. 'Need not', however, suggests that Ryle agrees that there are *some* occasions upon which the light *does* 'burst', and one feels he is merely postponing the evil day when he will have to tell us what in his view happens *then*, if it is not to be the 'seeing of an implication'. But as Ryle's argument proceeds, and no special account emerges of light 'bursting', one is gradually forced to the conclusion that he really wants to say that the light *never* 'bursts' upon the thinker. It is *always* a case of 'dawning'. Now if *that* is his view, we must look more closely at his account of the light 'dawning'. We must ask especially whether the process so described is in fact, as Ryle appears to suppose, one in which the 'seeing of implications' is absent. Here is the relevant passage:

'Nor need there have been any occasion on which the light burst upon him. It might well be that the idea that the gamekeeper was the murderer had already occurred to him and that the new clues seemed at first to have only a slight pertinence to the case. Perhaps during some minutes or days he considered and reconsidered these clues, and found that the loopholes they seemed to leave became gradually smaller and smaller until, at no specifiable moment, they dwindled away altogether. In such a situation, which was the situation of all of us when we began to study the proof of Euclid's first theorem, the force of the argument does not flash, but only dawn, upon the thinker, much as the meaning of a stiff piece of Latin unseen does not flash, but only dawns, upon the translator. Here we cannot say that at such and such a moment the thinker first drew his conclusion, but only that, after such and such a period of chewing and digesting, he was at last ready to draw it in the knowledge that he was entitled to do so . . .' (pp. 299–300).

Now what does all this add up to?

In the example which Ryle has taken (and I do not quarrel with it) of a comparatively complex problem, it is of course true that we do not reach in a single, sudden, inspired flash the conclusion that is sufficiently strongly supported by evidence to be deemed the 'solution'. Before that final stage is reached, we have gone through a long, laborious process; searching for clues, testing the several alternative hypotheses which seem to have some initial probability, trying new hypotheses suggested by freshly discovered facts, and so on. These preliminary steps prepare the way for, and (positively or negatively) contribute towards the logical force of, the culminating insight. In that sense the process as a whole may fairly enough be described as one in which the light 'dawns' rather than 'flashes' upon the investigator. But surely this has no tendency to show that the process is one that is devoid of definite, dateable acts of seeing implications, whether *en route* or at the finish? All that it shows is something that no one disputes that the detective's ultimate solution did not arrive 'out of the blue'. If the light *as a whole* 'dawns' rather than 'flashes', this is perfectly compatible with countless individual *shafts* of light flashing upon the detective in the course of the enquiry, and contributing each its quota to the final illumination. And that is surely what normally happens? The whole prior process, impartially surveyed, would seem literally to abound in the 'seeing of implications'; and even in the seeing of them for the first time. How, for example, can the testing of the alternative hypotheses be carried out save in terms of 'seeing implications'? When we test an hypothesis X by observations directed to discovering whether a state of affairs *a* is a fact, this can only be in virtue of our seeing, or thinking we see, that if X is true *a* must be, or cannot be, the case. We are 'seeing implications' like this from beginning to end of any complicated investigation. Many of them are doubtless very simple implications, such as that if the gamekeeper killed the squire he must have been in the vicinity at the time the crime was committed: but the ease with which we may see an implication does not make this any the less an 'act of inferring'.

This seems to me a plain, straightforward description of what does actually happen in a typical case of seeking a solution to a comparatively complex problem, a description which anyone may verify for himself from his own experience. And I would emphasize that it is quite guiltless of the paradox which Ryle would apparently like to fasten upon all accounts of theorizing which stress the 'seeing of implications'. Our account is *not* 'like describing a journey as constituted by arrivals, searching as constituted by findings . . .' (p. 303). What *is* maintained in our account is that there are normally many intermediate arrivals preceding the terminal arrival in the course of the 'journey', many intermediate findings preceding the terminal finding in the course of the 'searching'. There is no question, for us, of the journey being *constituted* by arrivals, the searching *constituted* by findings. That would indeed be paradox; though whether anyone really holds a view which has this implication, I do not know.

K

Moreover, there would seem to be no reason whatever to suppose that these 'seeings of implications' throughout the course of an inquiry are not in principle 'dateable' acts. Often enough they are dateable in practice too. A detective narrating the progress of a case is surely sometimes able, and very willing, to tell us just when this or that important 'shaft of light' first flashed upon him? There seems even less reason to suppose that the detective's final insight, e.g., that the gamekeeper did definitely kill the squire, is reached, in Ryle's phrase, 'at no specifiable moment'. I should have thought it a commonplace occurrence for detectives, in fact and in fiction alike, to impart to suitably admiring audiences just what new fact, or what old fact viewed from a fresh angle, supplied the missing link to clinch his case, and at what point it did so. It seems to me that there is no better ground for asserting that the detective arrived at his final insight 'at no specifiable moment' than that the gamekeeper killed the squire 'at no specifiable moment'.

There is, I think, only one point that need detain us in Ryle's polemic against dateable acts of inferring; and it need not detain us long. Ryle takes some trouble over showing that inference is not the kind of thing that can be fast or slow. '. . . Reaching a conclusion . . . is not the sort of thing that can be described as gradual, quick or instantaneous' (p. 302). I entirely agree. I have indeed already had occasion to urge that if a conclusion is apprehended at a later time than the premisses are apprehended, then the conclusion is not apprehended as *implied by* the premisses, and the situation is therefore not one of 'inference' at all. But what follows from this that threatens the orthodox view? If I understand him rightly, what Ryle *thinks* follows from it is that 'dateable acts' of inferring are a myth. But this is surely wrong. The fact that in inference there is no time occupied *between* apprehending the premisses and apprehending the conclusion by no means entails that there is no time occupied by apprehending the premisses *as implying* the conclusion; i.e., by the *inference*. There seems to me no more danger from this than from any other quarter to the orthodox view that inference occurs at a time and occupies a time.

Let me very briefly summarize. I have sought to show (*a*) that

Ryle's attempt to discredit the orthodox belief in 'occult' intellectual acts which differ in status from publicly observable behaviour
breaks down all along the line; every one of the arguments he
uses can be effectively rebutted; and (*b*) that Ryle's substitute
account of intellectual acts, while adhering ostensibly to 'one
world' of publicly observable behaviour, gets whatever plausibility it enjoys by introducing elements incompatible with that
world. It not merely looks like, but is, giving the 'one-world' case
away when thinking is described as using words *heedfully*, and
when inference is described as proceeding from the verbal statement of premisses to the verbal statement of a conclusion *knowing
that one is licensed to do so*. Perhaps the ancient Mind-Matter
dualism may some day be successfully resolved. But I make bold
to assert that, if it is, it will not be along the lines of *The Concept
of Mind*.

INDEX

GEORGE ALLEN & UNWIN LTD
London: 40 Museum Street, W.C.1

Auckland: P.O. Box 36013, Northcote Central, N.4
Bombay: 15 Graham Road, Ballard Estate, Bombay 1
Barbados: P.O. Box 222, Bridgetown
Buenos Aires: Escritorio 454-459, Florida 165
Beirut: Deet Building, Jeanne d'Arc Street
Calcutta: 17 Chittaranjan Avenue, Calcutta 13
Cape Town: 68 Shortmarket Street
Hong Kong: 105 Wing On Mansion, 26 Hancow Road, Kowloon
Ibadan: P.O. Box 62
Karachi: Karachi Chambers, McLeod Road
Madras: Mohan Mansions, 38c Mount Road, Madras 6
Mexico: Villalongin 32-10, Piso, Mexico 5, D.F.
Nairobi: P.O. Box 4536
New Delhi: 13-14 Asaf Ali Road, New Delhi 1
Ontario: 81 Curlew Drive, Don Mills
Rio de Janeiro: Caixa Postal 2537-Zc-00
Sao Paulo: Caixa Postal 8675
Singapore: 36c Prinsep Street, Singapore 7
Sydney, N.S.W.: Bradbury House, 55 York Street
Tokyo: P.O. Box 26, Kamata

STUDIES IN THE METAPHYSICS OF BRADLEY

SUSHIL KUMAR SAXENA

Does Bradley deny the *existence* of things, or 'so patent a fact as (their) interrelatedness'? If we accept his thesis that relations involve an infinite regress, does it in fact become impossible to tie two sticks with a bit of string? Is Hume's attitude to causation, as developed today, unchallengeable? Do asymmetrical relations present a *special* difficulty to monism?

Dr Saxena's answer is negative. He shows where and how the critics of Bradley err, – from Cook Wilson and James Ward to Russell, Lazerowitz, Ayer and Passmore.

To misinterpret a metaphysician is not the right way to 'eliminate' metaphysics; and, though its primary aim is to defend Bradley, the book is sympathetic to metaphysics in general. 'It contains a reasonable and reasoned plea, modestly advanced, for an enlargement of current conceptions of the whole duty of philosophic thought'.

An attempt is here made to hold that, if metaphysics be regarded as an *interpretative* scheme, Bradley's doctrine of Immediate Experience, and of thought's *arguable* inability to recapture or dispense with the wholeness of such experience, may be preferred to the modern insistence on the mere actuality of the metaempirical.

LECTURES ON PHILOSOPHY

G. E. MOORE

G. E. Moore lectured at Cambridge every year from 1911 until his retirement in 1939. These lectures were often attended by philosophers from different parts of the world, and they were one of the chief means by which he exerted his influence on the philosophical thought of his time. Dr. Lewy has now edited a selection from some of these lectures. They discuss problems in epistemology, in philosophical logic and in the methodology of philosophy. They contain ideas which Moore did not publish elsewhere, and they should be of unusual interest to students of analytic philosophy.

GEORGE ALLEN & UNWIN LTD